Future Mind

Little, Brown Computer Systems Series
Gerald M. Weinberg, *editor*

BASSO AND SCHWARTZ
Programming with FORTRAN/WATFOR/WATFIV

CHATTERGY AND POOCH
Top-down, Modular Programming in FORTRAN with WATFIV

CONSTABLE AND O'DONNELL
A Programming Logic

CONWAY
A Primer on Disciplined Programming Using PL/I, PL/CS, and PL/CT

CONWAY AND GRIES
An Introduction to Programming:
A Structured Approach Using PL/I and PL/C, 3rd ed.
Primer on Structured Programming Using PL/I, PL/C, and PL/CT

CONWAY, GRIES, AND ZIMMERMAN
A Primer on PASCAL, 2nd ed.

EASLEY
Primer for Small Systems Management

FINKENAUR
COBOL for Students: A Programming Primer

FREEDMAN AND WEINBERG
Handbook of Walkthroughs, Inspections and Technical Reviews:
Evaluating Programs, Projects, and Products, 3rd ed.

GRAYBEAL AND POOCH
Simulation: Principles and Methods

GREENFIELD
Architecture of Microcomputers

GREENWOOD
Profitable Small Business Computing

HEALEY AND HEBDITCH
The Minicomputer in On-Line Systems

LINES AND BOEING
Minicomputer Systems

MILLS
Software Productivity

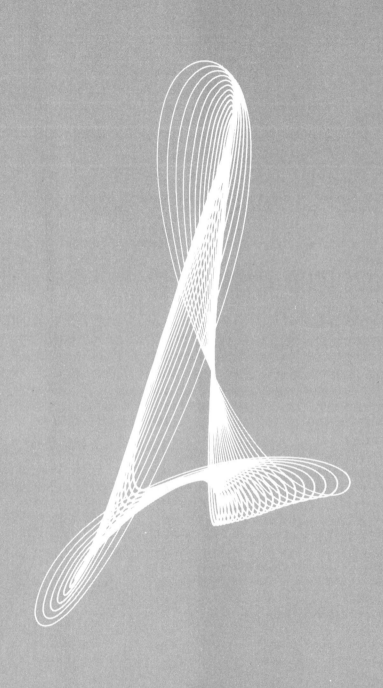

Future Mind

The Microcomputer—
New Medium, New Mental Environment

Edward J. Lias

LITTLE, BROWN AND COMPANY
Boston □ Toronto

Library of Congress Cataloging in Publication Data

Lias, Edward J.
  Future mind.

  (Little, Brown computer systems series)
  Includes index.
  1. Computers and civilization.   2. Microcomputers.
I. Title. II. Series.
QA76.9.C66L5   303.4'834   82–6542
ISBN 0–316–52422–0   AACR2

Library of Congress Catalog Card No. 82–6542

ISBN 0-316-52421-2

ISBN 0-316-52422-0   {PBK.}

9 8 7 6 5 4 3 2 1

ALP

Published simultaneously in Canada
by Little, Brown & Company (Canada) Limited

Printed in the United States of America

ACKNOWLEDGEMENTS

The author gratefully acknowledges permission to use material from the following sources:

Pages 29, 64–65, 216: Reprinted with permission, from Edward Rondthaler, *Life with Letters* (New York: Hastings House, 1981). *Page 36:* Reprinted with permission, from Eric Fromm, *The Revolution of Hope: Toward a Humanized Technology* (New York: Harper & Row Publishers, Inc., 1968). *Page 37:* Reprinted with permission, from Alvin Toffler, *Future Shock* (New York: Random House, Inc., 1972). Copyright © 1972 by Random House, Inc. *Page 37:* Reprinted with permission, from Martin Greenberg, *Computers, Communications and the Public Interest* (Baltimore, Md.: The John Hopkins University Press, 1971). Copyright © 1971 The John Hopkins University Press. *Page 38:* From J. Newman, ed., *1994: The*

Continued on page 287.

Foreword

SPACEGRAM

From: Willobyte 987.382.77

For: All shoulder-embedded transceivers and all archive capture devices

To: Earth satellites (globalnet)

Transmit hourly 15 times.
   Three of us amused ourselves today by reading a quaint book shelved in our sterilized memories room. Titled *Future Mind* it attempted to forecast the future of computer assisted media and communications between A.D. 1982 and 2020. The book is now 40 years old and seemed rather unimaginative. It carried details about early computer gadgets and other services that are now obsolete.
   People in that era were not yet embedding their communication devices inside their bodies, so their culture had none of the benefits of computer assisted thought or bio-trigger transmission, which generated this text. The *Future Mind* book used the 1982 Chaucer III style of spelling which, despite its absurd inconsistencies, we were able to read or in part translate to current speech through the print-to-voice machine.
   Although its contents were dated, a rowdy dialogue developed as we discussed the childlike level of awareness. What was it like, we wondered, when all earth people were unaware of the environment in which their minds were swimming? They appear to have been only half awake, for they were surrounded by the models of about 500 popular electronic media, yet failed to realize that these media formed the total environment for their minds. While staring, big-eyed, at the messages in their newspapers and on their television screens, they seemed unaware of the social and psychological effect of the media themselves as agents of change.

Their media fixed their limits and bounded their territory more than any of the trivial messages that rode upon those media. The fact that they had media such as paper, speech, alphabets, movies, radar, satellites, Citizen Band radios, computers, fiber optic cables, and FM radios fixed the social and cultural options of their lives and minds. Yet someone wrote this book to explain to them that without the media they would not be able to reason or coexist as rational beings.

We came to a friendly, non-judgmental appraisal of their naive awareness when someone reasoned that earth people had been similarly unaware of their *physical* environment for millenia. Their gradual awakening to the inter-relatedness of the physical globe between 1950 and 1970 was, for them, a gradual maturing that draws no criticism, so we reasoned that if our ancestors came to media awareness between 1980 and 1990, it simply marked the boundary of a new consciousness in the race. That our ancestors migrated through these stages of awareness seems natural to us after discussion, although we cannot remember ever being unaware of the ecology of our minds. All 3000 of us on the FRONTIER station use computer-based media exclusively. Never having been without them, and being committed to the growth and development of the central nervous system which alone makes our species unique, we give first attention to our media and secondary attention to the messages and services which these media convey.

It is good to be alive. We see our life spans easily averaging 130 years—in good health. The excitement we feel in our growing minds and the daily creative innovations we conceive give us a flair for existence both exhilarating and wonderful. Machines assisted man during his coming to physical awareness, and our computer-assisted media, implanted in our shoulders, are carrying us to surprising insights and conclusions which could not have occurred to the unassisted mind. Computer Ecology; Media Ecology; Mental Environments. These terms of awareness mark some invisible line that the race once crossed, after which consciousness was different.

In our discussion we agreed that we are not really capable of trying on the awareness of 1982. Our learnings from birth declared media to be the providers for thought, the basis for thought, the sacred carriers of our symbols. The *Future Mind* book, therefore, amused us as we simulated the feelings of its migratory readers.

—Willobyte 987.382.77
June 28, A.D. 2021

Preface

Computers seem to surround us on every side. They inhabit our wrist watches, our cars, our clothes dryers and soon our credit cards. Airplane pilots use them, along with airplane passengers, bus drivers, cattle farmers, and accountants.

Our survival may not be at stake, but our salaries are. Like it or not, the world of science and of space-age inventions cannot be separated any longer from the world of earning a living. Soon we may measure our personal growth in terms of how easily we adopt the latest computer-based tools and media.

Some of us will live through the eighties kicking and complaining. Some will abhor the unnecessary interference with proven, understandable inventions like the bicycle, the mimeograph machine, or the water faucets. Some people wish for less computer memory in the telephone system. They need no dashboard fuel computer in their cars, no calculator on their writing pens. Some people even prefer a watch with the convenience of hands. From their point of view, the mimeograph crank was carelessly dropped from the word-processing terminal.

This book probes the changing environment of the eighties. It could be a manual for bridging the innovation gap—a source book for coping with change.

There is probably not much choice. Anyone involved with work, recreation, art, or sport in this decade—and that means all of us—will have to adjust to the rapidly growing "surround" of push buttons, digital displays, and computer-generated speech.

Native drummers who adopt the rhythms they hear on radios soon move on to make a living in urban music ensembles. Similarly, the information and ideas in this book may directly affect your personal or professional life. In preparation for the day when every gadget in our culture contains a microcomputer, when every medium and communication device is optimized by computer controls, when every stereo set contains microcomputer links to global information banks, the reader will, I hope, be provided with a new perspective from which to view the changing world—and possibly a reason for adjusting to it.

The computer is a universal media manipulator. Computerized media form a new, and probably well-suited, environment for the human mind. This book tells why.

Edward J. Lias

Contents

Future Mind

Chapter One

New Medium,
New Message

□ The computer is a new medium in our culture.

□ Media create an all-encompassing environment for the mind.

□ The principles that apply to media in general can also be applied to the computer.

□ When we embrace new media, our options for relating to each other expand and change.

When President Rutherford B. Hayes was handed the first telephone for a trial conversation between Washington and Philadelphia in 1876, he had difficulty thinking of anything to say. After several sentences he disconnected the line and said, "That's an amazing invention, but who would ever want to use one of them?" Across the Atlantic a London paper commented that telephones might be an appropriate gimmick for Americans, but English society would never need them because England had a plentiful supply of messenger boys.

Few people seem to notice when a new medium is born. Unpretentious new media like the telephone enter cultures virtually unannounced. Later, when they become more visible, the public wonders where they came from. Who placed the order for a television set in every home? Was the long-playing record chosen by a committee? Who said "Let there be 35 millimeter slides"? Why do some colleges require that every student purchase a microcomputer?

In 1937 the League of Nations Research Council attempted to forecast the future of technological change. Its written report documents the difficulty of forecasting which new inventions will come to be accepted broadly. The council did not even extend recognition to inventions known at the time: almost every important discovery was missed, including radar, antibiotics, jet engines, atomic energy and computers.

Like telephones, computers entered our culture unannounced and unexpected. Today, small home computers are sold in almost every town. Local radio and hobby shops sell many types, such as Apple, Commodore's PET, Radio Shack's TRS-80, Atari and others. Looking at the business world, there were 88,000 computers in 35,000 corporate offices in 1978, after which year the sale of word-processing computers drove the count out of sight. By 1982 more than 900,000 desktop microcomputers had been sold; 5 million sales are anticipated by 1984 with no apparent end in sight for the coming decades. Some of these computers—those in TV games, for instance—cost less than $5, while others in government and business cost more than $3 million.

Where did computers come from? Who makes them? Why does anybody want them? What do people do with them? Are they good for people? Because of them do we play more? Laugh more? Invent more? Worship more? Dream more? Act more rationally? Act more kindly? Earn more money? Spend more money?

Traditionally these questions fall within the domain of sociology, because sociologists possess the best-known tools for analyzing the

Telephones did not become an accepted medium for business transactions until many years after their availability. There was some question whether anyone would want to use them. Similarly, computers were forecast to be of possible use to governments and the military. Four to ten computers were considered adequate for the needs of an entire nation. There was also some question whether anyone would want to use them. *(Photo courtesy New England Telephone.)*

impact of new inventions and the social changes which follow them. With questionnaires, polls, statistical analysis and trend theory the sociologist often provides useful materials toward a better understanding of a changing society.

Stanley Rothman and Charles Mosmann, James Martin, and Michael Arbib are the authors of books which bring social science and computer science together. This work complements theirs, but uses radically different, probing tools for analysis.

The computer is a new medium in our culture. Even if the word "medium" is taken to apply specifically to the ordinary magazine, radio, movie, or other popular communication media, the statement is still correct—computers *are* a new medium of communication, for nearly all of the world's messages are being passed through computers on their way from teletype to teletype, from copying machine to facsimile machine, from word-processing terminals to printers, from video-disk to television screen. Many more messages are passed through computers than through conventional mail or conventional electronic communication channels.

But the word "medium" has come to mean more than just the newspaper, the radio or the overhead projector. Because of the work of scholars known by such titles as general semanticists, general media theorists or media ecologists, the word "medium" can be used to include any system, formal or informal, which people use to relate to each other or to their social world. In this view, castles qualify as a medium. So do wood stoves, hair styles, religious rituals and architecture, for these all assist us in our communication with one another. Any environment of the human mind is a medium, by this definition, whether it is a printed page, a parade or a flag, for each of them enables one mind to communicate with another mind. Some of the principles of general media are stated formally—perhaps for the first time—in Chapter 2.

The opinions expressed by Marshall McLuhan in the seventies have developed into tentative conclusions as a result of the research of many scholars. Becausee of McLuhan's work, the definition of "medium" has become so broad that almost every artifact of the culture can be evaluated or reassessed by probing it with the newly formulated principles of general media theory.

The reader may find it presumptuous that certain principles can be proposed which are so general that they can assist analysis of almost anything in our culture, from computers to baroque music. The principles of media as they will be stated and applied in this study are just now coming into acceptance. Their final and

Teletext systems in the home, such as CBS's "Extravision," shown here, allow users to browse through hundreds of electronic pages which are always up to date. By pressing the buttons, any of the menu selections can be brought to the screen. Most of these systems use the normal home color TV screen. A small monthly fee buys the service. *(Photo courtesy CBS.)*

perfect statement is not yet formulated, but, as this study attempts to illustrate, they can appropriately assist in the understanding and prediction of the effects of technology on culture. Some day they may assist in the creation of policy and in the control of new inventions or new media.

What general arguments provide a ground for this study?

Thoughtful pioneers in the field of media and culture include Edward T. Hall, Marshall McLuhan, Edmund Carpenter, Neil Postman and Charles Weingartner. Their arguments are summarized here as a set of environmental statements which, as we shall see, are related to the mind of man and to the microcomputer scene.

1. The media provide an all-encompassing environment for the mind, just as physical surroundings provide an all-encompassing environment for the body. If all media were subtracted from a culture, the mind could not symbolize events or function rationally as we now know it. Our minds depend on a rich environment of media and symbols—even during silent thought or meditation. From the day of birth, most minds are imprinted with the sounds and subsequent meanings of syllables, words, gestures and other

A fish is probably unaware of its environment, being so immersed in it. Similarly, the environment of the human mind is seldom observed. Media are the environment of the mind. Reason has its life and being in the sea of media which surrounds it—words, speech, writings, gestures, tastes, sights and every cultural artifact which assists communication. The central nervous system swims in a sea of media.

symbolic events. The media of sound, smell, touch and vision are exploited from birth to death by the human mind.

2. Media largely determine the ways in which people relate to each other and to the world, because they surround our minds and supply all of our symbols. The media provide communication channels between persons, groups and agencies. All of our psychological and interpersonal relationships exist because of them. As the media change, our manner of relating to each other also changes. For example, in cultures which have no written language, the social organization will always be tribal. Speech (without writing) seems to be unable to hold more than 5,000 to 8,000 people together as a group. When tribal groups develop reading and writing ability, their writings can hold much larger groups together; tribes always become nations after they adopt a written form for their language. Media determine how we organize ourselves and communicate.

3. Society mimics its popular media. When media are added to or subtracted from a culture, various bureaucracies, institutions, and groups of all sizes will gradually reorganize into new relationships whose structure imitates aspects of the dominant media. That means that institutions and bureaucracies slowly evolve to become like the popular media. This suggests that, at a deep psychological level, we have become like books, like TV programs, like newspapers, and that our institutions do this as well. The reasons for this tendency will be explored in later chapters, as will the question, "Are we becoming like computers in certain respects?"

Computers, small and large, are a primary, startling new medium in our culture, and they have the potential of altering the day-to-day lifestyle of our society. Who would have thought a generation ago that graphic artists would be affected by integrated circuits? Or traffic flow by computer surveillance? Or secretaries by word-processing terminals? Or post offices by electronic mail? Or typesetters by computerized phototypesetting? As computers are adopted by corporations and by individuals, our concept of personality and values will be subtly modified. Computers radically alter the ways in which people communicate with other people, and they alter the ways in which corporations and governments manage their business.

The most innocent inventions, such as paper, the printing press, or alternating current were not seen, at their inception, to be globally significant or capable of altering the values of society. No

In certain respects, we have become like pages in books, like letters following each other in sequential rows. We unconsciously adopt the traits of the media which we jointly embrace. When new media are introduced in a culture, people will relate to each other in new ways. New media provide new channels for communication; hence new options for organization and symbol choice. New media shake up a culture. *(Photo courtesy Ford Motor Company.)*

research tools in 1800 could predict that light bulbs would not only replace lanterns, but would displace lamplighters, change nightlife, alter the pattern of crime, and change the form of theater through spotlight control.

When the fledgling principles of general media theory are applied to such inventions, however, the capacity of a new medium

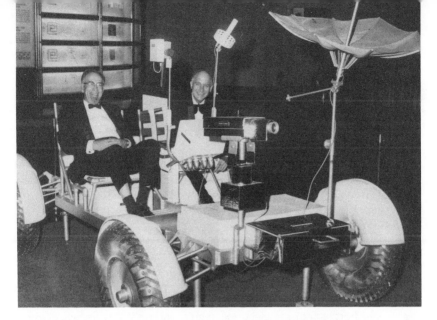

John W. Mauchly (left) wrote a memo in 1942 proposing the first electronic computer. J. Presper Eckert, Jr., (right) worked with him in its design and development. Their ENIAC, funded for $62,000, finally cost about $400,000. Thirty years later, hundreds of computers assisted this lunar Rover on the moon. *(Photo courtesy Sperry Corporation.)*

or invention for initiating an avalanche of change becomes more obvious, and almost predictable, not only because of hindsight, but because of their basic classification as *new media.*

When viewed as "media," each social convention and invention can be analyzed as to its likely impact, its basis for appeal, its inherent biases, its metaphoric lure, its demographics, its unique services, its vulnerability, its likely effect on organizations, its likely effect on individual users, its popularity rating, its versatility, its relation to other media, its variations, its effect on other media and its potential future.

If the general principles of media were used to analyze any medium in the culture, a book like this one might result. Important new media such as the laser, the communication satellite, the fiber optic cable, the video telephone, the video-disk, phototypesetting, xerography, or the citizens'-band radio could be analyzed with the same tools as those employed in this book.

In the chapters that follow, the word "computer" could at times be replaced by the phrase "digital watch, movie camera or compass." When the reader senses this interchangeability, the power of the general media concept will be underscored. At other times, when the uniqueness of the computer distinguishes it from all other media, the sense of separation will also have resulted from the application of the general principles.

Thus a dual thread is traced throughout the book. It is a case study in the application of media theory to one new medium in the culture. It is also an explanation and exposition of the newest environment of the human mind—the computer. When a new medium enters the culture, there is always a message: that life will be unsettled for a while, and made different; and that new options for communication will open new styles of relationships.

Figure 1.1
Miniglossary

Computer: An electronic device which can manipulate signals at very high speed from any of the electronic media, sorting them, merging them together, transmitting them and revising them in useful ways. It can also be used to control mechanical devices in flexible and surprising ways. It converts its messages to simple on-off pulses before operating on them: the pulses can then be rearranged according to preprogrammed formulas. Commonly referred to as digital computers.

Ecology: The study of an environment. Physical ecology embraces the study of the physical environment including the relationships between the elements of that environment. Ecological studies are not limited to a single branch of knowledge. Ecologists probe across many disciplines. Computer ecology is the study of the computer as an environment in which we live and communicate.

Medium: Any system that mediates between people's minds. Human gesture is therefore a medium of communication. Clothing and dress "say" something. Speech, print, radio, TV, movie film and computers are probably the most widely embraced media. Morse code, comic strips, opera, traffic signals and photographs are also media. In its most general definition, almost any human artifact is a medium.

Microcomputer: A computer which is embedded in a small ceramic rectangle one inch long and one half inch wide. Also used to refer to a desktop keyboard and screen which is sold as a complete working unit.

Program: A list of instructions which dictates the actions which a computer is to apply to some alphabetic or numeric set of data. The instructions are written by programmers who place them in the sequence necessary to achieve some goal or revision of data. As computers obey the instructions, they are said to be "executing the program."

Terminal: A TV-like device, or a typewriter which is driven by a computer. The computer displays its questions, for instance, on the screen and the user can type responses back to the computer.

Bibliography

Arbib, M., *Computers and the Cybernetic Society.* New York: Academic Press, 1977.

Carpenter, E., and M. McLuhan, *Explorations in Communication: An Anthology.* Boston: Beacon Press, 1966.

Gotlieb, C. C., and A. Borodin, *Social Issues in Computing.* New York: Academic Press, 1973.

Gottschall, E. M., ed., *U & l.c. Vision '80s* 7, no. 2 (June 1980).

Hall, E. T., *The Hidden Dimension.* New York: Doubleday, 1969.

Martin, J., *The Wired Society.* Englewood Cliffs, N. J.: Prentice-Hall, 1978.

McLuhan, M., *Understanding Media: The Extensions of Man.* New York: McGraw-Hill, 1964.

Postman, N., and C. Weingartner, *Teaching As a Subversive Activity.* New York: Delacorte Press, 1969.

Rothman, S., and C. Mosmann, *Computers and Society.* Chicago: Science Research Associates, 1972.

Chapter Two

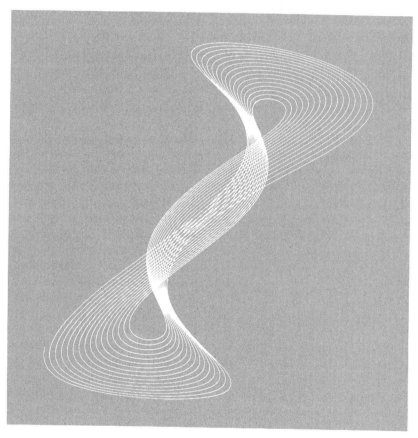

What Do We Know
About Media?

☐ Eight principles have been isolated which seem to apply to all media.

☐ Since the computer is a medium, the general rules of media can be used to trace or predict the social effects of computers.

Not everything is yet known about the effects of media on our minds, nor about how they affect our interpersonal relationships. Television and movies seem to have powerful effects on people, but researchers who attempt to measure these effects find them difficult to document or classify. Even less is understood about the effect of radios, cassette players, home movie cameras, computer games and LP records. But what is known is beginning to provide a new basis for understanding what happens when new media are introduced into a culture. In this chapter the eight principles which are common to all media will be presented. These principles can be applied to any medium in our culture, but when they are applied to computers their reasonableness and universality are illustrated in an exaggerated way, for the computer is an extraordinary case.

The principles will in each case be described in general, and then will be shown in their relationship to computers. The eight principles are the result of a distillation of the concepts of media theory as presented by numerous authors who are listed in the bibliography.

Principle One:
New media are accepted in each culture
with little forethought or planning

No society to date has ever established effective mechanisms for planning, controlling, or predicting the effects of new media. Whether illustrated by the Model T Ford (which was distributed broadly with little thought given to overall social impact), the Gutenberg printing press (which spread the concept of reading), or television sets (which are purchased today as a matter of course by nearly every American), the principle seems to exist universally.

An art director, for example, might invest $90,000 of his or her studio's money in a computer device which can set type, prepare line drawings and convert photographs to a dotted halftone version suitable for printing. Its abilities practically sell it without effort or justification.

But this is a new medium to enter the art studio, and it creates new dependencies and options. When it breaks down, will anyone remember how to prepare layouts in the old manual style? Are skilled operators available for hire? Will artists be willing to operate a machine? Will they demand higher wages? Will training programs and classes be required? Will turnover increase as skilled users migrate to other commercial users who pay more? New media need forethought and planning before we adopt them, for we are rarely prepared for the consequences and change which they bring.

Several factors converge to guarantee that new media are adopted with little fanfare:

1. The media are quite invisible compared to the messages they transmit or the functions they serve.

2. The principles media obey are only now being identified.

3. The newer electronic media evolve faster than legislative committees can control them.

4. The momentum of existing communication channels hides from us the power of new media when, seemingly with a will of their own, they replace their predecessors.

For all these reasons, we buy new communication devices blindly, expecting to learn how to use them later on. We plan quite carefully for new buildings, new organizations, and new marriages, but rarely for new media.

Who were the earliest users of computers? They were electronic geniuses, only partially conscious of the societal change which their inventions would trigger. Some foresaw the industry or wealth which might follow, but their inventive motivation arose primarily from the desire to solve various mathematical problems associated with military or scientific research. The energy which an inventor might wish to give to predictive planning or control is often channeled into a struggle for funding, the race to be first, and the physical details of the medium—regardless of the nature of the invention. James Watson's book *The Double Helix* illustrates this phenomenon perfectly. This is not a personal flaw of inventors, but a fact of media and invention. Media are difficult to predict or control.

How have computers changed the organization of computer-using institutions? Corporations often ordered computers without realizing the likelihood of change, let alone discussing the question, probably because the First Principle of Media operates reliably. For twenty-five years, with little forethought or planning, million dollar computers have been purchased by governments, businesses and colleges, usually with a hope for increased efficiency. Corporate organizational charts were painfully redrawn to accommodate the new medium. When large central machines were in vogue they were incorporated into the institution. When distributed processing became popular, management adopted this new approach to computing. Like hemlines moving up and down, various styles of computing become accepted in cycles of time. Social planning does not seem to guide the process. Even though heavy capital outlay was required, businesses did little to plan or control the growth or distribution of computers. Many corporate offices still do not know how many computers and service contracts exist in their branches. Chapter 13 expands and illustrates this idea.

How have computers affected the economy? The question seems strange because it is rarely discussed. When it *is* discussed, the automation of costly or boring tasks always seems to justify the rush to computerization. The possibility of recession, caused by extensive overcapitalization in thousands of businesses, has rarely been mentioned. Almost every large and medium business invests one to ten million dollars of "up-front computer money," and this has inflicted a tremendous economic surtax upon the cost of goods, although it is recognized only in hindsight. Recessions blamed on the falling productivity of the American worker and on the increasing price of oil may in part be the result of the billions of dollars required to install large computer systems, especially when the capitalization is repeated every six years in the major corporations for each new generation of computer. After 1984, a microcomputer will probably be part of nearly every office desk, representing further capitalization requirements in the decade of dwindling resources and recessions.

The question "What will this medium do to our culture?" comes after the fact for *every* new medium. We welcomed the Model T Ford, then wondered later about smog and road safety. We welcomed television sets into every room, then wondered later about its effect on crime and literacy. The recent formation of information planning committees in many businesses and universities reflects a new awareness that Media Principle One deserves serious attention. In the future, management is likely to exert more control over the purchase of large computers, but will probably be unable to control the number of personal desktop computers installed as office furniture, desired (or demanded) by every administrative employee to assist in mailing, word processing and the transmission of facsimile information.

What planning accompanied the growth of data-base management systems? These systems were adopted as "one more program on the system" when in fact they opened entirely new options for record management, wholly changing the nature of record-keeping. Thousands of government and business offices now use these advanced systems. There was no formal or informal inquiry about their social desirability. Their impact on personal privacy became a public issue twenty years too late, not because anyone in particular was negligent, but because Media Principle One was operating. Data-base systems were accepted with little forethought or planning.

What planning preceded the installation of electronic funds transfer (EFT) systems in financial institutions? Two million tax dollars were allocated in 1977 in an effort to set the stage formally for this important new economic medium. After eight months of weekly meetings, and after two years of work, the final report of the EFT committee contained so many dissenting opinions that its final plea was for more time, more money and more committee members. Meanwhile, EFT systems were being installed—planning or no planning. When the final EFT study was released in 1979, eleven national systems were already in operation.

What planning precedes the introduction of new data channels? The Federal Communications Commission, whose purpose is to allocate and control communication channels, is the official planning agency. Its decisions, which sometimes take decades to appear, often become irrelevant because new channels evolve faster than commission members can document or understand them. Meanwhile, users who are blocked from passing computer data on one channel simply switch to others—FM, microwave, fiber-optic, five types of satellite channels, infrared and the air waves. (See Table 17.1 on page 229.) Although we placed men on the moon, Congress passed laws which for a while prevented us from using satellites to communicate within our own country. Only international messages could be sent by satellite for many years.

In the future it seems likely that we will attempt to predict the impact of new media, especially electronic ones. Canada has attempted to plan for teletext systems in its Telidon standard, adopted by the American Telephone & Telegraph in May 1981. But the media evolve very rapidly. And it will be some time before the principles of media can be understood or appreciated sufficiently to allow predictive control of the process. Therefore, if computer uses continue to grow without formal planning, as seems likely, the chaotic variety of standards and procedures will cause the costs of computing and network exchange to be significantly higher than they otherwise would be.

On the other hand, the proliferation of standards in computer languages, the transmission codes, the data protocols, the data standards, the security and encryption standards and the network architectures, etc., serve to fertilize the individuality and spur the decentralization which most users see as good and valuable. Individual users enjoy their own unique ways of doing things, and computers allow for hundreds of approaches to any problem or program. Every medium barters from both hands; perhaps computers most of all. The lack of standardization is detrimental to corporate values, but not necessarily to individual values.

Environmental impact studies have become popular as a method of predicting what physical changes can be expected when a bridge or dam is erected. Media are our mental environment, affecting our social and cultural relationships probably more than any other factor. Perhaps media impact studies should precede the introduction of new media into a culture. It was tried once, in the case of electronic funds transfer, and it should be tried again and again until we learn how to do it. New media always seem to grow like Topsy, without conscious planning or purposeful control. Historically this seems to be true in all cultures and places and may therefore become known as Media Principle One.

Principle Two:
New media always carry older media
as their content

Photographs became the content of movies, movies became the content of television. Poetry became the content of music, music became the content of LP records. With a little thought, nearly all media can be traced backward or forward in this manner. Each medium of communication has to have some type of content in order to justify its existence. Radios would never be purchased unless, when turned on, some speech or music could be expected. Each medium is a channel for something else, and the something else is always some prior medium. Speech is the content of the telephone. With partial humor it has even been observed that the planet earth is now the "content" of our thirteen hundred man-made satellites, their orbits spinning an electronic cocoon around the earth.

If many common media are to become the content of the computer, that is, if older media become the messages which the computer manipulates, then we should define them. In later chapters a full list of such media will be presented, ranging from the mimeograph to the classroom. The computer can imitate speech, graphics, photographs, print, music, and teachers, as we shall see.

In addition to the computer's ability to make old media its content, the computer gives rise to several wholly new communication channels. Electronic record management is one such new medium; the marriage of the computer with the file cabinet, brought to life by the giant data-base management programs and embraced broadly by the business community and government. Electronic funds transfer is another wholly new medium which has the potential to make obsolete, or to greatly modify, paper-based financial systems. The marriage of computers and credit cards produced this new medium. Electronic information retrieval is also a new medium, resulting from the marriage of computers, libraries and video-disks.

Are there any media which cannot be subsumed by the computer? The universality of the binary coding system of on-off electric pulses will be seen to provide a new "universal encoding system" into which all other coding systems can be translated. Once the messages of any medium are digitized, they can be sorted, rearranged and then converted back into any other medium. The answer to the question is "No."

The significance of Media Principle Two becomes clear when it is applied to computers. Computers can embrace all prior electronic media, enhance, empower and automate them, speed them up, recombine them, and output the results in any desired alternate medium. It may be an evolutionary ultimate; the final gene switch in the evolution of media. Though in the future other new media will be developed, they will always be children of the computer, either because of the digital coding system which new media will henceforth conform to, or because of the microcomputer which spawns them. Chapter 18 will present evidence to support this idea.

Principle Three:
New media seem to move from general uses to specific uses

This principle observes that most media in their early years serve generally homogeneous audiences but increasingly move toward more heterogeneous and specialized audiences. For instance, there were only three major television networks between 1950 and 1970. Today there are dozens of strongly competing networks, both cable and satellite, which serve specialized audiences such as the religious, the sporting, artistic, educational, etc. The same principle is true of radio, or magazine publishers. Many general purpose magazines that were popular between 1950 and 1960 have been hard-pressed to survive in the face of proliferating specialist journals. Gary Gumpert first proposed this theory in the *Journal of Communication* (September 1970), after which the idea could be traced through many other media.

Who have been the major users of computers? First came government. Then business and manufacturing. Then universities. The common functions which attracted these users were typically the automation of payrolls, budgets, accounts receivable, personnel data files and mailing lists. The large general-purpose computing machines served generally homogeneous types of audiences. Between 1954 and 1970 individuals could not easily execute personal projects on the big mainframe computers—not unless they had a personal relationship with the people in the computer center.

As time passed, the user groups became more specialized and the computer software became more individualized. Entire (large) computers began to be devoted to single functions such as information retrieval, research or timesharing. From 1970 onwards, timeshared computers allowed each user to imagine that he or she was the only user of the machine—that it was designed specially for the particular use to which he or she put it. The minicomputer extended this specialization further—a computer solely for typesetting, solely for assembly-line automation, solely for optical character reading, solely for chemical analysis, solely for libraries, specially designed for courtroom automation, etc. Chapter 7 attempts to document this evolution.

The personal microcomputer rounds out this trend toward ever more specialized personal use, each microcomputer being put to use in homes and offices in ways never previously envisioned. Just as the mimeograph made everyone a publisher, so the home computer will spread the awareness of how personal data can be manipulated. Energy and thermostat settings, household payments, even personal wine lists can all be input and recalled. Commodore's VIC computers and the Sinclair, selling for $99, are typical of popular home microcomputers.

The trend from general to specialized use can also be seen in the way in which computers have been accessed. Early access methods made computing seem difficult. Computer power belonged to those who could pay and who could get past the complexities of job control languages, operating system monitors, keypunching,

The low-cost home computer terminal rounds out the trend toward ever more specialized and personal uses for the computer. 800,000 home computer terminals had been
sold by 1981. The average home contained three microcomputers in various appliances
and games. This VIC 20 Commodore computer sold for about $300 in 1981. It featured
full-color graphics and three octaves of synthesizer sound. *(Photo courtesy Commodore
Business Machines.)*

etc. In the big central computer shops the flying card decks, spinning reels of tape and flashing lights would frighten the layman
away. Chapter 8 describes the move toward "user-friendly" microcomputers.

Access methods have gradually become more favorable. Small
jobs could not be run on computers in 1969, when the price was
$13 per minute. Today home microcomputers with their type-
writer keyboards can dial through the phone line into various
specialized computer networks such as pediatric data, legal data,
sociological data, available grants, and other data banks. Or the
microcomputer can operate locally to sort the home wine list or
scan the attic inventory.

Projecting to the future, as little home computers proliferate a
sudden "publication explosion" may be experienced, in which gov-

ernment and institutional files about people become accessed in so many ways by so many home computers that most personal information becomes public knowledge. If this happens, a rapid decentralization of power could occur, with the lay person having considerable influence on the functions of business, government and legislation. Chapter 15 describes this likely phenomena.

Principle Four:
Old media fade away unless adopted
by the newer media

Like elevator operators who were phased out of employment as automatic controls were installed, so do some old media pass away in the presence of newer communication channels. The quality of sound recording was so improved with vinyl LP records that few remnants of the older medium of Edison cylinders and discs can be found. The stereopticon is now an antique curiosity, because high quality three-dimensional slide machines replaced it. And the Pony Express went bankrupt about two years after the telegraph system reached to the West Coast.

Morse code, for instance, is still used, but it has not been adopted by the newer media; it is probably a dying medium. Ship-to-shore radio and citizens'-band radio have made it obsolete. Similarly, the use of computer-punched cards is declining now at the rate of 30 percent a year. But up to about 1972 computer users rarely sanctioned any other way of passing data to a computer: keypunching was thought to be the best method of data entry. Today, many computer centers have no card readers or card punches. These devices have become unnecessary in the presence of home microcomputers, online terminals, page scanners, bar-code readers and laser scanners. The punched card is probably a dying medium. Semaphore (communicating through flag signing) has its final use in parades and on aircraft carriers. It is probably on the list of endangered media.

Hundreds of media have been accepted for a few generations, only to be forgotten and lost in the presence of newer communication options. Like Latin, the media which we abandon take on a final romantic overtone. Somewhere there is probably a society forming to pursue the lost art of communicating through smoke signals.

Not all the older media fade away, however. Many of them take on new vigor and usefulness—especially when they are adopted or incorporated into the newer media. Movies were not made obsolete by television, in part because movies became a major content of the television medium.

Many of the older media do live on, and even take on new powers as they form relationships with the newer media. And the computer provides a boost for many of the older media. It offers them new reasons for existence; new functions to perform. Typewriters become word-processing terminals. Pianos become music synthesizers. Post offices become electronic mail stations. X-ray machines become digitized depth viewers.

What older media are activated or empowered by the computer? In later chapters this question will be applied to the medium of record-keeping—a medium as old as writing itself. The standards of paper width, file cabinet sizes and filing methods have not changed much over the years, but data-base management systems can put the data from file cabinets into electronic files and relate the diverse bits of data to each other in structures and hierarchies, allowing for search and navigation through the data. Reports can be creatively requested in ad hoc style. The science of record-keeping is likely to be given new power, new reasons for existence.

The world economy has relied on an economic system of paper money, paper checks, bank transfers and stock markets. These media of exchange have remained the same over the years, but will be speeded up by the computer and made to serve new functions. If electronic funds transfer becomes widespread, the use of paper-based systems will seem archaic, maybe romantic. But the principle suggests that money will probably not disappear; it will take on new uses and functions as it is integrated with the electronic financial systems.

In Chapter 17, Principle Four will be applied broadly to the cultural scene. Radio, the oldest of the speed-of-light media, serves a new, exciting role when it transmits digital signals from Mars to earth, the signals becoming photographs after computer decoding and translation. Other media are also empowered for new uses under the umbrella of this ultimate medium.

Projecting from this principle into the future, if surviving media live on by becoming computerized, and if media exist as communication channels from mind to mind and from institution to institution, then more than half of the labor force in the United States may be employed in information-processing or communications by 1990 or 2000. In 1980 approximately 30 percent of the labor force was thus employed.

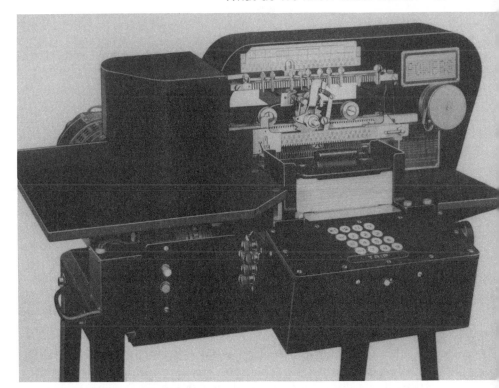

The Powers keypunch machine was used by the U.S. Census Bureau between 1920 and 1930. A model card is held at the top of the machine where forty-five columns and round holes are visible. Notice the absence of letters on the keyboard. Eventually the IBM 026 and 029 keypunches changed the standard to eighty columns, rectangular holes and twenty-six letters. Cards were a continuing means of supplying data to computers. Mainframe computers could not be ordered without card readers between 1954 and 1972 except for special installations. Today most data enters computers through terminals or optical character readers. *(Photo courtesy Sperry Corporation.)*

Principle Five:
Each medium biases or distorts the messages it passes

Since no medium can present the full range of sensory experience which humans enjoy, each medium distorts its messages with a particular bias, which is often difficult to observe. The media scholar asserts that the "common sense" notion that media are neutral servants, obediently passing messages to and fro, is not to be trusted. So subtly do the media bias their messages that it takes considerable scrutiny to see this point.

Even movies, which seem to present high-fidelity images of the world—including sights, sounds, motion, gesture, color, speech and music—still bias their messages heavily. If one adds three-dimensionality through holography or 3-D glasses, even if the screen surrounds the viewer, even if *smells* are released into the cinema at appropriate moments, the biases are still present.

The missing, unseen parts of the world are part of the bias, but the larger part is caused by the medium itself. For instance, all of the camera shots are selected. Someone determines the camera focus, zoom, frame, length, angle and duration of every shot. Someone selected who would be in the scene, what clothes they would wear, what type of cloud or sun should appear, etc. Viewers have no option regarding these things: it is done for them. They are manipulated. The theatre viewer cannot stop the film to examine a certain frame, or "read it backwards." The viewer cannot ask the cameraman to give a closer or rear view.

Such biasing factors in each medium are believed to be the crucial, though generally unobserved, distortions that are built into every medium we use. (Readers who wish to pursue this theme will enjoy McLuhan's book *Understanding Media: The Extensions of Man.*)

This principle raises questions in relation to computers. What special biases does the computer impose on its messages? What distortions does it introduce? Users "know" the accuracy of computer output and are therefore unlikely to notice or believe that the computer, too, can bias the messages which it seems to process so obediently.

A primary bias whereby the computer modulates its message is its instantaneous functioning. The computer's speed is usually part of its guise of efficiency: each job processed by the computer appears to work more efficiently, on account of the sheer speed of the operation. Most individuals would agree that there is more to life than speeding it up, but we behave privately and corporately as though speed is our ultimate mission in life. Million dollar computers are bought and maintained in order to capture this bias and put it to work in favor of the corporate annual report. As a result, many computer centers cannot feed paper to all of their printers as fast as the computer can generate the data. Therefore Computer Output on Microfilm (COM) units have become a popular recording medium, typically providing 10,000 "pages" on microfilm each hour. Citibank records 100 million frames each year in this manner.

Few counterforces to this bias can be identified at this time. The trend towards speed and efficiency in all things—a basic force in a competitive economy—will probably extend itself into the wish that *everything* should be computerized and thus made more "efficient." This will affect record-keeping, banking, the law, libraries, hotels, food production, sports, education, hospitals, airports, trucking: if something *can* be computerized it *will* be, for the sake of "efficiency." Byproducts of automation may give the process some redeeming value but the primary urge to computerize stems from the widespread drive for speed and efficiency in all things. The efficiency bias of the medium is enjoyed, corporately and privately. Why else would files of computer data be burgeoning? Why else would assembly lines be automated with robots and computers? Efficiency is considered beneficial by most computer users. It is something we might pay extra to get. And we do.

Principle Six:
New media reshape societies, their governments,
businesses, and educational systems

Education was profoundly reshaped by the invention of paper and the printed word: the main thrust of education for the past 500 years has been intimately tied to print and literacy. It is evident that the media of paper and print reshaped the purpose and goal of formal education. Every college library and bibliography attests this fact.

Television radically altered the business world with its potential for mass advertising and mass markets. Try to picture our culture without TV or radio commercials. Government processes were also reshaped by television, because politicians realized that their elections had more to do with television charisma than with their actual platforms. That is why 12,000 media people were assigned to cover 2000 delegates at the 1980 political conventions. Political processes were radically changed when war was seen in real time on the nightly news. New media have the power to reshape a culture.

This principle, in general terms, suggests that we are deeply altered and regrouped by each new dominant medium. The slide projector, the hand calculator, the citizens'-band radio, the digital watch, the tape cassette—these seemingly innocuous inventions initiate rapid change and new relationships among people and institutions in those cultures which embrace them.

When this is applied to the computer, several issues are raised.

The Johnson Space Center in Houston receives a continuous stream of data from space which must be reduced by computer and converted into photographs or other useful information. These multiple UNIVAC 1108s processed information from the Apollo and other NASA space projects.*(Photo courtesy Sperry Corporation.)*

How is the computer reshaping government, business, education, other media? Will the organization of business or government be affected? Will individuals inherit more decision-making power, or less? Will society experience increased centralization, or a decentralization of power?

These questions are addressed in many of the chapters of this book. The radical change in government organization is illustrated by the new Department of Defense, whose very existence is made possible by the worldwide communication systems which are now computerized in war rooms throughout the country. Generals now make decisions about details of battle far removed from direct experience of it, thanks to the computer.

Similarly, credit bureaus and banks make decisions about people based on several dozen details in a dossier, never actually meeting the individuals whose lives they affect.

The concept of individual privacy is hopelessly lost under the eye of computerized questionnaires, lie detectors, credit bureau networks, burgeoning government files and global satellite channels for computer-to-computer data transfer. Court decisions, it will be shown, clearly warn individuals not to expect privacy in their banking records. Insurance and medical information is often derestricted by the individual who signs the release that accompanies his or her insurance or medical questionnaire.

As media go, the computer is likely to generate more change in society than books, radio, movies or television, for it embraces all of these media, and society has embraced it, as installation statistics reveal. The computer will clearly become the dominant medium—the trend is certain and obvious. Electronic mail, word-processing and electronic funds transfer guarantee it. Credit cards with computers inside arrived in 1980, the computer reducing the account with each transaction. So did paging beepers carried on the hip—with memories and message display.

Using keyboards attached to TV sets, individuals will soon interact with each other in simple networks of communication—for bird watchers, coin collectors, war historians, physicists, water skiers, car salesmen, employment seekers—for every special interest which attracts mind to mind across the communication channels. It will make life different, publicly and privately.

Principle Seven:
New media often generate their own markets, their own need to be used

The tape recorder, originally thought to be of service only to radio studios, generated spin-off uses for such unexpected groups as teachers, spies, churches and psychiatrists. Multi-channel tape decks in cars and planes are commonplace, although they are not essential to travel.

Principle Seven observes that the original reason for embracing a new medium may be lost as the medium "suggests" other uses for itself. Some media seem to generate their own markets.

The computer is a classic example. Many corporate officers will state that when they first ordered a computer they didn't know what would be done with it. Ten years later they don't know anything of a business nature which it cannot do. Microcomputers are bought as Christmas presents, even when the recipients have no clear use for them.

Is the computer suggesting uses for itself beyond our rational intent? Are the towering computer files maintained by government really necessary? Governments functioned for years without computer assistance. But in a 1977 census, 6,739 files of information were carried by federal agencies, averaging 18 records for each person in the country. Since then many millions of dollars in computer equipment have been added each year to carry more and more files on the computer, for easy access and cross-reference. Such record-keeping could not be managed manually, but with computers, since it *can* be done, it *is* done.

Are the hundreds of data elements carried in payroll files or other business files really necessary? The pay check is an almost forgotten side-product in a vast state and federal reporting system, whose requirements increase each year precisely because the computer is assumed to be present in most businesses and schools. Therefore, since it *can* be done, it is *required* to be done.

This operates towards an outcome of total utilization of a medium. In the case of the computer, it points towards total computer dependency, because the more a medium is used, the more uses it suggests for itself. The microcomputer's capacity for new uses may be as rich as the universe which it models.

Principle Eight:
New media cause underlying
social values to change
through the metaphors they instill

People come to value the dominant traits of the media they rely upon, say the media scholars. The printing press and the alphabet universally impose a metaphor of sequentiality and linearity. Industrial revolutions have always followed in cultures which adopt phonetic alphabets. Assembly line events flow along sequentially, in a manner similar to the flow of letters and words in a book. In China, which historically used pictographic recording systems, and in tribal cultures, assembly lines make little or no sense, for the people have not yet adopted the metaphor "life is a series of sequential events like letters on a page or pages in a book." Our compartmentalization of jobs, or our job descriptions, do not make much sense to people unskilled in reading sequential letters on a page. In countries which have pictographic (non-sequential) styles of writing peasants usually drift back to their fields unless Westernized (print-oriented) foremen keep the assembly lines running.

Marshall McLuhan described the differences between cultures

that use phonetic alphabets, those that use non-sequential, pictographic alphabets, and those that have no alphabet. The presence or absence of these primary media etch the entire culture with a tell-tale impression. Edward Rondthaler, in *Life with Letters*, describes the changes which the invention of the phonetic alphabet triggered:

> Today we take it for granted that symbols—letters—can be strung together one after another to make a written word just as sounds are put together to make a spoken word. We take it for granted that if each letter represents a single sound, then our hands can write for our eyes to read any word that our ears can hear. Five thousand years ago this brilliant idea . . . doubled man's power of communication. It gave him the ability to write *anything* he could say and to make a permanent, accurate, visual record of speech.
>
> The phonetic alphabet, along with its equally remarkable numerals, is the major man-made miracle that underlies our Western Civilization. It gives us a reliable way to pass knowledge from generation to generation; to teach; to broaden the knowledge of the learned, and to transmit information and ideas from the learned to the unlearned—efficiently and accurately. Without phonetic symbols the West could never have overtaken the headstart of ancient Eastern Civilization. In the Orient, China's adherence to dead-end pictographic writing flagged its progress for 5000 years, ever widening the gap with the West.
>
> A short dispatch from Peking recently appeared in our newspapers: "The Central Committee of the People's Republic of China, announced this morning that a phonetic system of writing using the Roman alphabet, will be introduced into Yunan Province." If a similar dispatch had been issued in 3000 B.C. we'd be living in a world vastly different from the one we now see around us. Our science, technology, education, art, ethics, political and economic systems, race relationships, and probably our religion and philosophy would all have strong Oriental overtones. It is fascinating to picture what the world would be like if both East and West had shared in the use of phonetic symbols. Nothing man-made has been more influential than letters: their magic keeps speech from vanishing into thin air; their magic makes speech stand still; their magic passes on to us the speech, the knowledge, the wisdom of earlier generations. (p. 2)

Japan developed a phonetic alphabet for documenting its technology during the World War II. It was taught in schools and provided the basis for Japan's rapid industrialization. Without the sequential metaphor which letters of the alphabet quietly provide, the Japanese mechanical genius would not have emerged, according to Media Principle Eight. Industrial revolutions and assembly lines only come to cultures which adopt phonetic alphabets.

What new metaphors might the computer instill? If we embrace some of its basic features and become like it, what will those selected features be? Will our discursive, reasoning powers be promoted or diminished? Will our capacity for dreaming, loving or worshipping be promoted or diminished?

The dominant features of the computer, those most easily capturing the imagination of the public, are its instantaneity and simultaneity, its equal respect for every letter or word presented to it, and its solution of problems through the "systems" approach of rationality and logic.

If we picture a culture in which many individuals accept these traits as being valuable because they are fundamental to their beloved medium, what new values may be expected?

Because of its speed, the instant results which we get on our home computers may cause us to want all of our goods and services to be here *now*, instantly, just like our information. The pattern of instant food, speed reading and instant-on TV sets, when projected, indicates that people may never be satisfied with events which occur at less than the speed of light. Normal jets are too slow and the Concord jet will, eventually, also be considered too slow—it doesn't measure up to computers in speed. The dial phone causes delay in getting a connection, but the push-button phone is also becoming too slow for us. Cards inscribed magnetically with commonly called numbers can be inserted in a telephone for instantaneous connection—if you pay $200 to get the device.

Computers accept all instructions and data as equally authoritative. Does this mean that prejudices and bigotry might be more abhorred, more clearly seen for what they are? Does it mean that respect for alternate life styles, religions, skin colors, mores, might be promoted?

If the metaphor "life is an exercise in system design" is adopted, it will probably be applied to social problems, psychological problems, economic problems, political problems, pollution problems, poverty and every other problem in contemporary life. The results can sometimes be redeeming but more often may be humorous. Weizenbaum suggests that "since we do not . . . have any way of making computers wise, we ought not to give computers tasks that demand wisdom."

The trend toward new personal values can already be seen and, unfortunately, can be projected forward with no observed counterforces likely to divert them. Even the act of exposing these metaphors is unlikely to reduce the drive for efficiency. To say "You people are adopting efficiency and speed as a primary value because your computers and electronic media process things at nearly the speed of light" will probably not diminish the public's urge to speed. Ellul's exposure of the bad side of automation (*The Technological Society*, 1950) did not slow our rush to computerization. We read his book, agreed with him, but went ahead and automated our factories.

The computer has already presented itself and it has been adopted widely—without much public discussion. We are already becoming like computers in certain respects.

In summary, the eight general principles of media are:

1. New media are accepted with little forethought or planning.
2. New media always carry older media as their content.
3. New media seem to move from general to specific uses.
4. Old media fade away unless adopted by the newer media.
5. Each medium biases or distorts the messages it carries in significant ways.
6. New media reshape societies, their governments, bureaucracies and institutions.
7. New media often generate their own market, their own need for existence.
8. New media cause underlying social values to change through the metaphors which they instill.

The value which human beings place on information processing has its origins in both private and social instincts. *Privately,* each human possesses an inner desire to communicate, to extend internal brain waves and thoughts outside the body. The various media (speech, photographs, recordings) assist us in executing this urge. *Socially,* man produces electronic devices which manipulate and amplify the various communication media. Citizens'-band radios, telephones, computers, data communications, satellite networks and all of the media devices illustrate this cooperative, social endeavour.

The media are here to stay. Our minds need them, enjoy them, and constantly grope for new variations on the theme of communication. We bargain constantly with the universe, wrestling from it new styles and methods of communicating. Our future mind can be glimpsed in the evolving media. When such new communication channels alter our values, change our lifestyles or have an impact on society, we hardly notice. The mind will communicate, regardless of the change it imposes on our relationship. Deep in our cells, communication must be more important than security, for when we communicate, relationships change.

Bibliography

Ellul, J., *The Technological Society.* New York: Vintage, 1950.

Gumpert, G., "The Rise of Mini-Comm," *Journal of Communication* 20 (September 1970).

Martin, J., *Future Developments in Telecommunications,* 2nd ed. Englewood Cliffs, N. J.: Prentice-Hall, 1977.

———, *The Wired Society.* Englewood Cliffs, N. J.: Prentice-Hall, 1978.

McLuhan, M., *Understanding Media: The Extensions of Man.* New York: McGraw-Hill, 1964.

Postman, N., and C. Weingartner, *Teaching As a Subversive Activity.* New York: Delacorte Press, 1969.

Rondthaler, E., *Life with Letters.* New York: Hastings House, 1981.

Silver, G. A., *The Social Impact of Computers.* New York: Harcourt Brace Jovanovich, 1979.

Watson, J. D., *The Double Helix.* New York: Atheneum, 1968.

Weizenbaum, J., *Computer Power and Human Reason.* San Francisco: W. H. Freeman, 1976.

Zambino, M. P., "Microimage Technology and Practice," *Datamation* 10 (October 1977).

Chapter Three

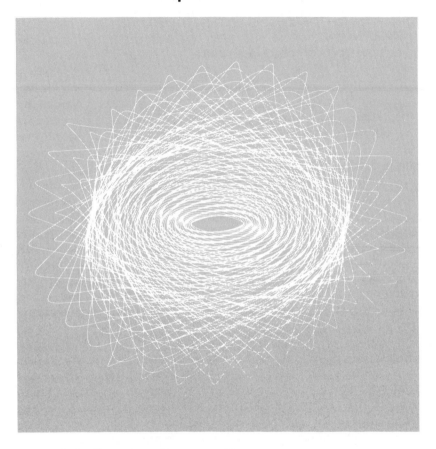

What Are Computers
Doing to Us?

- Computers have been integrated into society more rapidly than any other medium.
- In one view, technology and computers will lead the planet to eventual doom.
- In another view, only technology can enable the planet to support humanity in comfort and health.
- Nearly every process in society and in technology is now dependent on computer assistance.

General Electric Corporation installed the first publicly owned computer in its Louisville, Kentucky plant in 1954. Twenty-five years later approximately 1,800,000 computers of all sizes above the microcomputer were functioning throughout the United States. By 1980, 8,000,000 computers of all sizes were being shipped in a single year to federal and state governments, game manufacturers, appliance makers, car dealerships, homes and offices, schools, banks, and factories.

Computers and computer services have been accepted in our society with unparalleled speed. Nearly every area of our life and culture seems to have been influenced, and in some cases radically changed, by computer technology. With very little planning or prediction, our culture has moved from general mechanical automation in its factories to specific electronic automation—most of this occurring within the first twenty years of the new invention's life.

The state of our computer consciousness in 1955 might be judged now as infantile, given what we know today of the impact of computerization. In the late 1950s it was projected that one IBM 7090 class computer could accommodate all U.S. Government needs and that approximately ten such machines would satisfy the total requirements of the entire United States. Today tens of thousands of computers are installed which are hundreds of times more powerful than the early machines.

Unlike the case of the sewing machine or the multilith press, the acceptance of computers meant that personnel had to be retrained, office procedures and business cycles restructured, new professional groups of computer "experts" created and consulted and sizable funds committed. In terms of its scope and scale, and the brevity of the period in which it was accomplished, the computer revolution has no precedent in the history of our culture, or of any other.

The computer now has a broad impact on American life and

In 1955 the Metropolitan Life Insurance Company on Park Avenue in New York City installed a UNIVAC I computer. Fifteen segments of the computer were hoisted to the 29th floor. The street was blocked for two days. *(Photo courtesy Sperry Corporation.)*

culture. This impact of computers and other electronic technology upon society is recognized in both scholarly and popular literature. James Martin provides an excellent statement of our fear that simple human warmth is being caught up in a technological maze which we cannot control:

When my father visited his father, he walked to the other side of town. Now, to visit my father, I have to talk to the airline agent who communicates with a world-wide reservation computer network of great complexity. The plane I fly on is directed through the crowded sky above the airport by . . . computers, and then descends to foggy London airport under control of its on-board navigational computers. If I give flowers to my mother, I no longer pick them in the fields near home. I telex an international agency which delivers them wrapped in cellophane and uses computers for organizing its billing and inventory control of flowers grown out-of-season in greenhouses with artificial climates adjusted to market demand.*

This tendency for machines to replace friendly processes with impersonal formalization seems to have begun during the industrial revolution. Today it is vastly extended by the electronic media. What are the effects of machines and technology on people and their behavior? What dependencies develop as a result of computerization? What arguments support computerization as a useful activity? What arguments accuse it of being the cause of problems in society? Who is in control?

The effect of machines and technology on people and behavior

George Orwell published his widely read novel *1984* in 1949. In it he envisioned a society which had become a prisoner of its own technology and bureaucracy. As 1984 arrives, the prospects in this country do not seem to be quite as gloomy as the novel predicts, although the question of government surveillance of citizens' affairs and the issue of lost privacy is of great concern. In other parts of the world, government control is probably worse than Orwell predicted.

One feared effect of technology is that it will cause people to behave like the machines they tend. Eric Fromm summarizes the potential psychological impact of technology. Referring to society he suggests that we are already

a specter; a completely mechanized society, devoted to maximal material output and consumption, directed by computers; and in this social process, man himself is transformed into a part of the total machine, well fed and entertained, yet passive, unalive, and with little feeling. (*The Revolution of Hope*, p. 1)

---

* James Martin, *Design of Man-Computer Dialogues*, p. 5. © 1973. Reprinted by permission of Prentice-Hall, Inc., Englewood Cliffs, N.J.

Other writers regard the mechanical inventions of man as blessings whose impact for good or ill is ours to control. Alvin Toffler asserts:

> Only romantic fools babble about returning to a "state of nature." A state of nature is one in which infants shrivel and die for lack of elementary medical care, in which malnutrition stultifies the brain. . . . To turn our back on technology would be not only stupid but immoral.
>
> Given that a majority of men still figuratively live in the twelfth century, who are we even to contemplate throwing away the key to economic advance? Those who prate anti-technological nonsense in the name of some vague "human values" need to be asked "which humans?" To deliberately turn back the clock would be to condemn billions to enforced and permanent misery at precisely the moment in history when their liberation is becoming possible. We clearly need not less but more technology. (*Future Shock,* p. 428)

This focuses on the economic improvements which occur through technology. Technology brings antibiotics and comfort to the world. It also promises to ease those areas of life where routine, mechanistic, repetitive tasks are performed.

However, the results of automation sometimes trade one liability for another. For instance, the paperwork required for the design and construction of a jet bomber usually weighs more than the plane itself. Similarly, after 400 miles of computer tape were recorded from a single space satellite, scientists realized that it would require five men 500 years to analyze the data and convert it to useful information.

Martin Greenberg, writing of the impact of technology states:

> Many find it profoundly disturbing when, in their eyes, they see the country become a city and the city a social sore; nature's waters turned to waste and the air to ashen smog; the hopelessness of war and a world population out of control. They ask, what is technology's role in this modern tragedy, Satan or savior? (*Computers, Communications, and the Public Interest,* p. iv)

Technology has deeply affected society. Its evaluation and worth-assessment is the unanswered question. If the question were local to one culture or land, it might not be so critical. But the problem now affects the globe. The National Academy of Science reports:

> Most of the undesired effects of technological change are still reversible, (although) at ever higher costs, by yet further applications

of science and technology, or by changes in habits, attitudes, and institutional arrangements. But as these effects become more nearly global in scale we may . . . find ourselves faced with consequences that are truly irreversible—for example, profound climatic changes, or permanent alterations in ecological regimes. . . .

One unnamed scientist, quoted in the book *1994: The World of Tomorrow,* edited by J. Newman, states that:

No one—not even the most brilliant scientist alive today—really knows where science is taking us. We are aboard a train which is gathering speed, racing down a track on which there are an unknown number of switches leading to unknown destinations. No single scientist is in the engine cab and there may be demons at the switch. Most of society is in the caboose looking backward. (p. 27)

The relentless advancement of technology is portrayed in the work of Samuel Florman in his brilliant and respected work *The Existential Pleasures of Engineering.*

The newspapers report that the Bulgarian government, bowing to consumer discontent, is attempting to provide more and better washing machines. This is not "technique" run wild or "the suave technocracy" exploiting the people. *This is Bulgarians wanting washing machines.*

It is common knowledge that millions of underprivileged families want adequate food and housing. What is less commonly remarked is that after they have adequate food and housing they will want to be served at a fine restaurant and to have a weekend cottage by the sea. People want tickets to the Philharmonic and vacation trips abroad. They want fine china and silver dinner sets and handsome clothes. The illiterate want to learn how to read. Then they want education, and then more education, and then they want their sons and daughters to become doctors and lawyers. It is frightening to see so many millions of people wanting so much. It is almost like being present at the Oklahoma land rush, except that millions are involved instead of hundreds, and instead of land, the prize is everything that life has to offer.

People seem to be willing to enter into partnership with machines even though the ends of that relationship are undetermined. Florman's statement suggests that the will of humanity, its urge for beauty, affluence, travel and comfort, seems to demand technology. Hence the impact of technology is broad and pervasive.

What dependencies result from computerization?

Our dependence upon technology is not disputed. Less obvious is the dependence of nearly all technology upon the computer. Computer services are so versatile and subtle that the day-to-day operations of most government and business agencies now rely upon the reports, terminals, data-links, comparisons and data-banks of the computer service centers.

Several suggestive examples may be mentioned. Rocket and satellite technology could not develop into a serious or successful program until computer technology was sufficiently developed to compute orbits and other rapidly changing factors within the dynamic time frames which space travel required. Rocket technology had existed for many years but had to await the electronic support on which it now depends for full realization of its potential. Neither man nor machine could land on the moon until there were computers to coordinate the event.

Telephone and other communication services are similarly dependent on computers for their day-to-day operations. The functions of line switching, message switching, satellite tracking, signal conversions from one national standard to another and even the conversion of dialling conventions from one nation to another are all computer automated. Half the population of the U.S. would have to work for the telephone companies in order to maintain today's level of telephone services if computers were removed from the scene. A telephone bill is printed (by computer) each month for every telephone owner in the country, an event made possible by the computer log which enters every call day or night.

Similar illustrations could be drawn from medicine, science, hospitals, schools, libraries, transportation, and nearly every cooperative human activity in the culture.

The arguments for and against computer dependency

What good or evil is likely to result from our dependency upon electronic assistance at so many levels of life? Rothman and Mosmann describe two conflicting viewpoints:

> Our society is in the midst of a debate to determine whether technology can be controlled and directed toward the achievement of

sound goals and the betterment of man or whether its path must lead to the restriction and destruction of human liberty. In no field has this choice been viewed with more alarm than in the development and use of the modern electronic digital computer. The computer has emerged as one of the most revolutionary inventions of this century. Hardly two decades old, its impact is so little explored that its full impact . . . cannot be foreseen.*

The debate centers on the question: can computer uses be directed so as to achieve positive social goals for the betterment of man, or will technology, made ever more efficient through computers, lead mankind into decline, reducing freedom and liberty? Will computer automation make us more dependent on government and bureaucracy, or less dependent? More centralized as a culture, or more decentralized? Will human relationships become more warm and thoughtful, or more distant and uncaring? Will the rational heritage of mankind be enhanced, or threatened? Both sides of this debate are represented in the extracts from writings that follow. Lewis Yablonsky amplifies the negative impact of automation in his work *Robopaths*. One representative statement summarizes his point of view:

> Modern mass society, the technocratic state, and their machine domination of people have grossly altered the patterns and styles of human interaction. Their ultimate impact has been the dehumanization of people to the point where much of their social interaction is machine-like. People's emotions, spontaneity, creativity, personal identity, and ability to be compassionate are increasingly reduced to a set of robopathic responses. This subtle social pathology infects all levels of human interaction, from interpersonal relationships in a primary group, such as family or love relationships, on through secondary groups, such as corporate and political associations. I am alleging, therefore, that technocracies and the machine way of life have transformed human groups partially . . . into social machines. A social machine is a dehumanized interaction system wherein people's relationships are relatively devoid of sincere emotions, creativity and compassion. (p. 91)

This negative view of technology and automation was first made respectable in 1964 when Jacques Ellul's book *The Technological Society* was translated from French into English. In this famous

---

* From *Computers and Society*, p. 1, by Stanley Rothman and Charles Mosmann. © 1972, Science Research Associates, Inc. Reprinted by permission of the publisher.

work, Ellul personifies the abstract concept of "technique," attributing to it a personality, will, drive and personal power of its own, against which mere humans have little to say or do.

> Technique integrates the machine into society. It constructs the kind of world the machine needs and introduces order where the incoherent banging of machinery heaped up ruins. It clarifies, arranges, and rationalizes; it does in the domain of the abstract what the machine did in the domain of labor. It is efficient and brings efficiency to everything. Technique . . . leads to a more rational and less discriminate use of machines. It places machines exactly where they ought to be and requires of them just what they ought to do. (p. 5)

During the period of Professor Ellul's authorship (1950–53) there were few if any computers in France, and only a few computers installed even in the United States. Ellul could not have had the foresight to predict the widespread global trend toward electronic automation, and given his view of society's ills in the presence of mere mechanical and industrial automation, such a foresight might have caused him to redouble his gloomy prophecies. The book arrived just in time to catch Americans in the act of computerization. Why did it elicit such a wide reading audience and yet have such little influence? Despite Ellul's dire predictions of negative sociological impact, we went ahead into the computer years seemingly assured that the benefits of automation would outweigh the ills. Perhaps it was due to the other voices who spoke positively of the urge to automate. Buckminister Fuller recognized that negative outcomes might result from the applications of technology but he wrote of the *political* origins of those ills, arguing that the fault does not lie with technology, but rather with the political management of techology. In his view, the benefits of automation and technology when properly managed far outweigh the faults. His general plea was for the public to demand non-political control of the technology.

> The comprehensive introduction of automation everywhere around the earth will free man from being an automaton and will generate so fast a mastery and multiplication of energy-wealth by humanity that we will be able to support all of humanity in ever greater physical and economic success anywhere around this little spaceship earth. (p. 362)

Arguing positively that computerization will assist the betterment of society, Marshall McLuhan isolates the computer as the final technology needed to fill out the trend of electronic media toward the "global village." He writes:

> Men are suddenly nomadic gatherers of knowledge, . . . informed as never before, free from fragmentary specialism as never before—but also involved in the total social process as never before; since with electricity we extend our central nervous system globally, instantly interrelating every human experience. . . .
>
> It is possible to "fly" unbuilt airplanes on computers. So with new organizations of many kinds. We can now, by computer, deal with complex social needs with the same . . . certainty. (*Understanding Media*, p. 310)

The central, unique thrust of computer and media ecology is that computers and computer services should be respected for their ability to augment and empower the entire spectrum of communication media. Not only do computers utilize all other media as input and output devices, but they are a communication medium through which we pass transactions of all types, including financial, mathematical, medical, business and many others. Thus, as a medium of communication computers are likely to follow those laws or principles which other newly introduced media have followed.

Who is in control?

Increasing public attention is being given to questions of data-privacy and computer dependency. The press has at times published sensationalized stories of computer errors and operator crimes, not always balancing these stories by reporting the social good which also accompanies computer services. The alarms have not noticeably slowed the computer installation rate, however. In Chapter 12 the question of personal privacy and legal safeguards will be analyzed.

Congress has sponsored various investigations related to the computer's impact on society. Gerald Ford chaired the "Domestic Council Committee on the Right of Privacy." As president he signed into law the Privacy Act (Public Law 93-597) in September 1975.

Computer programmers, system analysts and other professionals are not themselves in a position to affect the social impact of the technology they work with, although they frequently see the issues more clearly, being closer to the details of computer activ-

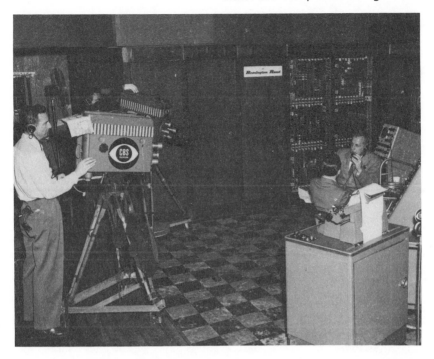

In 1952 this primitive UNIVAC I computer predicted early in the evening that Dwight D. Eisenhower had won the presidential election by a landslide. Thinking that it was wrong, programmers changed the mathematical formulas to make the predictions less radical. By the next morning, with the results in, the programs were restored to their original formulas, which had been correct. *(Photo courtesy Sperry Corporation)*

ities. The largest computer professional organization is the Association for Computing Machinery. In 1972 the members formed a special interest group known as "Computers and Society." The occasional publications of this group are of interest to those who care about the long term view. (ACM, 1133 Sixth Avenue, New York, New York 10036)

Computer services began to be utilized between 1952 and 1954. Policies to govern the flow of information from business to business and from nation to nation were still not in place in 1980, but will probably be brought into existence in the next decade. The issues are at least as complex as the electronic circuits which give rise to them. Our legislators will be making rules on issues whose effect is not currently predictable or evaluated. By viewing the computer as an environment, we may be able to sharpen the issues and contribute, through the collection of basic data and the application of media theory, to an eventual control strategy. Through better planning we can optimize the outcomes, making the future more predictable and life more comfortable for later generations of our society.

The outcomes of computerization should not be the result of accident and drift. Our culture should not be directed only by the commercial drive of salesmen, whose purpose might be to install ever more computers regardless of their uses or social effects. There are things the computer can do which should be prohibited from being done. Can we agree what they are? Should laws be passed to support our opinion? The social impact should be foreseen, planned, controlled and predicted as a logical and desired goal of the whole society. Computer ecology, as an evolving discipline, should be able to clarify further the issues and principles through which positive outcomes can be achieved.

Bibliography

Ellul, J., *The Technological Society,* translated by John Wilkinson. New York: Knopf, 1964.

Florman, S., *The Existential Pleasures of Engineering.* New York: St. Martin's, 1976.

Fromm, E., *The Revolution of Hope: Toward a Humanized Technology.* New York: Harper & Row, 1968.

Fuller, R. B., *Utopia or Oblivion: The Prospects for Humanity.* New York: Bantam, 1969.

Greenberg, M., *Computers, Communications, and the Public Interest.* Baltimore: Johns Hopkins University Press, 1971.

Greenspan, L., ed., *Protecting Your Right to Privacy.* Washington, D.C.: U.S. Government Printing Office, 1975.

Gumpert, G., "The Rise of Mini-Comm," *Journal of Communication* 20 (September 1970).

IBM and the Courts: A Six Year Journal. Waltham, Ma.: International Data Corporation, 1976.

Laurie, R. D., *Computers, Automation, and Society.* Homewood, Ill.: Irwin, 1979.

Martin, J., *Design of Man–Computer Dialogues.* Englewood Cliffs, N.J.: Prentice-Hall, 1973.

McLuhan, M., *The Gutenberg Galaxy: The Making of Typographic Man.* Toronto: University of Toronto Press, 1962.

————, *Understanding Media: The Extensions of Man.* New York: McGraw-Hill, 1964.

"National Academy of Science," *Report on Technology Assessment.* Washington, D.C.: National Academy of Science, 1969.

Newman, J., ed., *1994: The World of Tomorrow*. Washington, D.C.: U.S. News and World Report, 1973.

Orwell, G., *1984*. New York: Harcourt Brace Jovanovich, 1949.

Pritchard, A., *A Guide to Computer Literature*. London: Clive Bingley, 1972.

Rothman, S., and C. Mosmann, *Computers and Society*. Chicago: Science Research Associates, 1972.

Spencer, D. D., *Fundamentals of Digital Computers*. Indianapolis: Howard W. Sams, 1969.

Toffler, A., *Future Shock*. New York: Random House, 1972.

Yablonsky, L., *Robopaths*. Indianapolis: Bobbs-Merrill, 1972.

Chapter Four

How to Recognize a Medium When You See One

- Communications media possess five common features.
- These features are embedded in computers in uniquely flexible ways.
- The computer is able to manipulate, control or amplify all of the other electronic media.
- The computer is a universal media manipulator.

Not every stick and stone qualifies as a medium. Our definition of the word "medium" has been very broad, but it does not include the whole universe. How is one to recognize a medium? What distinguishes a medium from the rest of the world? In this chapter the outward characteristics of media will be identified.

The early computer designers had a problem of symbol manipulation to solve. Lengthy, complex problems in mathematics—often dealing with the aiming of guns or the splitting of the atom—made them wish for a calculating machine that could be varied or "reprogrammed" according to need—one week to solve equations, the next week to handle problems in theoretical physics. In the early 1800s the Jocquard loom was devised, which used cards with holes to "program" the loom for different types of tapestry, and that idea made many inventors hopeful that a calculating engine could someday be reprogrammed with similar ease. If an electronic "universal engine" could be designed to perform any sequence of mathematical operations, then its list of operating directions could be changed from day to day, making it a universal problem-solving machine. Thus it could be set to add, then add again, then multiply by the first number squared, then pull in numbers from a storage device, add them to the list, and so on. The next day this flow of instructions could be completely changed.

It was not until calculators began to use *electronic* pulses to do their computations that this hope of readjusting them from day to day became more feasible. This concept was implemented by several inventors, and they called their machine a "computer." In 1944 Howard H. Aiken's Harvard Mark I Sequence Controlled Calculator received its instructions from a long loop of punched paper tape, allowing it to calculate trajectories, and with a change of tape it could calculate Bessel functions. It was driven by relays.

The early designers were forced to look closely at the medium of mathematics. They were attempting to "empower" the medium of mathematical notation. They wished to make the various uses of mathematical formulas more flexible and more rapid in their execution. Somewhat by accident, with a few modifications, the

Computer tapes are shelved in fire-proof areas. On such tapes are stored the financial and business details of entire corporations. The magnetic tape is half an inch wide and is similar to audio tape except that magnetic spots represent numbers and letters rather than sounds. Human operators mount the tapes in the central computer room when the computer requests them.

digital computer was able to control or coordinate other electronic media, even those unrelated to mathematics. The arithmetic engine described above came so close to fulfilling perfectly the criteria of features common to all media that the step from it to a *universal media manipulator* was made without any other inventive effort.

What *are* the outward features that characterize all communication media?

1. Each medium must have a set of symbols with its own grammar of relationships, syntax, sentences or agreed-upon relationships.

2. Each medium must have a way of receiving messages from outside communicators. Ears, microphones and eyes are typical input devices.

3. Each medium transmits messages to receivers outside itself.

4. Each medium uses some other medium as a communication channel for 2 and 3 above.

5. An advanced medium uses some other medium as a recording device for storage and replay.

The universality of these features can be seen in Table 4.1, which fits particular media into the framework of these five features.

Since the computer provided for all five of these features, it was quickly used to handle media other than mathematical symbols. Alphabetic materials of all types quickly began to be sorted, compared or rearranged in delightful discoveries of the computer's potential.

For instance, since computers were built to provide any of the math functions (for example, add, subtract, multiply) at any time in any sequence, it was relatively easy to invent other functions which would allow the manipulation of alphabets. The "concatenation" function is typical, as when one word or group of letters is added on to another group of letters. Thus, if commanded to concatenate A with B the result would be AB. If 12 is concatenated with 301 the result is 12301. If "Hello" is concatenated with "John" the result is "Hello John." If the payroll file is concatenated with the personnel file, the resulting file carries both sets of data. Many other such functions were made integral parts of computers and their languages.

In 1954, nearly all of the popular communication media had an electronic recording base. Tape recorders, LP records and magnetic cards on business machines made it easy for computers to access the contents of any of these devices, rearrange the data and send it back to any other recording medium. The computer empowers these media, giving them new levels of usefulness and new options for playback and revision of data. Consider the functions of selection, sorting and reformatting, and how these functions apply universally to any medium.

Selection

Pick out all places on this video tape where red is the dominant color.

Table 4.1
Five features of all media

Medium	1. Unique symbol set	2. Input device	3. Transmitter for output	4. Secondary medium for communication	5. Storage and replay medium
Speech	The sounds (phonemes) of words and sentences of a language	Ear	Mouth	Air waves and vibrations	Human brain, writing, print, tapes, records
Gesture	Socially assigned meanings of movement or stance	Eye	Body	Light and shadow	Brain, painting, TV tape, movie, photo
Home TV set	Camera scene choices, event choices, screen size, color fidelity	Antenna and channel selector	Picture tube and speaker	Radio signal of electromagnetic vibrations	TV tape
Telegraph	Morse encoding of alphabets from any language	Telegraph key	Buzzer	Copper wire or radio channel	Printed dots or audio tape

Telephone	The sounds of speech plus telephone manners and voice fidelity	Vibrating mouth piece	Vibrating ear-phone	Copper wire or microwave channel	Audio tape
Movie film	Camera scene choices, event choices, makeup, dress choices	Movie camera	Movie projector and screen	Light and sound	Film, TV tape, video-disk
Adding machine	Symbolic representation in arabic numerals, or other base	Key in numbers	Paper tape or screen	Screen or paper or internal memory	Printer tape with visible numbers
Printed book	Symbolic representation of speech sounds, sequentially arranged	Typesetter or photocomposer	Reader viewing light and dark shapes of letters	Ink on paper	Paper, computer tape, microfilm
Computers	On or off switches or bits; binary representations of any letter or number	Any other desired electronic medium; often cards, tape or typewriters	Any other desired electronic medium; often printed paper, tape or disk	Any communication channel: radio, telephone system, microwave, copper wire	Computer disks or tapes, cards

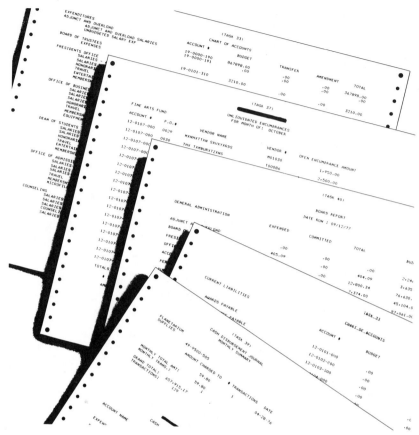

These budget reports are typical of thousands of printouts produced by high-speed computer printers at the rate of one page every one to three seconds. The reports were produced by a budgetary accounting system which a comptroller uses in the financial management of a college.

Or where speech occurs without music.

Pick out all places on this audio tape where the phoneme "eek" occurs.

Or on this typesetter's tape where the word "cult" appears.

Or on this typesetter's tape where misspelled words occur.

Sorting

Resequence this video tape into an ascending sequence of frames by the total amount of light projected from dark to light.

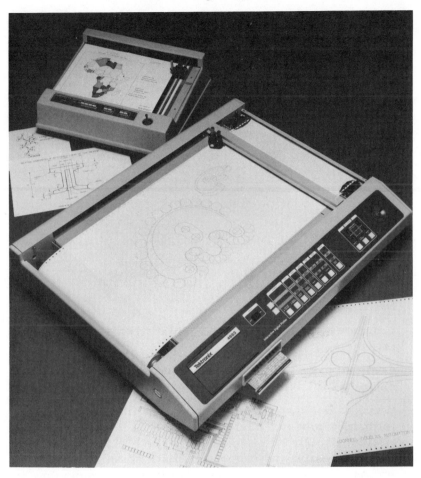

Plotting devices like this one from Tektronix allow governments, small engineering firms and graphic artists to apply the computer to a wide variety of tasks ranging from aircraft design to election district mapping. *(Photo courtesy Tektronix.)*

Or into dominant color groups starting with yellow.

Resequence this computer tape of words into alphabetic order and count the number of uses for each word.

Resequence this computer disk file into zip code order.

Reformatting

Tally all of today's sales and graph them by product line on a TV screen.

Print a report with company names on the left instead of the right.

Read a magnetic tape of data and print it in alphabetic order.

Media conversion or translation

Convert radio signals coming from Saturn spacecraft into photographs.

Convert letters on drivers' licenses into computer disk records.

Convert TV camera images into a typewritten picture.

Convert telephone pushbutton signals into banking and financial transactions.

Convert copying machine images into a telephone signal and transmit to another copy machine in another city. Along the way, reduce it to half size.

Comparison

Compare records from banks with records from internal revenue.

Compare today's newspaper to yesterday's newspaper. Which one refers to China more often?

Compare one disk file to another. (The files may contain information from any other medium.)

Computers satisfy all of the criteria for classification as a medium. As we shall see, as universal media manipulators they are the new foundation on which all other electronic media must sooner or later begin to depend.

Chapter Five

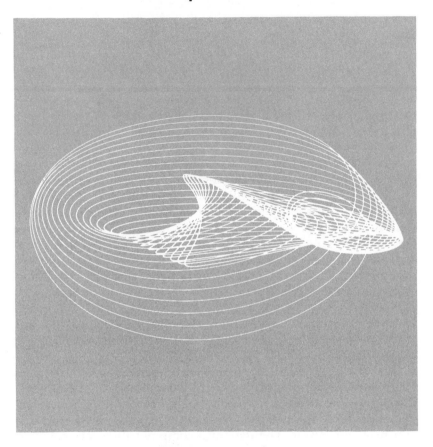

The Birth
of the Computer

- ☐ It is impossible to locate the very first phonograph record, car or computer.
- ☐ A long history of converging ideas preceded the birth of the computer in 1946.
- ☐ New media are quite invisible compared to the messages they pass and the things they do.
- ☐ The computer became available to corporations in 1954.
- ☐ The microcomputer revolution started in 1974.

The history of computer usage spans only a few decades. Yet the precise dates of the inventions that gave birth to it are subject to question. When were computers first used, and at what point of their development did they become a significant social innovation? Many historians have remarked upon the difficulty of tracing the origins of historical innovation. A phenomenon of "invention evanescence" (the phrase is coined here) seems to occur whenever an attempt is made to pinpoint the facts concerning social innovations. At the time of writing, two of the inventors of the computer are still living, but in their speeches and in personal conversation with me they have difficulty remembering the dates, and even sometimes the partners, of their inventions. In 1975 John Atanasoff won a federal lawsuit in which he claimed to be equal with J. P. Eckert, Jr. and J. Mauchly in the invention of the computer. New textbooks will include Dr. Atanasoff's name among the primary inventors, although the early writers and inventors who were close to the event do not include him.

D. D. Spencer and H. D. Huskey differ by four years (1949 and 1952 respectively) in stating the operational date of the EDVAC computer. The difference probably results from the delay between the receipt of funding of the project and the public demonstration of a problem solved. The date of a computer discovery could be the date of the first electric current passing through it, the date of its first test run or the date of its first published solution.

Some of the early hardware still exists in museums. At the Moore School of Electrical Engineering in Philadelphia parts of the original ENIAC computer are preserved. Other parts of it are in the Smithsonian Institution in Washington, D.C. Of course, the ENIAC is in pieces, abandoned after four years of development and revision. The original ENIAC is lost forever. One of the first assignments given to ENIAC, in 1946, was a problem in nuclear physics. It produced the answer in about two hours. Early users

ENIAC, invented by J. Mauchly and J. P. Eckert, Jr., in 1946, filled this room at the Moore School of Electrical Engineering in Philadelphia. It is believed to be the first programmable computer. The concept of main memory came later when Mauchly and Eckert built their BINAC in 1948. *(Photo courtesy Sperry Corporation.)*

observed that one hundred mathematicians using mechanical calculators would have had to work for a year to get the same result. Their accuracy, of course, would have been in doubt.

Several of the pioneers of the early years were interviewed for this book, including Drs. Eckert and Mauchly and Captain Grace Hopper. The facts gleaned from these interviews are almost less important than a realization of the sense of subjectivity that surrounds reflections about the past.

New beginnings are delicate. The bud of most flowers gives little hint of the brilliant colors that will follow. Teilhard de Chardin observes in *The Phenomenon of Man* that the first artifact of any era or species is usually lost:

Close as they are to us, where are the first Greeks and Romans? Where are the first shuttles, chariots or hearthstones? And where . . . are the first motor cars, aeroplanes or cinemas? In biology, in civilization, in linguistics, as in all things, time . . . rubs out every weak line in the drawing of life. Except for . . . consolidated achievements, nothing . . . subsists of what has gone before. . . . All the terminal enlargements of the fans [species] are only prolonged into the present by their survivors or their fossils.

When we look back, . . . everything seems to have burst into the world ready made. (p. 121)

In order to probe the birth of the computer, one might begin with the year 1954 since the public had access to computer power for the first time in that year (at high price). The General Electric Corporation was the first commercial firm to engage in business data processing. In 1954 it installed the UNIVAC I in its Louisville, Kentucky facility, using it for business purposes until 1972. Since it was the first private user of computers, G.E.'s installation may mark the beginning of the social acceptance of computers and the beginning of the computer era. A lot of experimentation preceded the year 1954, but after it government, business and education began to purchase computers for a variety of problem-solving tasks.

The early inventors of programmable computers improved their discoveries very quickly, across a five-year period. Just as at conception an embryo shows little evidence of later growth to come, so these early users of computers could not predict the multi-billion dollar business which would descend from their patents within fifteen or twenty years. The idea of a computer on a half inch square chip, or a $300 computer for the home, could not be projected from the computing experiences of the years 1950 to 1960.

Figure 5.1 indicates that computing has its origins in various calculating devices which, in their time, represented significant social innovations.

In 1642, the mathematician Pascal published this advertisement for his solution to an accountant's drudgery.

Dear reader, this notice will serve to inform you that I submit to the public a small machine of my invention, by means of which you alone may, without any effort, perform all the operations of arithmetic, and may be relieved of the work which has often times fatigued your spirit, when you have worked with the counters or with

Figure 5.1
Inventions leading to the idea of computers

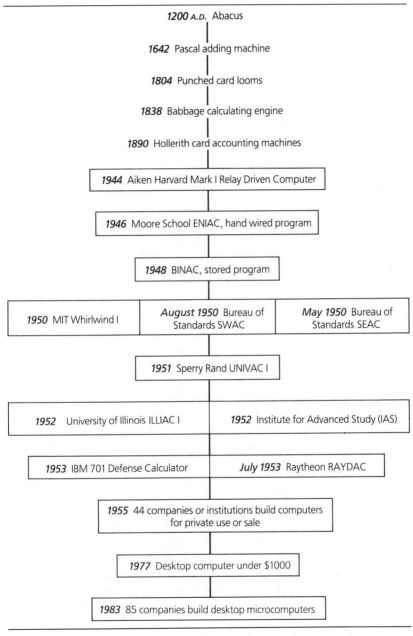

the pen. (Pascal, quoted in D. E. Smith, *A Sourcebook in Mathematics*, p. 166)

The card-processing machines which H. Hollerith created for use in the 1890 census analysis gave credence to the idea of mechanical manipulation of numbers. But the actual creation of a programmable machine was a task awaiting the arrival of vacuum tubes and later technology. The idea for a "calculating analytical engine" was presented by Charles Babbage in 1838, but the idea could not be fully executed with mechanical constructs. Later, using electronics, it was fully implemented, permitting a desired program or sequence of directions to be stored within the machine in the same electronic form as the calculations themselves. This idea of a stored-program computer was the converging result of many previous ideas and it soon gave birth to a new medium of communication, to a new industry, and to a new alternative for human culture and for the human mind.

Table 5.1 presents a chronology of the early computers, their settings and the uses they were put to which justified the tremendous investment required.

Brainerd, Eckert, and Mauchly built the ENIAC computer in 1946 at the Moore School of Electrical Engineering in Philadelphia. The components from which it was made had existed for 15 years. No new materials were required. They claim that it was the first stored program computer. If a different sequence of tasks was requested, the reprogramming process commonly took one to five days, even when the program was known. (Today most computers load their programs in less than one second.) Two years after, the ENIAC the EDSAC stored program machine was demonstrated in Manchester, England, and output from it was mailed to interested parties in the United States.

The stories behind these historical triumphs are dramatic, paralleling in excitement the discovery of the double helix DNA molecule. The 18,000 vacuum tube machines generated tremendous heat compared to their modern hand-held equivalents. They sometimes ran for twenty minutes between failures. Today certain hand-held calculators are programmable and are as fast and powerful as the early ENIAC, but the idea of building an electronic machine which would do nothing until it received instructions supplied by a program was a new idea, established in theory by Babbage and in reality by the pioneer computer users.

Prior to 1954 nearly all computer uses were centered on research to make computers better, or were geared toward war-related prob-

Table 5.1 Early computing machines and their inventors

Year	Machine	Place	Persons	Use
1944	MARK I	Harvard	Aiken	Relay driven calculator
1946	ENIAC	Moore School, Philadelphia	Eckert, Brainerd, Mauchly	Missile trajectories Hydrogen bomb
1948	Williams TUBE	Manchester University, England	Williams	Store TV images digitally
1949	EDSAC	Cambridge University, England	Wilkes	Mathematical calculating
1949	EDVAC	Moore School, Philadelphia	von Neumann, Eckert, Mauchly	Ballistic and weapons study
1949	BINAC	E M Corporation, Philadelphia	Eckert, Mauchly	Mathematical problem solving
1949	SWAC	Los Angeles	IBM Corporation	Electronic calculator
1950	SEAC	Washington	Bureau of Standards	Air force logistics Hydrogen bomb
1951	UNIVAC	Sperry Rand Corporation, Philadelphia	Eckert, Mauchly	Bureau of Census: 15 machines made
1952	ILLIAC I	University of Illinois		Research
1952	IAS	Princeton	Goldstein, Neumann, Burks	Mathematical research
1953	IBM 701	New York		Defense calculating
1954	IBM 650	New York		Most widely used computer prior to 1959 Sold to government and industry
1955	IBM 702 IBM 704 IBM 705	New York		Sold to research laboratories and service bureaus

In 1948 J. P. Eckert, and J. Mauchly formed a company to sell their BINAC computer. Only two were made; both for Northrop Aviation. The concept of main memory was incorporated using mercury delay lines for the memory. Notice the drum, vacuum tubes and extensive air-conditioning. *(Photo courtesy Sperry Corporation.)*

lems. The Manhattan Project, which brought the atomic bomb into existence, utilized card-processing equipment to great advantage in reducing nuclear theory to a physical and chemical possibility. Electronic computers were invented and demonstrated one year later, and immediately were put to use to assist in the refinement of the nuclear sciences, and to hasten the development of the hydrogen bomb.

A few writers attempted to forecast the future of computing, and their works are available to the curious who wish to examine snapshots of the state of scientific awareness between 1948 and 1954. Probably the best-known prognosticators were Edmund Berkeley, John von Neumann and John Diebold. Only a few were brave enough to view computers as an ultimate or revolutionary discovery. Edmund Berkeley's book *Giant Brains,* published in 1949, was one.

New media have always been difficult to forecast. Their applications and services are so visible that the medium itself can hardly be observed. The environment of the human mind is *all of the media of communication.* And of all the media, the computer will come to be seen as the ultimate media manipulator. Only now is this awareness developing: when the computer was born, the concepts of media ecology were undeveloped. Since our mental environment was largely invisible to most people in 1950, the computer can be said to have been born in a manger, with little fanfare or promise.

The rapid acceptance of computers and the rapid cycle of im-

Card processing machines were introduced by Hollerith to the Census Bureau in 1890. In 1910 this device sorted cards by mechanically identifying where the holes were punched. Many passes of the cards were required to obtain a final sorted card deck. This type of processing became known as "unit record" or "card processing". It was used extensively between 1900 and 1965, lending credibility to the concept of data processing. It helped to ready the culture for the computer years which followed. *(Photo courtesy Sperry Corporation.)*

IBM's SSEC (Selectric Sequence Electronic Calculator) was introduced in January 1948. It was IBM's first large-scale electronic machine. 400,000 digits could be referenced on the large hanging loops of paper tape. Main memory was invented a few months later in the Mauchly-Eckert BINAC. *(Photo courtesy IBM.)*

provements on them has never been equalled by any other medium. In popular terms, four generations of computers have been begotten in the forty year period between 1950 and 1990. Compare this to the improvements in the printing industry as described by Rondthaler in *Life with Letters:*

> More than three and a half centuries passed by after Gutenberg with no significant change in the printing industry. Then the giant began to stir. Between 1800 and 1875 the speed of printing presses increased from 250 impressions per hour to 12,000. Papermaking was mechanized. Bookbinding machines were introduced. Electrotypes, stereotypes, collotype, Senefelder's lithographic press, mechanical type casting devices, and aids to punch cutting and matrix making all came into being. Yet typesetting itself—the very heart

of the printed word—remained unchanged. Progress in typesetting methods had scarcely moved an inch since 1450. It was still a totally manual operation; still so drearily slow that the average compositor spent most of a week setting and distributing a single newspaper page. After 400 years, the typesetter—not the scribe—was now the industry's bottleneck.

It's easy to picture the urgent drive for a more mechanized method of typesetting. New York newspaper publishers offered prizes totalling half a million dollars—tax free and uninflated—to any inventor who could save even 25 percent of the work of hand composition. This challenge brought 127 different proposals for composing machines. The Patent Office was inundated. We are told that the complexity of these inventions caused one examiner to lose his mind. (p. 5)

Four hundred years of evolving improvements in the printing industry may be contrasted with the forty years of gigantic improvements in the computing industry. The computing hardware soon began to draw upon space-age materials, replacing "core" memory with integrated circuits and reducing the size of the machines by magnitudes while increasing their speeds beyond the layman's ability to grasp. The prices of modern computers range from eighteen dollars to thirty million dollars, as shown in Table 5.2.

Table 5.2
What computers cost, in dollars

	Low end of price scale	High end of price scale
Calculators, hand-held	4	75
Programmable calculators	18	900
Personal microcomputers		
Small memory 4 to 16 K size	149	2,000
Medium size 16 to 64 K size		
with floppy disk	800	4,500
Large memory and disk	3,000	7,000
Desktop business microcomputer		
with disk and printer	4,000	20,000
Minicomputers	10,000	100,000
Mainframe computers	80,000	2,000,000
Multiple linked large processor		
systems	2,000,000	30,000,000

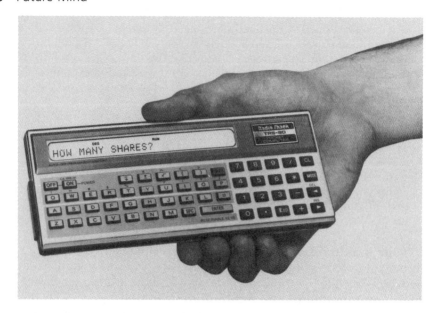

Radio Shack marketed this hand-held computer-calculator nationally in November 1980. Its power of computation exceeds many times the power of the early computers discussed in this chapter. Price: $249. *(Photo courtesy Radio Shack, a division of Tandy Corporation.)*

The chronology of development reads like a speeded-up movie. In 1971 Intel produced the first computer on a single silicon chip. This was the 4004 computer and was incorporated into cash registers, assembly line controls, and so on. Then, in 1974, Intel produced the 8080 microcomputer chip, which made the personal computer feasible. In a few months Motorola produced the 6800 chip and the microcomputer revolution was born.

MOS technology produced a competing computer chip, the 6502, and it became the heart of all Commodore and Apple computer terminals. In 1975 Altair began to sell the 8800 computer with screen and keyboard as a hobby computer. In 1976 Zilog produced the Z80 chip which competes with the 6502 in its various performance features.

In 1977 the popular personal computers were introduced to the larger marketplace. The Apple, the PET and the TRS-80 became household terms and names. By the end of the year, the color version of the Apple computer which attached to the home television screen, was introduced.

By 1981, a few computers were priced at $250. Commodore introduced its VIC-20 computer for $299 which included color and synthesizer sound. In 1981 Commodore introduced its Super-Pet which provided five computer languages on a single desktop computer for $1995. Nearly every magazine and newspaper carried ads for the user-friendly home personal computers. The world was the marketplace; every desk, car, kitchen, business office, library, game room and waiting room was a potential home for a computer.

Bibliography

Annals of the History of Computing. Montvale, N.J.: AFIPS Press, 1980.

Berkeley, E., *Giant Brains.* New York: Science Editions, 1961.

Burks, A. W., "Electronic Computing Circuits of the ENIAC," *Proceedings: Institute of Radio Engineers* 35, no. 8 (August 1947).

Gleiser, M., "Analog Inventor Vannevor Bush," *Datamation* (October 1980).

Huskey, H. D., "The Development of Automatic Computing," in *The Compleat Computer,* ed. Dennis van Tassel. Palo Alto, Ca.: Science Research Associates, 1976.

Metropolis, N., J. Howlett, and R. Gian Carlo, *A History of Computing in the Twentieth Century.* New York: Academic Press, 1980.

More About the Computer. Armonk, N. Y.: IBM Corporation, 1971.

Progress Report on the EDVAC, I and II. Philadelphia: Univeristy of Pennsylvania, 1946.

Rondthaler, E., *Life with Letters.* New York: Hastings House, 1981.

Rosen, S., *A Quarter Century View.* New York: Association of Computing Machinery, 1971.

Smith, D. E., *A Sourcebook in Mathematics,* vol. 1. New York: Dover, 1959.

Spencer, D. D., *Fundamentals of Digital Computers.* Indianapolis: Howard W. Sams, 1969.

Teilhard de Chardin, P., *The Phenomenon of Man.* New York: Harper & Row, 1959.

Watson, J. D., *The Double Helix.* New York: Atheneum, 1968.

Weik, M. H., *A Survey of Domestic Electronic Digital Computing Systems.* Maryland: Aberdeen Proving Ground, 1955.

Chapter Six

How Many
Would You Like?

- The U.S.A. possesses more computers than the rest of the world combined.
- The cost of computer hardware dipped below the cost of the people who operated them in 1973.
- Hundred of companies manufacture computers.
- Slow computers can add 19,000 numbers per second, fast ones can add 800,000,000 numbers per second.

How many computers are out there? The rate of growth between 1954 and the present cannot be appreciated until a count is taken. Statistics about the numbers of computers vary because they are purchased and exchanged so frequently. Questionnaires arrive in local computer centers about once a month, asking for the latest count. Unfortunately, the purpose of each census differs so the questions are rarely the same. Therefore the findings are useful only for trend analysis. Small computers were counted with large ones until about 1973, after which minicomputers and later microcomputers were counted separately.

In 1974 the United States contained within its borders more computers than all the rest of the world combined. The value of mainframe computers in 1974 is shown in Table 6.1.

Even by the year 2000, the United States' total of installed general-purpose computers is likely to match that of the rest of the world combined. By then, of course, the monster mainframe com-

Table 6.1
Millions of dollars spent on computers
(cumulative to 1974)

Country	$ millions
United States	$29,942
Japan	4,922
West Germany	3,772
United Kingdom	3,231
France	3,012
USSR	2,195
Canada	1,530
Italy	1,329
All others	6,020
Total	$55,953

Source: U.S. Dept. of Intelligence

puter will have shriveled to the size of a cement block. It may operate on pen-cell batteries and have a lifetime free-maintenance guarantee.

The facts presented in Table 6.1 reveal an extraordinary rate of acceptance of computerization in the United States. In Figure 6.1 notice that the relationship between funds spent on hardware and funds spent on salaries remained nearly constant until 1973, after which hardware costs began to decrease and salary costs spiralled upward with inflation.

Something about the life and culture of the United States speeded up our embrace of computers. A vacuum was waiting to be filled. A fortunate combination of capital for investment, drive to efficiency and a deep belief in the helpfulness of machines prepared Americans for the new medium, so that we adopted it with unprecedented speed.

Our stories about inaccurate phone bills and mixed-up book

Figure 6.1
United States' expenditures for computer hardware and salaries

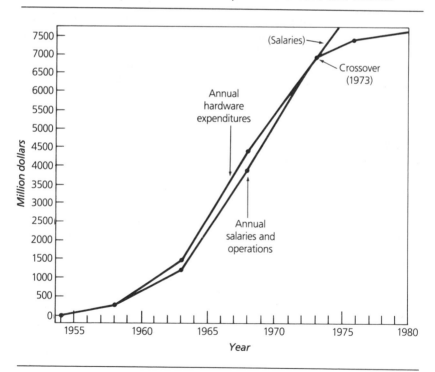

Source: Projected from EDP Industry Report

club bills were flimsy masks. Back at the office we were ordering more computers, hiring more programmers and writing five-year expansion plans for computing. In 1975 word-processing had not yet become a buzzword, nor had electronic mail become a serious possibility. But even without these services the rush towards computer power can be seen in the graphs and tables of this chapter.

The International Data Corporation of Waltham, Massachusetts, serves as a research agent for *Computerworld* newsweekly and published a computer census in 1980. It was distributed as a public service and contains a fascinating overview of the industry—who bought computers, who sold them and what types of customers buy them. The installation analyses which follow are drawn from this source.

The growth in the United States computer population between 1958 and 1980 is presented in Figure 6.3. The facts were gathered

Figure 6.2
Processor use by industry groups

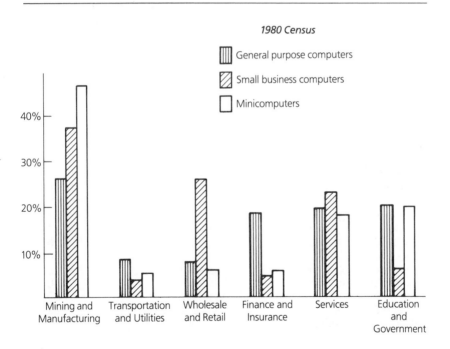

Source: Data courtesy IDC Corporation

Figure 6.3
Growth in United States computer population

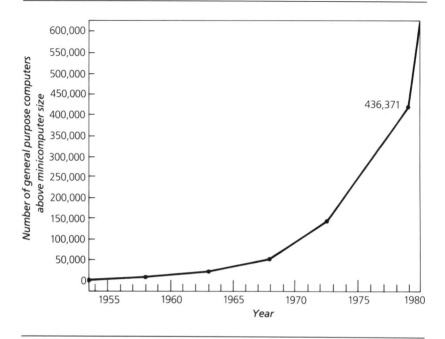

Source: Data courtesy International Data Corporation.

Table 6.2
Small business computer census (1980 snapshot)

Name of manufacturer	Most popular model	Total, all models
Anderson-Jacobsen, Inc.	1400	440
Basic/Four Corp.	400	3,515
Basic Timesharing, Inc.	4000/25	782
Burroughs Corp.	B700	5,500
Business Controls Corp.	System 80	180
Business Systems Products	Advisor	100
Cado	System 20, 40	800
Cascade Data, Inc.	Concept II	320
Century Computer Corp.	Opus III	930
Cincinnati Milacron	George	630
Clary Data Systems	404	100
Computer Hardware, Inc.	2130C	249

Table 6.2
(continued)

Name of manufacturer	Most popular model	Total, all models
Computer Interactions,Inc.	Compo II-8	485
Data General	Design Data N312	670
Diablo	3200	400
Digital Equipment Corp.	Datasystem 300	6,200
Display Data Corp.	Insight	440
Educomp Corp. (Quodata)	All models	237
Financial Computer Corp. (Fedder)	System III/10	490
General Automation, Inc.	DM-130/2	265
General Robotics Corp.	FD/X3	160
GRI Computer Corp.	System 99	196
IBM	System/32	22,300
Infotecs	Imp	270
Jaquard	J-100	250
Lockheed Electronics Co., Inc.	System III	440
Logical Machines Corp.	ADAM	341
Martin Wolfe, Inc.	Mesa Two 7000	143
Microdata	Reality	2,000
Mini-Computer Systems, Inc.	Micos	785
Mylee Digital Sciences	3000 Series	110
NCR Corp.	8200 Series	2,475
Pick & Associates	Evolution	122
Q1 Corporation	LMC	900
Quantel	950	1,394
Randal Data Systems	R-200	664
Sperry-Univac	BC-7	700
Wang Laboratories, Inc.	2200	13,110
Warrex Computer Corp.	Centurion III	640
All others		1,741
	Total	71,474

Computers in this category are used by small businesses in ways that imitate the larger general purpose machines. They are smaller, however, and their channels which reach to disk are slower and less expensive. Their operating systems are less mature than the expensive mainframe machines. Small businesses often use them as turnkey solutions for their inventory or accounting problems. Application programs are usually provided with the computer. The census included vendors who had installed at least 100 computers. *Source:* Data courtesy IDC Corporation.

by the International Data Corporation. Updates are from 1980 data.

How fast do these computers operate? Mainframe computers were for some time measured in KOPS, meaning thousands of operations per second. Table 6.5 shows an amazing speed range among mainframe computers, the lowest being 19,000 operations per second and the highest (in 1980) being 800,000.

Table 6.3
Minicomputer census for 1980

Name of manufacturer	Most popular model	Total, all models
Artonix	PC-12/7	135
Bytronix	Series 1000	50
Century Computer Corp.	C-200	150
Cincinnati Milacron	CIP Series	3,835
Computer Automation, Inc.	LSI-2 Series	23,205
Control Data Corp.	Cyber Series	1,435
Data General Corp.	Nova-3/12	46,295
Digital Equipment Corp.	PDP-11/03, LSI 11	117,085
Digital Scientific Corp.	Meta-4/4000	160
Electronic Associates, Inc.	Pacer-1000	150
General Automation, Inc.	SPC-16	14,963
GRI Computer Corp.	99/30, 38	1,282
GT&E	Tempo II	3,110
Harris	Slash 5	1,210
Hewlett-Packard	2100A	23,630
Honeywell	700 Series	6,787
IBM	Series 1	3,000
Keronix	IDS-16 Series	1,800
Lear Siegler	VDP-410	100
Lockheed Electronics Co.	SUE	5,037
Microdata Corp.	1600	12,067
Modular Computer Systems	Modcomp-II	3,211
New England Digital Corp.	ABLE Series 40	60
Perkin-Elmer Corp.	7/16	8,761
Prime Computer Corp.	300	1,306
Raytheon Data Systems	704	1,704
Redcor/Sperry-Univac	V-73	7,965
Systems Computer Corp.	1,000	400
Systems Engineering Labs	32/55, 57	540
Tandem Laboratories	T16	245
Texas Instruments	990/4	15,250
Unicom	CP-8	343
Westinghouse Electric	2500	612
Xerox	Sigma-2	205
All others		849
	Total	306,937

Minicomputers are similar to small business computers except that they often perform specialized tasks in laboratories or factories. Unique programs are usually written so that the machines can be applied to local tasks. *Source:* Data courtesy IDC Corporation.

Table 6.4
General purpose computer census for 1980

Manufacturer	Number of models	Value in millions	Number of 1/79 installations
Amdahl	4	476	150
Burroughs	19	3,078	4,260
CDC	30	1,614	605
Cray	1	40	6
DEC	8	650	636
Honeywell	37	3,096	4,233
IBM	46	34,597	38,808
ITEL (NAS)	4	307	228
Magnuson	2	8	6
NCR	22	1,040	3,309
Singer	1	20	1,400
UNIVAC	42	3,313	3,846
Xerox	9	425	473
Totals	225	48,664	57,960

General purpose computers are more costly than minicomputers because they have high speed channels reaching to the disk storage devices, enabling powerful file handling services. Their operating systems often have a 5,000 person-year investment, causing the machine to be more secure, able to handle 50 to 2000 tasks simultaneously and to be efficient in the control of all peripheral devices. *Source:* Data from IDC Corporation.

Table 6.5
Selected list of computers and their
processor speeds

Mainframe	Thousands of operations per second	Mainframe	Thousands of operations per second
UNIVAC 9200	19	DEC 1040	165
IBM Sys 3/32	20	NCR V-8455	179
IBM 360/30	36	Burroughs 1728	200
IBM System 3	55	Honeywell 64 DPS 320	213
Burroughs 1830	70	IBM 4331	213
Honeywell Level 62	75	UNIVAC Sys 80 mod 5	250
IBM 370/125	80	Honeywell 66/05	270
RCA 70/46	83	UNIVAC 9060E	295
Burroughs 2700	95	IBM 370/145	300
UNIVAC 9400	110	CDC Imega 480I	321
UNIVAC 90/30	139	Magnuson M80/3	321
IBM 360/50	158	Burroughs 6807	340
UNIVAC Sys 80 mod 3	160	Nanodata QMX 6333	380

Table 6.5
(continued)

Mainframe	Thousands of operations per second	Mainframe	Thousands of operations per second
NCR V8570	383	Burroughs 6822	1260
UNIVAC 1100/11	392	CDC 73	1300
Burroughs 6700	425	UNIVAC 1100/62	1496
Honeywell DPS 8/20	473	Burroughs 7760	1528
DEC 1070 KI	497	UNIVAC 1100/81	1800
CDC 171	520	CDC 173	1870
Magnuson M80/32	531	IBM 370/165	1900
Burroughs 6808	545	Burroughs 7770	1950
UNIVAC 1106-II	571	Honeywell DPS 8/70	1987
National Adv. Sys AS/4	595	UNIVAC 1100/62H1	2244
DEC PDP 11/70	600	CDC 74	2500
UNIVAC 1100/61 C2	672	IBM 370/168-3	2500
Honeywell DPS 8/44	710	Burroughs 7780	2535
IBM 4341	758	NCR V-8650	2650
Burroughs 6810	765	UNIVAC 1100/62	2800
NCR V-8585M	779	CDC 174	2805
UNIVAC 9080-3	800	Amdahl 470V/5-II	2850
IBM 370/158	829	National Adv. Sys AS/6	3000
DEC 1090KL	829	UNIVAC 1100/82	3360
DEC VAX 11/780	831	CDC 6700	3700
Nanodata QMX 6343	880	Amdahl 470V/7B	3825
Honeywell 66/40	900	IBM 3033N	4000
IBM 370/158-3	900	NCR V-8670	4293
CDC Omega 480-III	950	IBM 370/195	4750
CDC 72	1000	UNIVAC 1100/83	5040
UNIVAC 1100/12	1044	IBM 3033U	5900
IBM 3031	1045	Amdahl 470V/8	6375
UNIVAC 9080-4	1100	UNIVAC 1100/84	6400
UNIVAC 1100/61 H1	1120	CDC 176	9360
Burroughs 6818	1150	CDC 7600	10000
Honeywell DPS 8/52	1200	CDC Cyber 205 Vector	800000
CDC 172	1230	Cray 1-S Vector	800000

This list is condensed from 238 mainframe computers which were available for purchase in 1980. The list reveals the tremendous range of speed which is available to the computer buyer. See *Datamation,* November 1980 for the complete list. Compared to human senses, computers seem to operate at the speed of light. The slowest machine above can add (or subtract) 19,000 numbers in a second. Only mainframe computers are included in this table.

The field of microcomputers is so dynamic that it will be reviewed separately in later chapters. As a preview, in 1979, 478,000 small business computers and desktop computers were installed.

By 1984, shipments are projected to grow four to sixfold, meaning that about one million desktop computers will be sold in that year. The five leading microcomputer manufacturers in 1981 were Apple, Radio Shack, Commodore, Atari and Texas Instruments.

International Data Corporation anticipates that 3,200,000 desktop computers will be in our homes and schools in 1984. How many computers have *been* installed? Not as many as *will be* installed. There's more to come.

Bibliography

EDP Industry Report. Waltham, Ma.: International Data Corporation, 1974.

IBM and the Courts: A Six Year Journal. Waltham, Ma.: International Data Corporation, 1975.

Infosystems. Wheaton, Ill.: Hitchcock Publishing, 1976.

Lias, E. J., "Tracking the Elusive KOPS," *Datamation* 25 (November 1980).

Chapter Seven

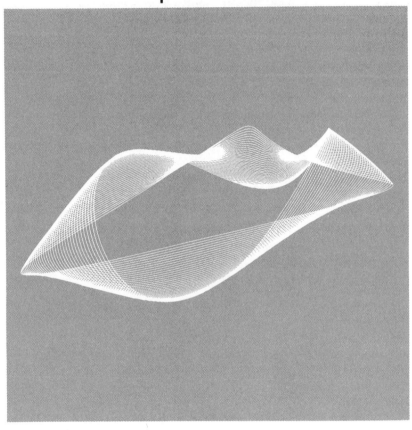

Hey,
Big Spender

☐ Governments (federal and state) were the big spenders on computers until about 1975.

☐ Business and industry now form the largest computer-using group.

☐ Universities and schools are in third place.

Since almost everyone uses computers—directly or indirectly—sociologists enjoy the challenge of dividing us into groupings that can assist their understanding of the social areas affected by computerization.

Divided according to their motives for acquiring computers, the following groups of users are identified by Gotlieb and Borodin.

1. Users who desire to achieve economy in some operation. The goal here is to utilize resources more effectively or to reduce production costs.

2. Users who desire to accomplish a new operation or service which is not feasible without electronic computer assistance.

3. Users who desire to analyze a complex process at a deeper level than common rational thought permits.

Mowshowitz identified five groups:

1. Clerical: routine tasks such as payrolls or accounting
2. Information processing: airline reservations, library circulation
3. Control: traffic flow, assembly-line monitoring
4. Design: computer-aided airplane design, car design
5. Decision-making: summary reports from many data bases for managers*

Divided according to the social groups using computers, the federal government's *Standard Industrial Classification Manual* provides this breakdown:

1. Government
   a. Federal
   b. State
   c. Local
2. Private sector
   a. Manufacturing
   b. Finance

* A. Mowshowitz, *The Conquest of Will.* © 1976 Addison-Wesley Publishing Company, Inc. Reprinted with permission.

    c. Wholesale and retail trade
    d. Services and education
    e. Transportation, communication and utilities

Computer vendors such as IBM, UNIVAC, Burroughs, Digital Equipment Corporation and Control-Data divide the nation into geographical marketing sectors which become the territories for sales representatives. Sales personnel are trained to market to specific audiences. Commonly, these groups are government, education, industry (business) and others.

The Association for Computing Machinery publishes the following categories of computer users in its conference book *Computers and Crisis:*

    1. Education
    2. Finance (Securities, Insurance, Banking, Accounting)
    3. Government
    4. Health and Welfare
    5. Industry (Apparel, Automotive, Food distribution, Petroleum, Plant automation, Power, Printing and publishing, Retail)
    6. Transportation
    7. Urban Development
    8. Engineering
    9. Humanities
    10. Law
    11. Management
    12. Medicine
    13. Science

Divided according to dollars spent, up to 1975 the biggest spender was the government, followed by business, education and other users.

Government

The federal government was by far the major user of computers in the country, until about 1975, after which trends changed. Within government the military ranks as the biggest spender. The U. S. military, unlike those of Japan and Canada, whose use of computers was negligible, utilized more than 8,000 computers in 1976, twenty of which cost more than $1.5 million. (*Inventory of Automatic Data Processing Equipment in the United States.*)

Infosystems Journal observed in 1976:

In 1969, when the inventory of computers in the federal government approached 4,700, there were some data processing people in the General Services Administration who believed the number would not grow very significantly.

Recently, the inventory for fiscal year 1975 was published. Beliefs voiced six years earlier went by the boards. The number of digital computers totaled 8,649, a 350 percent increase in the last decade (analog and digital computers built or modified to special governmental design and part of a weapons or space system were not included), and 7,504 were owned by Uncle Sam. The figures relate exclusively to central processing units. The value of totally owned equipment, CPU's and components was placed at nearly $3 billion.

The government's computer inventory book is 605 pages long and carries listings for each computer owned or leased by the government, including its location, year of purchase or lease, manufacturer and classification as to general or special application use. One table is included here to show the scope of government computer utilization. (See Table 7.1.)

Table 7.1
Business computers by federal government agency, 1975

Agency	Total
Agriculture	56
Commerce	82
Energy Research and Development Administration	285
General Services Administration	24
Health, Education, and Welfare	82
Interior	32
National Aerospace Administration	188
Transportation	50
Treasury	150
Veterans Administration	36
Other Civil, Labor, and Justice	122
Department of Defense	2,515
(Army, 703)	
(Navy, 586)	
(Air Force, 1047)	
(Other DOD, 179)	
Total	3,622

Source: Inventory of Automatic Data Processing Equipment in the United States Government, Washington, D.C.: General Services Administration #022001000663, 1975, p. 211.

The government buys computers for many reasons. In the armaments field, computerized electronics help to produce weapons and deliver systems which could not be created otherwise. In the day-to-day business operations of the various branches of government, economy of operation is the dominant motive. In their review of federal computer use, Nyborg, McCarter and Erickson state:

> While the federal government is the largest single user of computers, accounting for approximately 6 percent of total usage in the U. S., federal usage is not increasing as fast as in the United States at large. Nonetheless, the number of computers owned or leased by the federal government grew from 5,900 in 1971 to 9,600 in 1976; the Department of Defense accounts for almost half of federal computer usage. (p. 4)

To the federal government must be added all of the state and local computers, which are similarly widespread and increasing in such uses as automated jury selection, voter registration recording, tax assessing, billing and collecting, motor vehicle registration, criminal data files and welfare administration.

After 1975, other groups of users began to overtake the federal government in computer use. Table 7.2 uses 1980 data to reveal a more recent distribution of users.

Business

Industrial and corporate users of computers do not count or analyze their computer use with the openness displayed in the government's inventory. Private business has every right *not* to publish the cost, make or model of its computer services. Some sprawling companies do not even know how many computers they have. One mark of computer growth in the 1960s was having one or two computers at every branch of a company, with no central authority responsible for the results.

Education

Educational institutions are the third major community of computer users in the U. S. In chapter 9 the types of services which they utilize will be analyzed. Here, the *number* of educational computer users is the subject.

Table 7.2
General purpose computer distribution, 1980 census

Industrial group	Percentage of computers owned by group
Computer Services Industry	15.5
Manufacturing (Durables)	15.3
Manufacturing (Non Durables)	8.3
Banking	8.1
Insurance	7.3
Education	6.9
Federal Government	6.7
State and Local Government	6.4
Utilities	5.6
Wholesale	4.4
Other Financial	3.9
Retail	3.3
Transportation Carriers	3.3
Medical Health and Other	2.8
Agriculture	2.2
Total	100.0

Source: IDC Corporation

John W. Hamblen's *Inventory of Computers in Higher Education* provides a continuing census of educational computer users in his four volumes covering 1965, 1967, 1970 and 1977. In the 1969–70 volume, Mr. Hamblen states:

Approximately 1700 institutions (or campuses) of higher education are now spending nearly $500 million annually for computer facilities and their operation. This amounts to approximately 2 percent of estimated total expenditures for higher education during 1970–71. Computers have become an integral part of and an expected tool in higher education. (p. I.1)

Converting Hamblen's findings into table form, Table 7.3 shows the increases he records. In Figure 7.1, trends are projected for total expenditures based on the four census outcomes.

The dollar figures in Figure 7.1 indicate that educational institutions are primary users of computer services. In 1980, more than $990 million was budgeted for computer services throughout U. S. colleges and universities. If the microcomputer users in elementary, middle and high schools are added to these figures, the

Table 7.3
Numbers of computers located at educational institutions

	1964	1966	1969	1976	1985
Institutions with computers	707	980	1681	2163	2650
Institutions without computers	1512	1497	1126	950	600
Total number of institutions	2219	2477	2807	3113	3250

Source: John W. Hamblen, *Inventory of Computers in United States Higher Education: 1969–1970.* Washington, D.C.: National Science Foundation, Office of Computing Activities, March 1972, p. V–5.

academic world would rank as the third major user of computers in the country. In 1980 alone, the schools below college level spent fifty million dollars for desktop microcomputers and associated equipment.

The EDUCOM network of computers should be mentioned in this context. Founded in 1967, EDUCOM consists of a large number of colleges and universities which allow their computer resources to be pooled and accessed through a national network of communication lines. Researchers at one university are able to request the use of programs run on the computers of any of one hundred other institutions. The Telenet switching computer directs terminal users into the computer and location of their choice. (EDUCOM is run by the Interuniversity Communications Council, located at Box 364, Rosedale Road, Princeton, N. J. 08540.)

We saw in Table 6.1 that the number of computers installed in the U. S. is significantly larger than the number elsewhere in the world. In 1977 the U. S. used as many computers as the rest of the world combined. If all sizes above the microcomputer are included, more than 436,000 computers were installed in the U. S. in 1980. Machines larger than the IBM System 32 total more than 378,411. The 1980 census of general purpose mainframes counted 57,960 of the large machines.

As for microcomputers, if we include all varieties, eight million were shipped in 1980 alone. This includes desk-top computers together with those used in video games, terminals, music synthesizers, graphic arts devices and automobiles.

A pattern can be seen here. Federal computer use is growing, but in the industrial U. S. at large, computer use is growing much faster. Thus, business and educational uses are catching up with

Figure 7.1
Expenditures for computing hardware in U.S. higher education,
through 1984

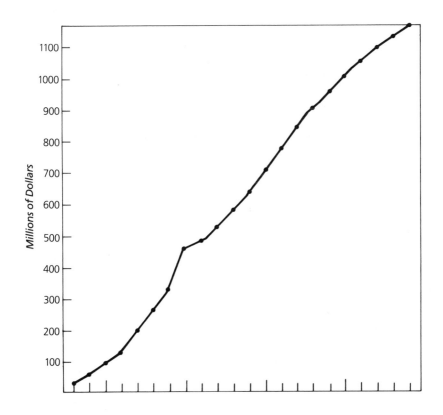

Source: John W. Hamblen, *Inventory of Computers in United States Higher Education: 1977, 1978*. Washington, D. C.: National Science Foundation, Office of Computing Activities.

the government, which began to automate earlier. Whether these computers are applied in effective and efficient ways is another question.

The data above were drawn from various sources. Each source, while credible, collected the data using different techniques and categories. In this dynamic field, one should view computer population figures as snapshots, general aids for broad understanding of relationships. On this basis, the trends shown in Figure 7.2 can be cautiously charted.

Our use of computers displays that they have proceeded beyond the stage of mere acceptance into our culture of mechanical automation. There is a deeper commitment to electronic automation in almost every area of business and government. All of the figures in this chapter reveal that the numbers of computer installations are increasing sharply together with allocations of money for them. No levelling off is in sight. Even in those years where recessions have occurred, the rate of computer increases has been little affected. No evidence of saturation can be detected from the data currently available. The computer, like other popular media, has successfully suggested new uses for itself. Extended to its ultimate conclusion, the trends point toward eventual usage within the USA as follows:

95 percent of all federal agencies will have 95 percent of their office functions fully computerized.	c.1990 to 2000
95 percent of all state and local government agencies similarly.	c.2000 to 2020
95 percent of all businesses and schools will have 95 percent of their office and manufacturing functions computerized.	c.2000 to 2020

Figure 7.2
Computer use increases

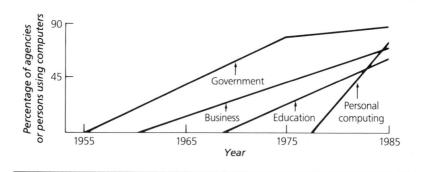

90 percent of all homes will have personal computer terminals in their TV consoles (and knowledge of how to use them).	c.2020 to 2040
90 percent of all schoolchildren will receive courses in the use of computer terminals and programming.	c. 1990 to 2000
60 percent of the labor force will be employed directly or indirectly in data-processing or data–communication-related jobs.	c.2010 to 2050

These predictions can be extended to the rest of the world, if the effects of war, energy crises and hunger are seen as factors which will *hasten* our rush toward total computer dependency.

I have witnessed the expenditure of $800,000 for a computer which serviced twenty-five terminals concurrently. This was in 1970. In 1977 $800,000 was spent to purchase a new computer; it serviced sixty-five timeshared terminals concurrently. Then, in 1980, $600,000 was spent for a UNIVAC computer which serviced 150 concurrent timeshared users.

Home microcomputers became available in 1974, priced between $3,000 and $6,000. In 1977 they cost $1,000 and came with unparalleled ease of access. Purchasers did not have to build or comprehend it—they merely had to use it. By 1980 computers in cars, elevators and game rooms operated unnoticed as people pressed the buttons and enjoyed the instant results. Some microcomputers for the home now cost less than $100.

Bibliography

Bemer, R. W., ed., *Computers and Crisis*. New York: Association of Computing Machinery, 1971.

Computing Newsletter. Colorado Springs, Co.: EDP Industry Report, 1975.

Gotlieb, C. C., and A. Borodin, *Social Issues in Computing*. New York: Academic Press, 1973.

Hamblen, J. W., *Inventory of Computers in United States Higher Education: 1976–1977*. Washington, D. C.: National Science Foundation, Office of Computing Activities, 1978.

IBM and the Courts: A Six Year Journal. Waltham, Ma.: International Data Corporation, 1975.

Inventory of Automatic Data Processing Equipment in the United States Government. Washington, D. C.: General Services Administration, 1975.

Mowshowitz, A., *The Conquest of Will: Information Processing in Human Affairs.* Reading, Ma.: Addison-Wesley, 1976.

Nyborg, P. S., P. M. McCarter, and William Erickson, eds., *Information Processing in the United States.* Montvale, N. J.: AFIPS Press, 1977.

Pullen, E., and R. Simko, "Our Changing Industry," *Datamation* 49 (January 1977).

Standard Industrial Classification Manual. Washington, D. C.: U. S. Government Printing Office, 1972.

Chapter Eight

Take a
Ticket and Wait
Your Turn

☐ No medium will have much influence if it is not made available to the masses.

☐ No medium will gain significance if it is too complex or costly to use.

☐ Computers were once costly and difficult to use. Now they are on every toy counter and in every mall arcade.

When only scribes could read and paper was made by hand, the written word had very little influence on the larger culture; people had almost no access to the medium of paper and print. The development of paper and the printing press eventually provided for broad access to alphabets and books. When this access was provided and the medium embraced by the culture, an industrial revolution inevitably followed, say the media scholars, because the print medium promotes logical, rational, sequential discourse.

Cultures often model themselves, metaphorically speaking, after the likeness of a printing press or book, once these media are widely adopted. Just as letters flow across a page, and just as pages follow each other sequentially, so also, it seems, the specialized events on assembly lines begin to make sense for people who have learned to read. Thus, industrial revolutions have always followed wherever print and literacy are adopted. Depending on the culture you live in, you have differing opportunities for accessing books, films, television sets, citizens'-band radios or other media.

In our culture, it has not always been easy to gain access to a computer. For many years it was a case of paying a heavy fee, taking a ticket and waiting in line. Only the super-serious would bother to do it. Sometimes users would wait days for a call from the computer center stating that their job was ready.

Some readers may never have had the experience of submitting a job or problem to a large computer. (Others have certainly used computers without knowing it, as in electronic toys and games, elevators, check-out counters and elsewhere.) This chapter briefly outlines the changing procedures which people have had to follow in order to gain access to a computer. From 1954 to the present we have moved from an era of difficult access methods to an era of easy, cheap and instant access for almost anyone who wants to use a computer.

Ideally, any medium, whether electronic or mechanical, is designed to be foolproof and forgiving in its operation, like television sets or typewriters. Users generally do not want to know how media work, but rather desire a few simple knobs by which to get immediate service.

Like some other electronic devices, the computer does nothing when turned on. The TV set must have an active channel tuned in. The tape recorder must have a reel of tape inserted. And the computer must have a program placed in its "memory" and instructions given for some activity to occur. Thus, to present some problem-solving task to the computer, the user is required to initiate one of the following actions: Ask a knowledgeable friend to obtain certain results from the computer. The friend must take one of two steps: use a previously written program and supply unique data to it when it runs on the computer; or reduce a problem to a list of formal instructions and personally write a detailed progam to submit to the computer. As another alternative, you can buy a computer that automatically begins to run its program when turned on.

Simple procedures have not always been available to computer users, because computer programs have commonly been written in a technical "language" consisting of fifty to two hundred English verbs, each given a precise meaning, thus enabling users to state their problems to the computer in lists of instructions. The problem may involve the manipulation of numbers, letters, or even the control of servo-motors in Disney World stage characters.

To obtain services from a computer, a user must observe the following conventions:

1. Push a button on a panel which loads a program, runs it, and produces some desired result.

Or:

1. Conceive a problem capable of solution by some logical process.
2. Write a program or use a previously written program whose execution will solve the problem.
3. Present the program to a computer for execution through one of seven access methods (described below).
4. Receive results back from the computer printed on paper, microfilm, computer tape, paper tape, plotter or television screen.

Simple programs are quite easy to write and present. Thanks to human engineering during the past fifteen years, access methods have improved so that even the uninitiated can have successful and pleasant experiences after twenty minutes of tutoring. Certain computer languages, such as BASIC, provide English-like verbs for easy programming. In BASIC, for instance, the simplest program is one line in length:

```
10 PRINT "Hello."
```

The 10 identifies the line as line 10. PRINT is the verb meaning "When executed, the letters enclosed in quotations should be displayed on the screen or typewriter."

If on the next line the user types "RUN" on the keyboard, the one-line program will run and on the screen will appear the word

```
Hello.
```

The "print" verb can perform more important functions, as illustrated below. Two variables known as A$ and B$ are created by the computer because the user names them in his program.

```
10 A$ = "  MS."

20 B$ = "  JONES"            (typed by the user on the keyboard)

30 PRINT "HELLO";A$;B$;"."

RUN

HELLO MS. JONES.                (typed by the computer)
```

This trivial example is typical of the ease with which simple problems can be stated to the computer. Eighth and ninth graders often learn BASIC on terminals in their classrooms. Many ninth-grade algebra books published since 1974 contain BASIC programs for children to correct, change or enter into a terminal and run. More time will be required before adults can confront the pleasures of such games and simulations, which many children now take for granted. When the school children of the seventies become adults, computers will be accepted even more broadly because children had early and pleasant experiences with them.

Unlike television, which could be accessed simply by turning a knob, computer access for many years required a more thoughtful, disciplined approach. The would-be user came to the computer with a problem already defined, thought-through, reduced to a step-by-step plan (commonly known as an algorithm) for its so-

The low-cost home computer terminal rounds out the trend toward ever more specialized and personal uses for the computer. 800,000 home computer terminals had been
sold by 1981. The average home then contained three microcomputers in various
appliances and games. *(Photo courtesy Radio Shack, a division of Tandy Corporation.)*

lution, and a list of instructions codified in one of twenty commonly
available computer languages such as COBOL, FORTRAN, BASIC,
APL or PASCAL. This procedure, which sounds complex and
even tedious, is in fact an enjoyable experience for most people.
The process of laying out a plan and then telling the computer to
obey it is likely to provide a basic metaphor to those who do it—
namely that a thoughtful, disciplined approach to any problem,
whether social, economic or personal is the realistic and productive
way to deal with it. (Later we shall look at the question of whether
this amplification of the rational side of life is altogether desirable:
can the perplexing inequalities of life and culture be solved by
applying a rational systems approach to them?)

The would-be user then had to obey another set of conventions
regarding the method of supplying the program to the computer.
He or she had to satisify all of the local rules for access, priority
of use, methods of handling error conditions, methods of supplying data to the program and methods of paying for the computer
time used. Because of these complexities, the evolution of computing displays a groping toward techniques of access which will
reduce difficulties for the user. A chronological survey of access

The National Bureau of Standards built its own computers—one for the East coast, the other for the West coast. This is the Standards Eastern Automatic Computer (SEAC) in about 1950. It featured direct human input using hexadecimal notation. *(Photo courtesy Sperry Corporation.)*

methods shows increasingly "humane" and user-oriented considerations becoming predominant.

Access Method One:
The single batch program run

Early computers ran one program at a time. Other programs accumulated outside the computer in a queue of card decks (for example), waiting for the current program in execution to run to completion.

In 1951 the UNIVAC I was delivered to the U.S. Census Bureau. It was the first main-memory machine to be purchased by a nonmilitary user. The unit shown bears serial number 1, and the occasion is the retirement of the machine in 1963. J. P. Eckert, Jr., and J. Mauchly, the inventors, are on the left. Luther Hodges, Secretary of Commerce, is in the center of the picture. *(Photo courtesy Sperry Corporation.)*

Between 1954 and 1960, the popular IBM 1401 and 1440 computers received their programs (typically) from card decks. An operator had to press a "load" button to initiate the loading of punched cards which contained the next program in machine-ready form. The term "batch processing" resulted from the observation that no matter when a job was brought to the computer center, an operator would put it into a queue or batch of other waiting jobs.

The batch access method required the user to submit his request and return later after the operator had loaded and run the job. A number of problems arose from this procedure, especially the tendency for the operator to run all of the small five and ten minute jobs ahead of those requiring six or eight hours of uninterrupted machine time. The person who scheduled the running of the programs was like a king, all users humbly desiring to stay in favor in the hope of a quicker turnaround.

Access Method Two: Multiprogram batch with operating system

As computers developed in speed and power, the manufacturers began to provide "operating systems" with the hardware. The operating system is a large program which is loaded into the computer each morning. Its purpose is to control the operation of the machine for the entire day, managing the use of memory and other resources to best advantage. The operating system decides when to load and run the waiting jobs, based on criteria such as job priority, resources required and the best fit of several programs into the available memory. The operating system predicts upcoming needs and it requests whatever it needs on a console. A human operator must resolve these needs, such as the mounting of tapes or disk packs.

With this access method, people who wanted a program run no longer talked with human operators. They approached a card reader, placed the program (on punched cards) in a hopper, pressed the button, watched the cards read in, put the cards back in a briefcase and awaited a typewritten estimate of when the job may be completed. Students in universities commonly use this procedure. Since the control program (operating system) is managing the resources, it may decide to run six or seven jobs at once.

Multi-partitioned batch machines began to be installed after 1965 with the IBM 360 setting the trend for batch operating system capabilities. By 1962, the technique for submitting programs through tape or disk media had been perfected and it greatly increased the ease of user access. Although the program to be run may have been punched on cards originally, it could reside on a disk device, making it available for loading into memory directly from disk in one or two seconds whenever requested.

With this service, the user who wanted to run a program could now submit one or two cards to the card reader instead of a large deck, those cards essentially saying, "Please run Program 17 (which is already on one of your disks) as soon as possible." The operating system would place this request into its queue, analyze the resource requirements of Program 17, schedule its upcoming run, report the likely time for completion and meanwhile continue without interruption the processing of six or eight other programs.

By 1968, it was possible to extend the memory on such machines so that fifteen or twenty concurrent jobs could all be executed at once, the computer going round-robin through the tasks giving one-tenth of a second to one-half second to each job. Multiprogrammed computers were often compared to a grocery store with one very fast checkout clerk racing between fifteen checkout stations, each station serving customers who were slow in placing their items on the counter.

Because of this ability to perform many tasks concurrently, the possibility of other access methods evolved. Today, in the case of large, expensive computers, the results may be coming off the high-speed printer before the user gets there to see them.

Access Method Three:
Remote job entry (RJE)

By 1968, the techniques for passing computer data through telephone lines had been perfected so that card readers and typewriters could be placed miles away from the central computer. So while the central computer was running ten jobs for local clients, jobs eleven and twelve could be dedicated to services requested through telephone lines and other remote devices. For example, a branch office in Detroit and another in Cleveland could both tie in by telephone line to a large central machine in Chicago.

This access method is still "batch" in that the jobs submitted through the Detroit card reader enter a larger queue in the central Chicago machine to be completed some time later. After completion, the results are automatically sent out on the proper phone line to the Detroit printer or terminal. This method gives users the illusion of having their own computing power, at a cost much lower than if the computer was rented locally. Also, the services (stock programs) available on the large host machines are much more versatile than those that would be available on the smaller machines which could be rented. Thus RJE became a method of providing scattered users with the power of a central host machine.

As an example of this system, all of the four-year schools in New Jersey had, as late as 1980, card readers and printers attached by phone line to a central computer at Rutgers University. These scattered RJE sites together with the central host computer are known as the Educational Computing Network (ECN). Similarly, sprawling industrial companies have been able to satisfy the computing needs of their engineers by installing RJE equipment in their branches.

Many computer service bureaus sprang into existence between

1965 and 1972 because of the financial profits to be realized by supplying computing power in this way to widely spread engineering firms, schools, hospitals, etc.

Access Method Four:
Special-purpose data networks

The Virginia Light and Power Company receives more than 10,000 telephone calls each day at various cities throughout a 9,000 square-mile, five-state area. The calls come from customers inquiring about their bills, or rates or payments. The company installed 300 video terminals throughout the five-state area, all tied to a central host computer. Calls were received by clerks who were sitting in front of the computer screens. By keying in the customer's name or bill number, the full history of transactions could be retrieved and displayed within three seconds. The clerks could then make adjustments to the central records as required. This service was operating stably by 1972.

This example of the data network access method illustrates how a computer can be dedicated to the service of many terminals all of which are doing similar functions such as accessing a large database or file of information. For this service, the computer was specially adapted to respond to 300 terminals. This arrangement provided an instant access approach for clerks to use. It was highly successful in certain business situations after 1970 such as police networks, state tax record maintenance, order-entry, inventory-stock control and warehousing.

Access Method Five:
Full-function timeshared terminals

Some of the large multi-batch sites began to modify their operating systems after 1970 to provide concurrent services to many remote terminals. This access method was called "timesharing" because the computer shared its processing time with all the terminal users at once. In this arrangement, instead of all terminals performing similar functions, each isolated user is given the illusion that he or she is the only user on the computer and that the entire variety of its services is available. The operating system on the host machine is arranged to go round-robin from phone line to phone line and for one-fiftieth to one–twenty-fifth of a second do whatever unique service is requested. One user may be keying

Two thousand people attend the DECUS conferences twice each year, this one being at San Diego in 1980. Their common interest is that they all use computers from Digital Equipment Corporation. Similar conferences are held by the users of UNIVAC, IBM, Honeywell, Burroughs and other companies. In the early years, the sessions dealt largely with hardware and operations. Today they deal with networking and software applications.

in a BASIC program, the next may be running a COBOL program, the next taking a computer-aided instruction course, the next running a large statistical crosstabulation, the next computing the tilt angles on a curving bridge, and so on.

Timeshared operating systems further simplified the user approach to the computer. On one popular network between 1967 and 1973 (Allan Babcock), the user could dial a phone number, press carriage return on the terminal and the computer would type:

LOG IN PLEASE:

The user would then type a brief identification statement. If the ID was verified, the user was immediately given the "ready" signal, and could request any of one thousand programs to be run, or enter any of fifty English verbs requesting special services (such as: list all file names under this account, enter the calculator mode or copy a file to a new place with a new name). Also, new programs could be written, run, tested and saved for later execution.

For the user, timeshared access method means that a small nine-pound terminal (keyboard) can be carried in a briefcase. Wherever there is a telephone, anywhere in the world, the terminal can access the power and services of the central host machine. The entire global grid of telephone networks becomes the servant of computer signals passing to and fro. The user has no knowledge that perhaps fifty to seventy other people are using their terminals at the same time.

Dozens of timesharing service companies sprang to life, appearing to the stock market as risky but attractive investments. University Computing, Applied Logic, Allan Babcock, Princeton Time-Sharing, Corporate Computing and many others were famous network names between 1968 and 1974. Such companies survived only if they diversified their access methods to include one or two other methods as well. Scattered timesharing users provided many short-term, low-income contracts to the host companies at a time when machine and support costs were relatively high. Only the fittest survived.

Schools, engineering firms, law offices and others took advantage of the dazzling instantaneity which the terminals provided. Games and demonstrations were popularized, and the mysterious jargon of earlier access methods was eliminated or greatly reduced. By the 1980s, several companies were designing computers just for this purpose, including UNIVAC's 9000 series, DEC's VAX, and others.

Access Method Six: Minicomputers and distributed data processing

Small computers costing from $10,000 to $90,000 are known as minicomputers. Digital Equipment Corporation produced one of the first, announcing its PDP-8 in 1961. It sold for $27,000. Data General followed, then Varian, Mohawk, Interdata, Nova, Prime and others. These minicomputers were about the size of a two-drawer file cabinet.

This access method enables a business to maintain private control of its data and programs, avoiding the risk of trusting a distant host machine with all of the company information. Also, if a business is spending $30,000 to $70,000 annually for RJE or time-sharing power, a local computer purchased for $50,000 is an appealing proposition.

The minicomputer is a strong product in the computer marketplace despite certain disadvantages not always taken into account by eager buyers. The initial purchase price does not include some hidden costs, a few of which are listed below.

1. The operating system program on small computers cannot

be as flexible or convenient as those on larger, mature computer systems. Their low purchase price usually precludes the investment of the two hundred-odd person-years to prepare the comprehensive operating system program that would go into a larger model. Therefore the local computer shop may have to write various services into its application programs which a mature operating system would have performed without effort or programming cost.

2. The true cost of establishing a local in-house computer shop is not clearly visible to the potential minicomputer buyer. The need for a programmer to maintain and enhance the operating system (system programmers earn more than some vice presidents), for operators to administer the system and safeguard the files, for programmers to write application programs, for insurance to cover the equipment and liability, for maintenance contracts to repair the hardware and for plans for additional peripheral devices and added memory, and so on, often become apparent only *after* a minicomputer is installed.

3. The repertoire of application programs, such as payroll, or accounts receivable, seldom fits the unique needs of the local buyer. Considerable time is required to design local software systems, code them, test them, maintain them and carry them through several versions. It is often frustrating and costly.

However, minicomputers have become a stable and growing product, partly because of the unique need they fill, namely the need for branch offices to retain some control over a portion of their data and programs which the corporate data center may not care about. Branch offices can satisfy their local data-processing needs on a local minicomputer. Then at night (or weekly) the minicomputer can transfer its collected files of data down a telephone line to the corporate machine for further integration into the larger management information system. This "distributed processing" style of computing is discussed in chapter 13.

Just as timesharing made personal computing power available to small users and individuals, minicomputers have made data-file management more local and more personally controlled.

Access Method Seven: Microcomputers everywhere

Microcomputers are miniature computers etched into the silicon surfaces of an electronic chip—often only a quarter of an inch square. This little computer, together with added memory chips

More than 100,000 components are crowded onto this Bell Laboratories computer chip. Smaller than a postage stamp, it is a BELLMAC 32-bit microprocessor. A memory chip, power supply, and keyboard would be added to make it function as a computer. *(Photo courtesy Bell Laboratories.)*

and other logic circuits, can be placed inside a typewriter or keyboard-screen terminal so that a language like BASIC can be made immediately available without any other attachment. Or, for instant use, a secondary memory chip can automatically provide a program which begins to run immediately when turned on.

André Vancroux described the surprising new technology in the May 1975 *Scientific American:*

> . . . a major conceptual advance in 1971, when the Intel Corporation, which had undertaken to develop a calculator chip, chose to design it as a more versatile, programmable, single chip micro-

processor. A microprocessor is equivalent to the central processing unit of a larger computer. Known as the Intel 4004, the device processes blocks consisting of four bits, or binary digits, at a time. It has 2,250 transistors on a silicon substrate measuring .117 by .159 inch, and it comes in a package with 16 pins, or leads. All that is needed to make the microprocessor into a minimal general-purpose microcomputer that could sell for $50 are two additional devices (a control memory and a temporary storage memory) and a master clock to time the system's operation. (p. 32)

This miniaturization generated the first possibility of "one person, one computer" because automated manufacturing methods can lower the cost and bring it to the mass market. The potential market for these devices parallels that of the record player and television set.

In April, May and June 1977, *Radio-Electronics* published the full plans for building a microcomputer costing between one hundred and three hundred dollars. Then, in August that year, three companies began to sell ready-to-use systems for the home. The Commodore PET computer was popular in 1977. It cost $995, complete with TV screen, typewriter keyboard and one standard tape cassette reader for storing programs or data. When turned on it was ready for immediate use. One cassette tape, supplied with the computer, provided ready-made programs for games and for home-management information systems.

Heath Company announced its microcomputer kit, and Radio Shack announced its assembled computer at the Atlantic City Microcomputer Fair on August 27, 1977. The two-day fair was attended by approximately 20,000 people.

Hobbyists had begun to form clubs and to hold state-wide conferences in 1974, but the microcomputers they used were usually homemade systems built from available components. In 1977, with the availability of assembled and tested systems, a major social innovation began. It was like the difference between ham radio fans and citizens'-band radio users. A box that worked, giving results without requiring technical knowledge, was suddenly available, and it began to outstrip all prior records for market penetration. The personal home computer is now available in computer stores across the country, at a price sometimes below $200.

Nearly all media in their evolution move from early general purpose mass media to more personalized and specialized media. Readers who wish to pursue such theories of media evolution will enjoy the writings of Maisel, Gumpert and Merrill.

While microcomputers will not eradicate large, central, general-

This small envelope contains a flexible disk of magnetic material on which small computers record data. Known as floppy disks, they typically cost five to eight dollars and can hold up to eighty pages of typewritten material. Any letter or word on the disk can be retrieved and viewed in less than half a second, after which it can be revised if desired. The equipment is IBM's Displaywriter. It can be purchased off the shelf from the company's Computer Stores. *(Photo courtesy IBM.)*

purpose computers, they will definitely service more people than the general-purpose computers ever could. The scope of this access method will be described in later chapters.

Microcomputers quickly became embedded in elevators, word-processing equipment, typesetting equipment, electronic mail equipment, copying machines and music synthesizers. By 1980 it had become difficult to obtain a Master's Degree in many fields without learning how to program and utilize a microcomputer terminal. Projections from International Data Corporation envision 3.2 million desk top computers installed by 1984.

Access Method Eight:
Push-button computers

The option of playing simulated tennis on the home TV screen, or space war at the shopping mall game room, was a great promotional event for computers. People hardly realize that they are using computers when they play these games. Just as comic books might lure a child into reading words and sentences, so the computerized games camouflage the new computer medium behind a colorful disguise of fun and pleasure.

The ability to bring computing to the public in a packaged, ready-to-use form awaited the perfection of the microcomputer. As the price of these computers on a chip fell to $200, then $100, then $35, then $11, manufacturers could package them in ever more creative and appealing ways. Drugstores sell $18 Christmas gift sets containing four TV games for the home. Players exercise their fingers and wrists, turning knobs to block the tennis ball or hockey puck "bleep" as it bounces around the screen.

In 1980 the Speak and Spell toy sent adults back to the toy-store to buy more and more options and boards for the device. It was good for the children—they learned from it—and good for the parents—they learned how to add the options.

Push-button computers require little or no knowledge of how the computer works. Children who never heard of programming or binary codes can use these computers. Today, many toys are packed with computer technology, most of it friendly in its responses and clever in its disguise.

Early television users were also electronic tinkerers. After a few years, however, the technology had matured so that TV sets came with only four or five knobs, at which point everyone could enjoy the new medium. Computers are now approaching this same maturity. In France, for instance, Phillips Data Systems has introduced a credit card which contains a microprocessor. It is not much thicker than an ordinary credit card, but it opens entirely new options. One can buy a card which "contains" 5000 francs, for example. At the grocery or department store, each purchase reduces the fund amount inside the credit card until it reaches zero. If you lose the card, no one else can use it because of the passwords which you alone possess.

Computers of this type contain a single program—already in place when you turn it on. It could never have been packaged without twenty-five years of experimentation and technological

The Commodore PET captured an early market in 1977 as the first low-cost, mass-produced computer terminal. Commodore dominated the European and Japanese markets, selling more computers to the public than several other vendors combined. The computer is inside the keyboard and it can be tied to mainframe computers as well as operating as a desk-top device. Its internal memory capacity is 32,000 characters, allowing it to hold a program of that size. *(Photo courtesy Commodore Business Machines.)*

development. The circuits in these computers are so miniaturized and microscopic that the average layman cannot even comprehend them. We just enjoy using them.

Eight distinct methods have evolved for allowing access to computer power. The first primitive method (running programs one at a time) was superseded, but eventually that first method returned as the most pleasant way to operate one's personal mini or microcomputer. Pleading with the director of a batch computer shop for a guaranteed two-day turnaround is no longer necessary; the home computer has nothing else to do but execute one program at a time, satisfying whatever task the user has defined.

In answer to the question "Are computers becoming more accessible to individuals?" the trend is clear. Personal home micro-computers can easily be operated by anyone. They are being sold to the public every day. Such terminals and toys are no match for the government computers, nor are they a threat to the large corporate machines, but they will spread to the masses of people a basic understanding of what computers do.

The internal speed of the Commodore CBM 8032 home computer is approximately three times faster than the IBM 360-25 which powered the early batch shops twenty years before it. Buyers of microcomputers will never know the agony of rule-keeping and the hours of waiting which older and slower systems demanded. Now we merely push a button to request one program or another, juke-box style.

Bibliography

Chamberlin, H., *Musical Applications of Micro Processors*. Rochelle Park, N. J.: Hayden Book, 1980.

Conway, R., J. Archer, and R. Conway, *Programming for Poets: A Gentle Introduction Using PASCAL*. Cambridge, Ma.: Winthrop, 1980.

Crowley, ed., *Acronyms, Initialisms and Abbreviations*. Detroit: Gale Research, 1979.

Gumpert, G., "The Rise of Mini-comm," *Journal of Communication* 20 (September 1970).

Lewis, T. G., *The Mind Appliance: Home Computer Applications*. Rochelle Park, N. J.: Hayden Book, 1978.

Lusa, J. M., "The Wave of the Future," *Infosystems* 24, no. 9 (September 1977).

Maisel, R., "The Decline of Mass Media," *Public Opinion Quarterly* 37 (summer 1973).

Merrill, J., and R. Lowerstein, *Media, Messages and Men*. New York: David McKay, 1971.

Nyborg, P. S., P. M. McCarter, and W. Erickson, eds., *Information Processing in the United States*. Montvale, N. J.: AFIPS Press, 1977.

Solomon, L., and S. Veit, *Getting Involved with Your Own Computer*. Hillside, N. J.: Enslow, 1977.

Vancroux, A. G., "Microcomputers," *Scientific American* 232, no. 5 (May 1975).

Weisbecker, J., *Home Computers Can Make You Rich*. Rochelle Park, N. J.: Hayden Book, 1980.

Chapter Nine

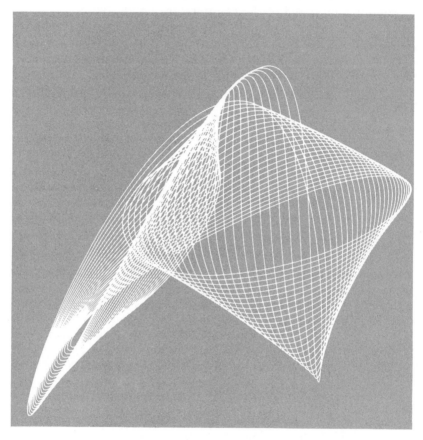

Who Would Ever
Want to
Use One of Them?

- ☐ Computers can solve the same problems as pocket calculators.

- ☐ Teachers use microcomputers to present personalized, interactive lesson and simulation materials to students.

- ☐ Manufacturers use computers to manage warehouses which ship goods on hourly schedules.

- ☐ Inventors can fly unbuilt aircraft on computers.

- ☐ Census data and election returns are analyzed statistically by computer.

Will it rain tomorrow? Does air pollution cause the ocean levels to rise? How much fertilizer is too much? What curve should a new camera lens have? Do sonar echoes indicate the presence of oil in certain geological strata?

No social security number or other personal identifier of the operator is required for a computer to solve these problems. The computer uses presented in this chapter are those which permit people to satisfy their computational needs and research goals. When used in this way the computer becomes an extension of man's arithmetical and logical mind.

What are the ways in which people use the computer to solve problems? As a problem-solving tool, does the computer operate as a neutral servant? In what areas are people or institutions assisted by the calculating and arithmetical abilities of the computer?

This chapter surveys five types of problems that the computer is often commanded to solve. Most of them could be performed on any type of computer—a desktop microcomputer or a giant million-dollar main frame. Any of them could solve these problems.

Problem-solving Use One:
Calculator types of usage

Pocket calculators are fine if you don't mind pushing the buttons. Anything a pocket calculator can do, however, the computer can also do, and sometimes more conveniently—especially if a lot of arithmetic is involved. Most timesharing systems and desk-top microcomputers provide their terminal users with a calculator with several memories such as X, Y, and Z, and they incorporate all of the trigonometric functions such as cosine, logarithm, etc. By simply typing the line:

((33-log4.701)/cos21)**2.035

and pressing return, the answer will be sent back immediately. (The two asterisks mean "raised to the power of," the dash means "minus.")

If the calculator program in the computer isn't good enough, the user can write a program for any other style of problem solving. Examples of such problem-solving uses of the computer are the following:

1. Programs that add, subtract, multiply and perform various trigonometric functions.

2. Programs to compute mortgage payments over many years given certain interest rates and other variables.

3. Programs to compute multiple regression or other statistical analysis for any set of numbers.

4. Programs used in electronics to compute optimal circuit design.

5. Programs used to compute changing orbits during space flights.

6. Programs used to simulate air quality, pesticide levels, the age of rocks or geothermal problems.

7. Programs used in blood analysis, biotechnology, medical diagnosis, etc.

8. Programs used in economic modeling, scheduling, critical path analysis and resource management.

9. Programs that analyze language, translate medium to medium, do typesetting, manuscript editing, etc.

10. Programs that assist music creation, choreography, sculpture, art or drawing.

11. Programs that play chess, hangman, backgammon, bridge, golf, star-trek, etc.

12. Programs that compute biorhythms, astrology charts, convert TV images to alphabetic printouts.

The problems to be solved may involve nuclear weapons or cancer research—the computer doesn't know the difference. The calculations could be performed (at greater length and cost, of course) with pencils, adding machines or calculators if computer use were forbidden. All of the access methods discussed in the previous chapter offer and encourage this common type of computer usage. Computer vendors often supply some of these programs free of charge when a computer is sold so as to make a good impression on customers who do not yet realize the many person-years of programming which are required to write more personalized application programs.

Several computer languages have evolved to assist the programmer in writing personalized programs to solve problems.

1. *APL.* "A Programming Language" was conceived by Kenneth Iverson as a means of expressing any of the events in the world in a consistent mathematical notation. His programming or notation conventions were published some years before computers were able to implement the concept. In about 1968 IBM implemented the Iverson language, to the delight of many engineers, mathematicians and researchers. Research laboratories and university scientists paid millions of dollars to the timesharing industry through their demand for this service. In 1981 three desk-top microcomputers were available which could execute APL programs; one from IBM, one from Vanguard Systems and Commodore's Super PET, which carries five languages on a 134K microcomputer.

2. *BASIC.* "Beginners All-purpose Symbolic Instruction Code," developed by J. Kemeny and H. Kurtz at Dartmouth College, was quickly adopted by all lovers of games, simulations, mathematical puzzles, and statistical reports. Most colleges and about 30 percent of high schools now offer courses in its use, and nearly all students at Dartmouth since 1968 have learned to use it. BASIC has been adopted by microcomputer users as the most common medium of communication and programming. As a computer language it has deficiencies, but it has become the de facto language linking all micro users.

3. *FORTRAN.* "Formula Translation" was one of the earliest computer languages, and is still widely used by people wishing to write programs to convert a mathematical formula into a program with a formal report resulting from its execution.

4. *Pascal.* This language came into acceptance between 1977 and 1979. It encourages programmers to write programs which are structured and therefore more understandable.

There are dozens of other computer languages, of course, forming the basis for thousands of textbooks and college courses.

5. *COBOL.* "Common Business Oriented Language" is re-

quired by the government to be available on any general purpose computer which it purchases or leases. A program written in COBOL should be able to run on any general purpose computer.

PL-1 (Programming Language One), ALGOL (Algorithmic Language), Assembler and others are used for various purposes as the method of telling a computer what it is to do.

Problem-solving programs are often given away as an incentive for signing up as a computer customer. Many useful programs have achieved some status by being published in magazines or books. Teachers can then give homework assignments which require the execution of several such programs. Certain textbooks from Dartmouth College professors (and others) assume that the Dartmouth library of BASIC programs is available to the teacher and students.

The home microcomputer provides every opportunity for this type of computer use to expand and flourish. BASIC is available when the switch is turned on. Neighbors and computer clubs can trade floppy disks of BASIC programs which contain innovative and personalized problem-solving programs. Mathematical drudgery can be transformed by the home computer into a playful activity like a crossword-puzzle, accompanied by laughter and pleasure.

Problem-solving Use Two:
Computer-assisted instruction

Hello Mary. Welcome back. It's been four days since you were here. So far you have spent 17.5 hours at the terminal for a total of 9 sessions.
Prepare for your typewriting warmup exercises.

Thus begins the tenth session of a college typewriting course taught entirely by computer with no teacher present. More than 4,700 students have passed through three such courses (typewriting, nursing math and computer literacy) at Ocean County College in New Jersey. Tutoring, drill, practice and testing is presented to the student by the computer.

In this use of the computer, a special type of problem solving is addressed: how to get a learner to interact with selected knowledge. The goal in writing CAI (Computer Aided Instruction) lesson modules is not necessarily to mimic what teachers do in front of a class, for normal teaching includes some negative aspects which CAI, when well implemented, can avoid. Table 9.1 compares the qualities of human and computer teaching.

Of course, mediocre CAI lesson materials can be delivered by computers, just as mediocre class lectures can be delivered by lecturers. But the primary justification for the CAI medium is that individual learners learn at individual rates, and that computers can sometimes be programmed to deal with this fact more easily than classroom teachers can adjust to it.

The students who passed through the three CAI courses at Ocean County College have provided interesting statistics regarding this method of learning. Toward the end of two of the courses the computer asked the students questions regarding the effectiveness of this mode of instruction. The statistics in Figure 9.1 reveal a significant positive acceptance of CAI. These statistics are based on the responses from about 2,900 students across a four-

Table 9.1
Contrast between two learning environments

Human instructor	Interactive electronic instruction
Instruction is directed to the average student in the group.	The learning rate for each individual is sensed by the computer and remedial or advanced themes are provided.
Teachers give lower grades to slower learners.	Computers will give endless hours of extra drill or dialogue to slower learners.
Teachers get their primary feedback at examination time.	Computers get feedback at every interactive point, minute by minute.
Teachers mean that class times must be scheduled at set hours.	Learners call in for appointments with a computer terminal at any time. Terminals in the home can provide all subjects at all hours.
Teachers are not at their best every time they perform.	Computer-based materials are tested and modified to obtain excellence in every module.
Teachers may not keep their lectures up to date.	Computer-based materials can be updated every hour or week if required.

Figure 9.1
Survey of 2,900 CAI students

QUESTION: *How do you evaluate CAI in general as a method of instruction?*

(70.6%) A. More satisfactory than a classroom situation.
(24.8%) B. About the same satisfaction as being in a classroom.
(4.6%) C. Less satisfactory than a classroom.

QUESTION: *In other classes there is much social interchange. In this course:*

(41.9%) A. Didn't want social interchange; happy without it.
(47.8%) B. Interchange with the terminal simulated a friendship.
(10.3%) C. Wished for more social interaction and missed it.

QUESTION: *Would you recommend this course to other students or friends?*

(77.6%) A. Yes, with enthusiasm.
(20.9%) B. Yes, but no more than any other course.
(1.5%) C. Would not recommend it.

QUESTION: *What impact did the course have on you?*

(26.4%) A. Hope to take more computer courses; a direct result of this course.
(58.6%) B. Thinking was stimulated. Interested in the subject now.
(14.1%) C. Conveyed necessary information; not turned on by the course.
(0.9%) D. A waste of time; collected credits—little worth.

---

year period; the students were aware that their names would not be associated with their answers when the questions were analyzed.

CAI means many things to different people, probably because it can be incorporated so many different ways into the curriculum. Figure 9.2 lists some of the many modes in which interactive learning materials can be released to students. Figure 9.3 (authored by J. Wolcott) illustrates a sample of the interaction which a typewriting lesson might provide.

Computer-aided instruction is only one strategy in a large spectrum of learning environments. Surprisingly, teachers often feel threatened by the idea of CAI and imagine that it might someday be used to displace them and teach all courses. These same teachers often welcome courses which are offered through TV tapes or audio cassettes with slides. CAI is merely one variety of general

Figure 9.2
CAI modes

Instructor highly involved ↑ ↓ Instructor minimally involved	1. Provide an interactive drill or simulation at a computer terminal. To be used as a homework assignment lasting 20 minutes to 1 hour. 2. Provide a lengthy set of drills. Students attend classes in the traditional way. Completion of the series of drills may comprise a significant part of the grade. 3. Continuous and lengthy work at computer terminals. Students report to teachers weekly or monthly. 4. Full course of instruction is offered on hard-copy terminals. Students build books from the terminal output. Final copy in book form is presented to the teacher at the end of the term. 5. A full course of instruction is offered on any computer terminal—screens are acceptable. All evaluations are performed by the computer. No teacher is involved. Grades may be deposited directly in the student record by the computer.

Figure 9.3
Sample CAI typewriting drill

We're ready to try some response typing again, Joan. Touch "return" as soon as you are ready. :

Here we go:

razor	:razor
quick	:quick
question	:question
size	:size
quiet	:quite
zipper	:zipper
querry	:querry
lizard	:lizard
quite	:quiet
dozen	:dozen

TIME: You may circle your errors while I check the score.

That took you 1 minute and 11 seconds.

You made two errors.

Do you wish to try this exercise again?: <u>NO.</u>

The right column is typed by the student.
Source: J. Wolcott.

systems for learning. It is no more likely to replace classroom teachers than film-assisted instruction or book-assisted instruction.

Home teletext systems, on the other hand, are likely to be a threat to the whole concept of college and learning as something occurring mostly in classrooms, accompanied by transcripts, testing, rigid scheduling and accreditation authorities. Chapter 18 will review these systems. By 1985 colleges will probably incorporate teletext systems into the course work of nearly all disciplines.

Learning systems are meant to be systems of support for the student, fueling the learning process. Regardless of the communication system used (human teachers or any other type), learning systems usually include strategies for accomplishing these processes:

1. Curriculum design and authorship.
2. Curriculum delivery.
3. Student contact and interaction with subject matter.
4. Retaining of student response data.
5. Adjusting to student needs or interests.
6. Reporting of student comprehension.
7. Demonstration of the system.

Most computer-aided instruction materials attempt to implement these functions through computer programs. There is no more likelihood that all courses might be taught by computer than that all courses might be taught by television tapes. In the repertoire of all possible learning systems, CAI provides one more variety of the whole spectrum of ways that learners interact with their subject matter.

CAI is operational at hundreds of schools and colleges. It rarely spreads to fill its potential, however, except where heavy government funding supports it. University administrators and teachers may see the folly of this neglect when the local cable companies and interactive video information systems bring language learning and other lessons directly into the home. Other agencies long ago began to reorchestrate certain learning materials into the new forms required by the computer-based media. The universities have lost valuable years of CAI and video-disk based development which could have put them into this business.

In a utopian college, if these learning tools were applied to the dispersal of knowledge and carried to their fullest conclusion, the features of Figure 9.4 would surround the student in a pleasant, interactive and learner-controlled environment.

Figure 9.4
Toward the College of Utopia

If the means become available for interactive learning materials to be received in the home, what new ways of life will be called "college"?

1. There will be no grades of D or F. Learners will be tutored until competence is demonstrated. "Provided you reach the end of the course, you will receive an A."

2. The "school" will be pleasing to the learner. If the student is ill, moody, or uninterested for any reason, the computer will not be annoyed. Take two months off for reasons of disinterest, nice weather or vacation.

3. The electronic tutors will be available round-the-clock. No more scheduling of history classes at 3 p.m. Tuesday and Thursday.

4. Textbooks will be unique for each student; each book adjusted in content to meet the interests and needs of the individual.

5. When five or ten national experts collaborate in writing a new CAI course, the user is interacting with the minds of these experts, reversing the normal student–teacher ratio.

6. Human encounters will be more meaningful. Lectures in old classrooms did not encourage conversation or social interaction. Students will relate to each other and to "experts" in new ways.

7. The tutors will be infinitely patient, staying with the student until every idea or skill is grasped, testing for both immediate and delayed understanding.

8. The electronic tutor will utilize colorful media like video disk, stereo sound, tape recordings, and other exciting source materials to make the instruction engaging. TV tapes of teachers lecturing will probably not be used because they are not interactive.

9. Learning will be pleasurable, even ecstatic, not painful. No threat of one's future hanging on grades or transcripts.

10. Learning will be available at home, on vacation, in community centers, on planes, in motels, in military barracks, anywhere in the world.

11. Learners will progress at their own rate of speed. Statements such as "We must reach the Civil War by Thanksgiving," will be unknown.

12. All age groups may demand lifelong learning privileges. They will desire to own the equipment and receive instruction with registration, admission, pretesting or tuition. The right to an electronic education may become an American right.

13. Feedback from the electronic tutors will be humane and supportive. No penalties for wrong answers. No long periods of inactive listening. The senses will be engaged, with user responses required frequently in the games, simulations, drills and other stimulating activities.

14. The unity of knowledge may be emphasized as the user chooses from cross-discipline themes rather than from narrow course subjects.

Problem-solving Use Three: Programs that audit and manage large revolving inventories

The moment-by-moment inventory status of a factory warehouse, whether it contains perfume, refrigerators or TV sets, cannot be known accurately without computers. When truckloads of washing machines roll in and out by the hour, the stock changes more rapidly than typewriters and paper are able to report. Thus the computer provides considerable relief to the warehouse manager who can call to his TV screen the current status of a complex inventory—even those items which are in transit.

Such systems treat the warehouse as a large dynamic data file which is constantly updated through a network of terminals. For example, factory assembly lines can constantly inform the computer of the accounting of goods flowing from the factory. The warehouse location of these goods is recorded through computer terminals there. The shipping data may include time, date, truck, driver, route, destination and mileage. They are all recorded in the computer. These records are constantly compared to the orders received so that any excess production at the factory and consequent storage problems can be avoided without a shortfall of goods. The savings which result can be significant, perhaps determining the difference between bankruptcy and success.

Problem-solving Use Four: Research uses of the computer

The history of invention and discovery provides many illustrations of new ideas for which it took someone between ten and fifty years to produce a real-world proof or working model. Atomic fusion, for instance, had many theoretical proofs, but the hydrogen bomb was its first actual proof.

The computer, when used in the problem-solving mode, accelerates by magnitudes the modeling and proving of theories. Someone who believes that a triplane with five jet engines will fly efficiently can model the idea in computer notation, "flying" the plane on the computer before it is built to determine how it will behave when it is built. Results of such simulations can be obtained in minutes, enabling the evolution of theories and hypotheses to occur faster and faster.

Every day people get hunches, ideas and theories about all kinds of things—how the weather can be controlled, how children learn, how the earth's crust moves, how planets are captured by suns, how house-dust causes allergies, how energy can be harnessed, how nations rise and fall, etc. Sometimes microcomputer terminals can be programmed to simulate or model such things. More often, researchers create large mathematical models of that portion of the world which they wish to control or modify and use the computer to prove or disprove their predicted results. Such programs are called "number crunchers"; typically, the researcher goes to the computer center late at night, taking over the entire machine and running the number cruncher until morning. The outcome might be a single number printed on a page, or a graph, or a list of relationships. But to the researcher, the result often represents new knowledge in the world.

Many false directions can be avoided by using computer research assistance. After eight hours of computer execution of formulas and mathematical functions, the scientist knows that 500 years of constant arithmetic performed by a roomful of slaves *might* have produced the same result.

Universities sometimes support one-third of their computer costs by obtaining grants to cover their research projects. The National Science Foundation awards about $12 million in grants each year to universities in support of various research projects. Readers interested in this use of computers can contact the National Science Foundation, Washington, D. C., to obtain lists of the institutions and research projects which have been funded each year. Other typical projects can be discovered by calling the director of research at any large university.

Problem-solving Use Five:
Statistical analysis of large files

The earliest expenditures on automated information processing were justified by the government by its need to analyze the census data. An event in 1890 represented a major turning point in the history of automating the statistical analysis of large files. Dr. Herman Hollerith was employed by the U. S. Census Bureau. In the IBM book *More About the Computer* we read that:

> . . . he devised a way to represent a person's name, age, sex, address and other vital statistics in the form of holes punched in paper cards.

This coded data then was counted electrically. During the 1890 census, his ideas enabled the government to tabulate the census data more than twice as fast as it had handled the 1880 census, even though the population had increased 25 percent during that decade. Without some such mechanized tabulation, the census data would have become obsolete before it could have been completely analyzed. . . .

During the first third of the twentieth century, punched-card machines based on Hollerith's ideas were modified, improved, speeded up. . . .

In the 1930s, punched-card equipment made it possible to handle a mountain of data which suddenly had to be recorded when the Social Security Act was passed. The same kinds of machines were also used to develop statistical tables, calculate the orbit of the moon more accurately than ever before and speed calculations. . . . (p. 5)

The idea of keypunching a data file of many millions of records and analyzing it statistically is still with us in the form of analytical statistics. Major computer programs are installed on most middle to large scale computers to perform all possible statistical analyses. Program packages such as SPSS (Statistical Package for the Social Sciences) or BMD (Biomedical) or SAS (Statistical Analysis System) are available to nearly all researchers.

The earliest government orders for computers (as opposed to mechanical card-handling machines) grew out of the continuing need to analyze large data files. The Bureau of Standards began to build its own computers in 1948, one on the East coast, the other on the West coast. The computers were named SEAC and SWAC representing Standards East Automatic Computer and Standards West Automatic Computer. SEAC in Washington, D. C., ran quite successfully at the Bureau of Standards between 1950 and 1960, performing statistical analyses of large data files.

Today, from anywhere in the United States, anyone can arrange to dial into various computers which provide various types of statistical services and all types of data files to analyze.

Also, the small home computers selling for a few hundred dollars will eventually permit anyone to use the computer for statistical research. Individual statistical programs are often written in BASIC and sold on floppy disks to users for five or seven dollars through the clubs and journals to which they subscribe. The data to be analyzed reside on other floppy disks which can be generated by the user or purchased from various suppliers. Thus, if a statistician wishes to perform multiple regression or chi-square anal-

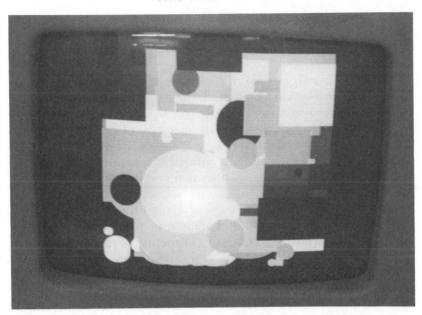

The GIGI computer color graphics system from Digital Equipment Corporation allows novice users to create graphs, cartoons, pictures and slides at very low cost. The system is marketed to business and engineering firms. By 1990 most statistical data will be dynamically displayed in color graphs. *(Photo courtesy Digital Equipment Corporation.)*

ysis with 50,000 records of data items, he or she first loads the multiple regression disk into the home computer and then the screen tells the user to insert the other disk which contains the data. The data records will then be scanned one by one and analyzed as desired. The results can be displayed on the video screen or on a typewriter-printer if it is attached. Mainframe computers can do this type of analysis less awkwardly—but at a higher price.

What data files are available to the public for analysis? A few sources are listed below, revealing the range of data files which hobby users or researchers can obtain. (None of these files contain Social Security numbers, names or other identifying information. They may contain such information as the city in which the data originated, or even the city-block. But personal identifiers are not released with the records. Such files are said to contain "blind data" meaning that actual individuals cannot be identified.)

Interested researchers can receive a list of the data files available from more than 100 federal agencies in a Department of Commerce book, *The NTIS Directory of Computerized Data Files.* Social and political scientists will enjoy the listings of 300 data files which have been collected and maintained by 220 colleges and universities, in the Institute for Social Research book *Guide to Resources and Services, 1980-81.*

Another directory of 800 machine-readable files, entitled *Government Data Banks,* is available from the Association for Computing Machinery. Persons who are engaged in stock market business analysis can receive analytical assistance from COMPUSTAT. (A 70-page description of this service is available from Investors Management Sciences, Inc., 1221 Avenue of the Americas, New York, N. Y. 10020. It documents the many data files that can be researched.)

The ability to research business investments through computer statistical analysis is a radical challenge to the armchair analyst. Those persons who are able to pay for the use of this new medium will benefit in significant ways—real dollar gains can result.

The question "Is the computer a neutral servant?" was raised at the beginning of the chapter. One possible threat deserves recognition, related to the so-called blind data files. Files such as those mentioned in this chapter do not carry sure identification of persons involved, and are easily analyzed with statistical computer programs. However, subtle but important changes to private individuals can result from such statistical treatment of these records. Statistics are created, and categories formed—of people who fall into groups tagged as "unemployed," "unmarried," "black," "under age 21," "South Bronx," "ninth-grade dropout." Sometimes categorization or generalization can go beyond all justification, based on what the statistics "prove." Thus, because of the pervasiveness of modern analytical statistics, individuals pay higher automobile insurance if they live on one side of a street rather than the other. The computer "maps" individuals into certain high risk groups based on statistical aggregates. The State Farm Insurance Company charges 10 percent less on automobile insurance to the person who drives fewer than ten miles to work, regardless of how many days he or she works. Life insurance premiums vary between men and women not because of individual appraisals, but because of refined computer analysis of volume data from each state and county. Bank credit often varies based on sex and age.

Milton Wessel, an attorney specializing in computer cases identifies the threat of what he calls data-in-gross:

Social scientists have achieved a high degree of accuracy in predicting future patterns of criminal conduct among children and recidivism among released prisoners predicated primarily on background information, to the point where one's belief in individual self-determination is shaken.

Unlike transactional data where individual rights have long been the subject of some common law concern, there is almost no legal precedent to help us handle data-in-gross. Nothing in present law, for example, prevents the politician from statistical research and analysis of voting patterns and instruction to his workers *not* to "get out the votes" of certain specific categories of person because a high percentage always votes the other way, nor prevents the stigmatism of a race or religion on the basis of patterns of mass behavior. The problem is that the computer makes so much more of this possible, that data-in-gross can ultimately become as much of a concern as individual data.*

The impact of blind data carried in computer files can be seen as a new factor in our social milieu, causing us to relate to one another in new, less personal ways.

Media impose biases on the simplest messages they carry. Computers, the newest medium in our society, have their own bias, and it can be seen even in such benign uses as problem solving and census analysis.

Bibliography

Birke, Y., ed., *Computer Applications in Management.* New York: Halsted, 1976.

Collected Algorithms from ACM. New York: Association for Computing Machinery, 1960.

Computer Programs Directory. New York: CCM Information Corporation, 1971.

Emery, J., *Networking for Higher Education.* Boulder, Co.: Westview, 1979.

ENTELEK CAI CMI Information Exchange. Newburyport, Ma.: ENTELEK, 1980.

Gepner, H. L., ed., *Datapro Directory of Software.* Delran, N. J.: Datapro Research, 1978.

Gottschall, E. M., ed., *U & l c. Vision '80s* 7, no. 2 (June 1980).

Government Data Banks. New York: Economic Research Institute, 1977.

Guide to Resources and Services, 1980–81. Ann Arbor, Mi.: Institute for Social Research, University of Michigan, 1981.

---

* M. Wessel, *Freedom's Edge: The Computer Threat to Society.* © 1974, Addison-Wesley Publishing Co., Inc., p. 38. Reprinted with permission.

Hamilton, D., ed., *ICP Quarterly Software Review*. Carmel, Ind.: International Computer Programs, 1978.

Hy, R. J., *Using the Computer in the Social Sciences*. New York: Elsevier North-Holland, 1978.

Levy, D., and M. Newborn, *More Chess and Computers*. Potomac, Md.: Computer Science Press, 1980.

Lias, E. J., *Establishing CAI in a College Environment*. Toms River, N. J.: Ocean County College, 1977.

More About the Computer. Armonk, N. Y.: IBM Corporation, 1971.

Nahigian, J., and W. Hodges, *Computer Games for Business, Schools and Homes*. Cambridge, Ma.: Winthrop, 1979.

Postman, N., *Teaching as a Conserving Activity*. New York: Dell, 1980.

Postman, N., and C. Weingartner, *How to Recognize a Good School*. Bloomington, Ind.: Phi Delta Kappa, 1973.

Pritchard, A., *A Guide to Computer Literature*, 2nd ed. London: Clive Bingley, 1972.

Rienhoff, O., and M. E. Abrahams, *Computer in the Doctor's Office*. New York: Elsevier North-Holland, 1980.

Rosen, S., *A Quarter Century View*. New York: ACM Publications, 1971.

Severino, E., ed., *Auerbach Software Reports*. Philadelphia: Auerbach, 1978.

U. S. Department of Commerce, *The NTIS Directory of Computerized Data Files*. Springfield, Va.: National Technological Information Service, 1975.

van Tassel, *The Compleat Computer*. Palo Alto, Ca.: Science Research Associates, 1976.

Wessel, M., *Freedom's Edge: The Computer Threat to Society*. Reading, Ma.: Addison-Wesley, 1975.

Wolcott, J., *Typewriting CAI Course*. Toms River, N. J.: Ocean County College, 1979.

Chapter Ten

Computers
and Filing Cabinets:
The Data-base Future

□ Until 1974, the official records of U. S. citizens were scattered in file cabinets throughout the country and could not be viewed as a whole.

□ Personal records can now be placed into computerized data-base systems, enabling privileged authorities to navigate through them in powerful ways.

□ More than ten thousand data-base systems are now used in the United States by government and corporations.

Sometimes computers are set to scan data files containing Social Security numbers and other personal identifiers, and these uses are far more threatening to the privacy of individuals than those touched on in Chapter 9. Nearly all large computers outside of research centers and laboratories are obtained for their ability to hold and manipulate data files of financial or other personal data. These computers are used to preserve records about people, sorting them, classifying them by formula, matching them to associated records and reporting them in any desired format.

Who collects personal data about us? Why do they do it? What trends in the evolution of data management can be identified? What data does the government carry regarding its citizens? What future directions can be predicted given the current trends?

The computer's effect on society is clearly seen as revolutionary in its manipulation of these giant files of personal data. However, all media, including speech, writing, radio, film, and television, are recognized as revolutionary, each providing new possibilities for social relationships and group rearrangements. They modify society silently but sweepingly. Media such as speech, books or movies may appear to be neutral carriers of messages or information, but we have overwhelming evidence that all media bias the messages which pass through them in a subtle but consistent manner. "Consistent" in that each medium will uniformly distort its messages in predictable ways; "subtle" in that the bias is usually hidden behind the messages being transmitted.

Computers are a new medium in our culture when they are used as data-base management systems for the processing of personal information. Automated record handling will equal television or print in its ability to restructure culture, as we shall see. Large-scale personal data handling by computer is predicted for the time period 1980 to 2000.

The evolution of data-base management systems

Just as radio signals speed up or amplify the medium of speech, so computers, when used to automate personal data files, speed up the medium of record-keeping. They thereby create a new, pervasive environment, whose influence will probably lure our culture into new behaviors and relationships.

A person, when speaking, cannot be heard outside the immediate environment, though on the radio he or she can be heard around the world. Similarly, folders in file cabinets have only had a parochial influence until now. When computerized, the same files and records can be linked together in surprising new ways.

In this context, consider the purposes of data collection. In a precomputer culture dominated by paper and print, the personal records and transactions of the populace lie hopelessly scattered in the file cabinets of government and business. In the years 1930 to 1955, records were gathered mainly for local offices. To collect or sort records into any meaningful or useful general or nationwide pattern would have been a costly if not futile undertaking. The data were present, but who could sort through them all?

Without computers, the FBI, the Census Bureau, the Internal Revenue and other agencies functioned largely as warehouses of file folders. Analysis of their information holdings was restricted to spot checking and crisis investigation. The sheer volume of paper limited the purpose of data collection to that of criminal surveillance and archival reference.

The computer, however, can automate the handling of diverse, large files of information. It is an invisible new medium for correlation of records. Programs can be written that scan many files of personal data, looking for general or specific linkages between events or persons. The resulting reports can reveal unexpected patterns, or yield the names of persons circumstantially involved.

Thus, computer data-base services are different from problem-solving services in that the latter can be solved by calculators or other means, but the automatic computer search of very large personal data-bases cannot be duplicated by any other known instrument, medium or method. In this single, widespread use we can see that the individual is a vulnerable bystander, at the mercy of a medium empowered to examine personal affairs without asking permission.

The evolution of this use of computers can be summarized as follows:

1. *1800 to 1950:* Paper records are carried in file cabinets for purposes of business or employee management.

2. *1940 to 1955:* More data elements are added to the records of each person due to governmental or business requirements. Office managers begin to select certain significant data from the paper records to be punched into cards so that calculators, punched cards, sorters and mechanical printers can help to manage the paperwork and reporting which is required.

3. *1955 to present:* Governments begin to merge personal data from various files, using computer assistance. Thus, Mr. Jones's insurance records, medical records, savings and loan records, credit records, tax records and payroll records can be compared or merged into one master record.

4. *1960 to present:* In response to the government's demand for more data elements to be carried for each person, businesses begin to utilize computers to maintain their private data-bases.

5. *1970 to present:* With automated data-base experience in industry and business, corporations begin to use this service to further their profit and loss margin, using market analysis and timely corporate business reports from the computer.

6. *1974 to present:* Computer vendors (IBM, UNIVAC, Honeywell, etc.), noticing that data-base management systems require the installation of many machines, begin to market entire computer systems (known as data-base management systems, or DBMS) designed for the express purpose of manipulating, updating, safeguarding and reporting large data-bases. Popular systems are IMS, DMS, TOTAL, RAMIS II, DL/1, ADABAS, MARKIV, IDMS, FORTE, IMAGE, and others.

Data-base management systems represent the newest and most dynamic product in the marketplace. Such systems were not available prior to 1970. Today 160 such data-base management systems are advertised for sale or lease and more than 10,000 of them have been sold according to a *Datapro* analysis.

What is the difference between older computer files and data-base files? Table 10.1 contrasts the two. Earlier business computer systems treated the company files as though they were separate file cabinets, just as they always had been. Although all of the data resided on computer disk or tape, the payroll file (for example) was totally separate from the other files and the programs which serviced or reported the payroll file could not easily reach any of the other data. Special programs could be written which culled through several of the separate files, and when such programs were written they were known as management information pro-

Table 10.1
Comparison of traditional vs. data-base systems
of personnel records

Traditional computer application systems (separate files)		
Inventory programs		Inventory files
Payroll programs		Payroll files
Personnel programs		Personnel file
General ledger programs	*maintain and report:*	General ledger file
Accounts receivable programs		Accounts receivable file
Mailing list programs		Mailing list file
Space utilization programs		Space utilization file
Management programs		Several files above

Data-base management systems (integrated files)		
One giant data-base manager program:		Giant corporate data file containing:
1. Updates and maintains all types of records.		1. Integrated data records of all types.
2. Reports by anticipation or ad hoc using English verbs.	*maintains and reports:*	2. Records which state where any data element can be found.
3. Limits certain users from accessing certain parts of the file.		3. Records which state the logical hierarchy of relationships between the data elements.
4. Provides automatic audit trails of all file activity.		

New medium-sized systems introduced in 1980 enabled local governments and small businesses to obtain data-base systems at attractive prices. Some buyers obtain these systems without knowing the difference between standard file systems and the powerful data-base systems. Once the conveniences of instant sorting and reporting are experienced, its usefulness assists the efficient operation of the office. *(Photo courtesy Sperry Corporation.)*

grams. If enough of them were written, they formed a system for management decision making. But the primary programming investment went into the business systems for the various day-to-day office activities in the payroll office, the purchasing office, and so on.

Because of the incessant demand for management information, special systems were developed which enabled a company to:

1. Place all of its data into a large integrated computer file.
2. Describe in that file where each data element could be found.

3. Describe in that file how each data element relates to every other data element.

Although data-base management systems are expensive, from $15,000 to $150,000, the benefit is that no more programs need be written to get combined information from separate unrelated files. The data is now essentially in one unified file, and the relationships between the records and data elements are known by the computer. With more than 10,000 installations of such systems, the trend toward integrating all important data is firmly advancing. These are sometimes called "integrated systems," as opposed to the "stand alone" systems.

Managers are clearly expressing their desire for the possibility of open-ended, creative searching of data-bases without waiting for costly new programs to be written. With DBMS, managers can, on their own terminals, request ad hoc searches of their files, such as: Find all those people who have been employed more than twenty years, all those who are single or widowed, all those whose salaries are over $25,000 and who belong to a minority group. When found, display the name, address, sex, age and driver's license number.

Simply by supplying search criteria, a data-base can be searched and reported in ways which no one ever predicted prior to the event itself. At the state or federal level a single file may carry diverse information such as an individual's income tax, payroll, real-estate, insurance, automobile, driving, court, criminal, hospital, bank and credit records.

The ability of the computer to manage large files of personal information permits business and government to accomplish what they have always wished, which is to relate widely diverse data records to each other so as to analyze, predict and control certain social phenomena for their corporate benefit. The Internal Revenue Service wishes to analyze income records *worldwide* for each U. S. taxpayer, and to compare these records to the 1040 income tax forms as reported. It would also be pleased to know the purchasing records of each person. Some people spend more than they report as earnings and their income tax reports could be scrutinized more closely if data-base management techniques could be applied to the nation's financial transactions.

Every business, government body and private organization must keep records of some type. Without records an organization cannot exist. *Record systems are an environment* and like any medium have contradictory effects upon the persons who are recorded in them. Table 10.2 lists some of the trade-off values.

When one analyzes the "undesirable" column in Table 10.2, it becomes clear that the computer is the primary new variable in the picture. It speeds up the record-keeping environment, making it a new medium (in the manner that movies elevated still photography to a new medium). Governments have always kept rec-

Table 10.2
Conflicting private vs. institutional values

Desirable for individuals	Desirable for bureaucracies but undesirable for individuals	Public service which justifies bureaucratic policy
To receive a paycheck each week.	To send a computer tape of all pay records to the state capital once each month, summarizing income by S.S. number. Required by most state governments.	To give back all tax money which is due. To reduce freeloading and tax evasion.
To obtain major medical insurance.	To sign on the application form that the medical records as they accumulate can be provided to other organizations without further permission.	Uncertain.
To obtain auto registration plates.	To be stopped by a policeman who consulted state computer files to see if parking violations are outstanding.	Can lead to the return of stolen cars.
To obtain auto insurance.	To be charged $80 more per year than people across the street because of a dividing line set by computer analysis. High-risk geographical areas are identified from statistical analyses of accidents.	Residents on the other side of the street pay less.

ords but until those records are automated by computer, each record-keeping system serves a limited purpose, that of easing the day-to-day functioning of the local office and providing a few summary reports to higher levels of the organization.

For example, a state can ask all its colleges to supply twenty new statistical reports annually, to which request the colleges would no doubt reply in unison that the price of education would have to rise sharply due to the increased staff required to meet the increased reporting requirements.

But if the colleges' business records are carried on computer, few programs will cull the information required in a few minutes. Additionally, the state can ask for the actual tapes of certain data-bases, in order to further analyze the data on its own computers.

This writer recalls the visit of the State Department of New Jersey to a computer network center in 1972. The meeting lasted ten minutes. After greetings and introductions, the visitors inquired about payroll and personnel records. Assured that they were carried in computer files, they produced a list of data elements which had to be written to computer tape in a certain format each month. Information about each employee was to be sent to the state capital each month; there the data from all counties was to be analyzed using these tapes. Such tapes have been mailed to the state continuously since that date.

Who is accountable for the use of such data after it leaves its home institution? Why is it solicited? What agencies access it? Who eventually disposes of it? Is it passed on to other states? To the federal government? What benefits accrue to citizens for allowing this? Answers are rarely provided to obedient contributors. Data sent to the state may, of course, help to ensure that proper tax monies are returned, or to reduce freeloading or tax evasion. It may also be used to diminish our privacy.

Not only can governments require more information from businesses, but they can install DBMS themselves to merge further the data which originated in diverse locations and settings.

It has been predicted that data-base management systems will be used more and more until nearly all business records in the United States are garnered into them. Such systems consume heavy processing power, allowing the computer to do few other things. And DBMS is expensive to obtain and install. But once it is operational, such a system then bypasses the slow programming process which requires a complex program for every report produced. Instead, with terminals in managers' offices, ad hoc reports can be generated on demand. They can search the institutional data-base because all the files of the institution are known to the DBMS. They can easily find all the employees who are divorced, over 37 years of age, live in certain zip code areas, are salaried full-time, are not tenured and whose employment is over seven years. And no one else may ever know that the search was conducted.

More than half of U. S. government agencies state in the book *Protecting Your Right to Privacy* that they have a DBMS in their organization. Ever more files will gradually be merged into these systems so that the use of data can be maximized and used in new associative ways.

Certain human values conflict with institutional values. Table 10.3 reveals that this conflict arises directly from the power of DBMS to navigate through personal files.

The future effect of such file management will be to transform business managers into data-base navigators. The history of business computing began with programs which brought data into the programs to be viewed or revised. Data-base management systems reverse this concept, focusing on one large program which goes into the data-base, searching, probing, associating and assisting the

Table 10.3
Private vs. corporate information values

Typical individual values	Corporate or bureaucratic values
Good business practice requires strict confidentiality of records.	All files and records should be sorted electronically so as to extract maximum associative information from them and open them to as many corporate uses as possible.
Government agencies should not share their information with other agencies whether by computer or in manual records.	All agencies should have access to all government files so as to prevent agencies attempting redundant maintenance of files.
Social security numbers should not be used by anyone except the Social Security Agency.	Diverse records can be brought together easily when SS numbers are used, or at greater cost using telephone numbers or addresses or full names.
Bureaucracies should not be allowed to use DBMS for government or business decisions.	Decision making without facts is inefficient and costly, especially when the data are available in various files.

would-be navigator to find his or her way creatively through millions of data elements toward some purposive goal.

Worldwide associations of data-base users will form and will promote the idea of international data-base systems. Worldwide DBMS files will be installed by the banking industry, the insurance industry, the travel industry, the energy industry, the United Nations and others.

The United States will probably form a new federal agency to govern the new automated information media. If formed, the chief of the agency will probably supervise the office of the national data-base administrator and the federal DBMS file.

Chapter 14 probes the privacy issue further and examines the non-federal uses of personal record keeping. When the combined statistics of both government and business DBMS are presented, the reader will understand better that we truly live in an informational "surround" and that it makes our lives different.

The presence of computers in the home will probably ease our transition into the data-base era. The innocence of the home computer, with its games and home management systems, will probably reduce public resistance to the encompassing environment of data files carried by counties, states, federal agencies, insurance companies, banks and grocery stores. Lulled into the belief that the computer is a fair, neutral medium, the public may not distinguish the results of DBMS as any different from the trivial household lists which they sort on little home computers.

Because of the versatility of the home computer and its ability to link through the telephone to other computers and files, the public will eventually demand the right to dial into specialized DBMS files for public information services. As computers become more widely available and their prices lower, ever more data will be requested and collected. It is a technological loop. As though the *World Almanac* were available online, researchers and the general public will be provided with spectacular lookup and creative search services through the telephone and their home microcomputers.

Eventually (the year is 2000) our civilization will be more alert to the nature of the data-base media and will probably demand that government files be opened for widespread access. If the tax payer pays the government to collect so much data, then the tax payer may insist on seeing it.

Because information is the most valued resource of any institution, it is predicted that the American public will eventually view the government data as worthy of publication and public computer lookup.

The idea of privacy will have been completely reversed, and a new age of information openness will have been born.

Bibliography

Abernathy, F. S., "The Poor Man's Guide to Automation," *Interface* 5, no. 2 (summer 1980).

Bachman, C., "The Programmer as Navigator," *Communications of the ACM*, 16, no. 11.

Berg, J. L., ed., *Data Base Directions, The Next Steps*. Washington, D.C.: National Bureau of Standards, 1975.

Carpenter, E., and M. McLuhan, eds., *Explorations in Communication, an Anthology*. Boston: Beacon Press, 1966.

General Services Administration, *Government Manual*. Washington, D.C.: U. S. Government Printing Office, 1976.

Greenspan, L., ed., *Protecting Your Right to Privacy*. Washington, D.C.: U. S. Government Printing Office, 1975.

Hall, E. T., *The Hidden Dimension*. New York: Doubleday, 1969.

Inventory of Automatic Data Processing Equipment in the United States Government. Washington, D. C.: General Services Administration, 1975.

McLuhan, M., and Q. Fiore, *The Medium is the Massage*. New York: Bantam, 1967.

Postman, N., and C. Weingartner, *Teaching As a Subversive Activity*. New York: Delacorte Press, 1969.

van Rijsbergen, C. J., *Information Retrieval*. Woburn, Ma.: Butterworth, 1979.

Chapter Eleven

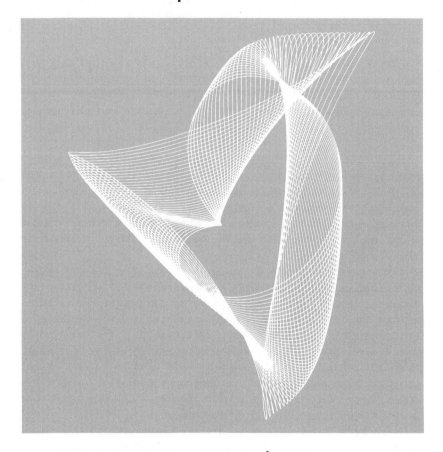

Computers and Money:
Electronic Banking

☐ The line at the window of the electronic bank teller is sometimes longer than the lines at the other windows.

☐ The lines at the grocery store checkout will get shorter if bar codes, laser scanners and credit cards are broadly accepted.

☐ Electronic mail systems could pass financial messages as easily as any other types of messages, thus merging the functions of post offices and banks.

Except for electronic funds transfer, nearly all other data-processing services grew like Topsy. No national symposium or presidential commission drafted legislation or guidelines for the emergence of computer data-base uses or problem-solving uses between 1954 and 1975. If something could be done by computer, it was.

Electronic funds transfer systems, however, represent what is probably the first coordinated effort at preplanning and predictive control; a sign that the nation is maturing in its awareness of the computer environment. Congress authorized $2 million to support a commission and in October 1974 the Senate confirmed William B. Widnall as Chairman of the National Commission on Electronic Funds Transfers.

What is electronic funds transfer (EFT)? It is a system under which individuals or businesses can purchase or sell goods and services without the direct use of money, checks or paper transactions. Such systems, when fully operational, can be a combination of: 1) computerized point-of-sale terminals in stores, with provision for reading the bar codes and inventory numbers instantly from the labeled goods; 2) online credit-card and password authorization; 3) automatic and immediate transfers of funds within computer files using online terminals; and 4) computerized communication linkage through telephone lines.

With EFT, at the grocery store checkout counter the soap, cereal, potatoes and milk are passed over a slot in the counter where a laser beam or light pen scans the bar codes, causing the terminal to flash the facts of the transaction to the checkout operator and customer, while at the same time the unseen computer adjusts the inventory records. The paper receipt from the terminal is the only visible record of the transaction. Since this terminal is online to the bank, the scanner also deciphers the ID numbers on the customer's credit card. As part of the approval process, the customer also supplies a six-digit personal password number. If the number matches the credit card information at the bank, the computer at the bank returns approval to the grocery store in about two seconds or less. The bill is subtracted from the customer's account at the bank and deposited in the store's account by the central bank computer.

This system is being implemented in stages and was installed as a working experiment in several communities in 1977. The EFT Commission was established before the systems became widespread, though sprawling EFT systems developed anyway. How does a new medium like EFT obtain a foothold in society? Who benefits from such systems? What methods of planning and control precede the installation of a new medium of exchange? Who grants permission? What future can be outlined for electronic banking and exchange?

The Electronic Funds Transfer Commission

By Senate edict the EFT Commission (1976) was composed of twenty-six members. The objectives of the commission were formulated by the members and published in their eight-month report.

1) To sustain and enhance competition among institutions, financial and non-financial, which might use EFT systems and to minimize government involvement as a regulator or operator of these sytems. 2) To protect the interests of the consumer, including his convenience, privacy and legal rights. 3) To understand the implications of EFT for other parts of the economic system—the availability of credit, the government's ability to carry out economic and monetary policy, the growth in telecommunications technology, and the international transfer of funds.

The commission met regularly—once each week during the first eight months—and eventually produced a final report which went to President Carter on October 29, 1977.

The virtues of EFT were quickly proclaimed: it provides users with convenience, confidentiality and credit availability.

The committee . . . supports the widespread use of electronic payment systems, including telecommunication facilities, computer processing and card access or other remote entry terminal devices, for the purpose of dispensing cash and the effecting of payments for goods and services. These dollar payments would otherwise be executed by a conventional paper check or cash.

Additionally, the commission agreed upon eight programs of study. The Providers Committee proposed an automated clearing house (ACH) organization which would aid the automatic disbursement of Social Security and other types of payroll payments. The ACH concept became a central part of the national EFT system envisioned by the commission.

Figure 11.1 is a map showing a new medium invading a culture with maximum impact. The familiar media of cash, checks and paperwork will be complemented with instantaneous electronic fund transferral any time, anywhere.

The results of planning for EFT

Given the serious mission of the EFT Commission, its final report was awaited with considerable interest. In this first attempt at rational preparation for the impact of a new financial medium, the results were expected to evidence humanity's ability to plan its future according to considered goals and values; an attempt to design the future.

When the report was made public, however, one-third of it contained dissenting paragraphs in which commission members disagreed with each other. These dissenting voices give insight into the problems encountered in attempting to plan for the implementation of a new medium.

1. Complaints centered on lack of time: too little evaluation, too much unfinished business, too much inadequate research.

2. Complaints about the membership being dominated by business interests. One person for instance, stated that some groups were not properly represented—consumers, the poor, minorities, civil libertarians and small business. Each could have made a valuable contribution.

3. Complaints indicating that no real legislation was drafted, but that only suggestions and recommendations could be made—and rarely in full agreement.

4. Complaints that the issues of privacy and security were not adequately addressed.

The actual recommendations of the commission are as follows:

1. The government should minimize the extent to which it requires an institution to maintain or report records generated by an EFT system.

Figure 11.1
System of relationships under the proposed Electronic Funds Transfer network
(Financial transactions conducted without money, checks, or any movement of paper)

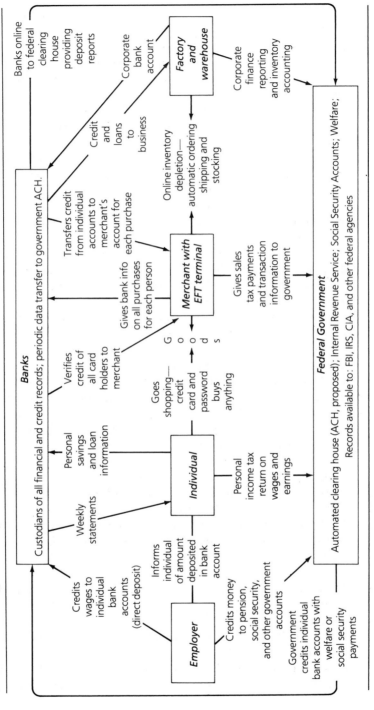

2. The government should minimize the extent to which it requires information to be collected by an EFT system that is not required as a matter of sound business practice.

3. EFT systems should not be used by government for surveillance, to learn either a consumer's physical location or his patterns of behavior.

4. Law enforcement agencies should be allowed access to personal records, with a subpoena. In some instances the individual investigated need not be informed in advance.

5. The local EFT agent or bank should treat all records as confidential and should not disclose to third parties any information without the consent of the individual.

6. Certain credit grantors, credit bureaus and credit authorization services could be given access to learn about an individual's credit rating.

7. EFT records should be open for use in finding the new address of someone who owes money at an older address.

8. Consumers should have the right to see and correct their records when denied credit.

9. Consumer statements should be provided monthly when transactions pass within that month.

10. No method of stopping payment should be provided, due to the immediacy of the system.

11. Consumers should not be held liable for the loss or theft of their card unless their personal identification number was also attached to the card.

12. Banks should be permitted to install terminals anywhere in the U. S. without calling them branch offices.

13. Debit and credit services should be offered by any bank to any location nationwide, even across state lines. If a New York bank has a terminal in Nevada, a card holder may deposit (credit) or debit his account in Nevada.

14. Security regulations should be developed uniformly from state to state. Heavier penalties for computer crimes should be legislated.

There were many open issues which the commission did not resolve:

1. Debit collection agencies, which trace missing persons, remain unregulated.

2. Reasons why credit has been denied can only be elicited by writing to the bank. Travelers are not secure under such a system:

if an individual's bank account is in good standing in his or her home state, the denial of credit in another state should be explained promptly.

3. Security measures were not viewed as real problems.

4. No penalties were suggested for the circulation of incorrect information by an EFT bank.

5. What will happen to stores and individuals who refuse to participate in the system?

6. European experiences with EFT since 1968 were not researched in depth.

7. No standards were drafted to permit information flow between EFT systems. Such standards would reduce the need for data conversion, multiple credit card readers, and other pieces of electronic hardware.

After another year of development, the EFT Act of 1978 was passed. It was enacted as "Regulation E" in May 1979. By then, eleven major national EFT networks were already operating. They will be subject to the act, of course.

The future of electronic banking

EFT has already become a major business. Fifteen or more large banks are offering EFT services as a local, in-state service. Their experiences are building a log of advance data on the public response to and evolution of such systems. Although the current installations are too localized to report in detail, the general public reaction demonstrates the trend toward quick acceptance of electronic banking.

In 1978, about 9,000 EFT terminals were in operation. In 1979, 13,000. In 1980 the estimate was 18,000, and climbing. The lines in front of the terminals are sometimes longer than the lines at the windows.

There are approximately 15,000 banks in the United States. More than 110 million checking accounts cause paper to be pushed in and out of cashier's windows, cash registers, desk drawers, mailboxes, and thieves' pockets. The American Bankers Association believes that operational savings of five to seven cents per check would be achieved under the proposed EFT system. Those savings are the key to economic survival in hard times. The Treasury Department states that half of its overhead would be eliminated under electronic banking.

High-speed printers like this UNIVAC model are attached to nearly all computers, allowing information to be printed at rates of 4,800 and 9,600 lines per minute. Faster output can be obtained by outputting directly to microfilm. Also, new laser printers can produce high-quality computer output, moving the paper through the machine at about 27 miles per hour. *(Photo courtesy Sperry Corporation.)*

The banks are the promoters of these systems. The public's need for the conveniences of EFT will be marketed to us. We will come to believe that we need such services just in time for their large scale arrival. Customer telephone bills can be paid directly from an individual's bank account to the phone company at about 300 banks nation-wide. A few will pay J. C. Penney and other department stores directly.

Following the commission's endorsement of EFT, President Carter asked federal agencies to use EFT to speed the payments of grant monies to state and local governments. Seventy-two billion dollars in grants are distributed each year, incurring tremendous paperwork. All agency heads were urged to use the Department of the Treasury to identify grant programs that might be paid by EFT. Part of the president's argument was that grantees usually have to advance their own money while waiting for federal money to arrive.

Clearly the government benefits from the instantaneous knowledge and control which EFT systems provide. Figure 11.1 displays a picture of a culture reorganized by bank computer networks into a willing supplier of information to the government, at several levels. Individuals, banks, merchants, employers and manufacturers all obediently submit records of all their transactions to the government's Automated Clearing House.

If the public accepts this, it will be because of the alluring display of bank advertisements promoting the benefits of reduced paperwork, instant loans, nationally recognized credit and personal financial convenience.

A surprising reaction was documented by the EFT commission, however. A wire service news item stated erroneously that the commission was seeking public comments on EFT systems. Six thousand letters arrived in Washington. Eleven letters favored EFT, 10 were uncertain, and 5,979 letters were solidly against it. The commissioners catalogued the areas of concern and found that an unexpected deterrent was the resistance on religious grounds to everyone needing to have a number in order to buy and sell. The number of letters making this point was surprisingly high. They may have been triggered by a church or denominational group which promoted a letter-writing campaign.

The speed of public acceptance of EFT, and its future, depends on several factors.

1. *Standardization.* Five different types of bar codes are now used, with many styles of credit cards and identification numbers. Protocols for interfacing terminals to banks and stores vary among computers. "Smart" credit cards which contain an internal computer did not exist when early standards were set.

2. *Economics.* By 1984 any banking system which still requires the physical movement of signatures on paper will have a serious problem of overhead. Meanwhile the descending price of computers and the accumulated knowledge of EFT will create a wide competitive bank movement into EFT.

3. *Data transmission capabilities.* The process of connecting 800,000 stores, merchants and businesses to bank computers via the existing Bell network of wires is unwieldy and probably impossible because of the resources required. AT&T, GTE and Bell Telephone are planning a separate data network system of wires and fiber optic cables designed to carry digital signals. Fiber optic cables, when laced between cities and countries could provide adequate bandwidth for all data communication needs. This technique is being used in Japan but is not likely to be widely available in the United States until 1990. Also, simple rooftop satellite an-

tenna systems will permit banks to communicate their transactions point-to-point across the country.

4. *Law.*   Since EFT systems will directly affect the lives of 200 million people, government intervention, control and supervision may be expected. Laws covering privacy, the right of access to records and computer crime must be enacted and tested before public acceptance will endorse the new medium of electronic funds transfer.

5. *The merger of EFT with electronic mail transfer.*   A few businesses have installed their own in-house electronic mail service which allows people to type messages on terminals to another terminal or person in the network. Although branch offices may be in separate cities, typewritten messages can be passed at a cost similar to that of telegraph or telephone without a two-day wait for delivery. When such networks are opened for public use at a six- or eight-cent charge for each page transferred, the more costly government mail service will be bypassed more and more. Where messages pass, money also passes. The passing of financial messages is not very different from the passing of other messages. In EFT, the financial transactions which pass from place-to-place could also carry a side-band of eight to twenty sentences of information. Another alternative is that the electronic mail networks could be connected to the banks, thus providing credits and debits as part of the mail service. Thus EFT will grow in parallel with electronic mail transfer and may eventually merge into it. One law of media suggests that two media will not exist for long when they provide the same communication functions. Thus EFT, electronic mail and graphic transfer systems will probably merge into a single network of communication services by the end of the century.

The maturing of EFT is not likely to be universally accepted until the next century, but it is likely to modify the behavior of all credit card users during the next twenty years. Some researchers anticipate a $22 billion market in 1985, largely because the versatility and wide recognition of certain online credit systems will cause EFT to grow in ways that grocery shoppers and jet travelers will welcome. Public dependence on computers will become solidified only when one or two "real" cash registers are left in the supermarket.

Since 1973, prices have been printed on products using the bar codes for inventory use. The public will gradually accept the ultimate use of computerized price recording and tallying. Shoppers will probably appreciate the more detailed receipts that EFT terminals provide. Such receipts list every item by name with its price, and show how it was paid for (cash, checks, credit card, food stamps or welfare account). The larger system in which these terminals participate is out of sight and out of mind as far as the public is concerned. Like other popular media, EFT is likely therefore to be embraced by the public long before its full implications are recognized by most people.

Bibliography

"Electronic Funds Transfer," *Communications of the ACM* 22, no. 12 (December 1979).

McCarter, P., *The EFT Act Is Law.* Pennsauken, N. J.: Auerbach, 1979.

Chapter Twelve

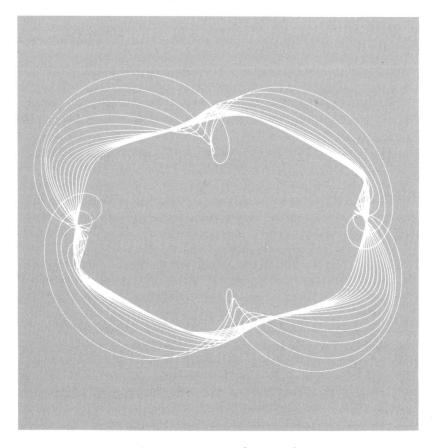

Is Privacy Obsolete?

☐ Our signature on an insurance or hospital form usually authorizes the publication or distribution of the data on it.

☐ Courts have ruled that we should have no expectation of privacy in our banking and checking records.

☐ We set up agencies whose purpose is to collect data about us and then we supply the data to these agencies. In these actions we act against privacy.

☐ Global satellite communication systems are in the anti-privacy business, broadcasting facts about us at the speed of light.

Personal privacy is the fracture point, the fault line, between society and computerization. More than any other topic relating to the impact of computers, the issue of privacy produces the most literature and the most debate. In this debate the opposing tendencies of private human values and corporate bureaucratic values can become a battleground.

Consider the case in New England. The Credit Bureau of Nashua, Inc., mailed letters throughout New Hampshire and Massachusetts, stating that it held personal information about individuals on its computer system. It stated that the data would be sold to a large computerized firm, and offered to remove individual records from the tape before releasing the data, for a fee of $7.50. The letter was published in several journals including "The Privacy Journal." It said:

> We have a credit file which contains all or part of the following information about you . . . your employment, income, marital (sic) status, credit references, how you pay your bills, mortgages, liens, attachments, divorces . . .
>
> We have decided to give you a chance to obtain sole possession of your complete file before it becomes part of a large computerized data bank which may allow unlimited access by thousands of people.
>
> It is your privacy. The choice is yours.

The Massachusetts Attorney General warned the company to stop. The company president, however, observed that he was providing the public with a useful service. In the future, individuals will not have an opportunity to protect their privacy, and many people might desire to pay the fee to have data on them removed from the tape.

Many credit agencies sell their credit information to other institutions; it is not illegal to do so. Questionnaires sent in the mail to private citizens often promise that responses will be "confidential." Questions about spending habits, salary, cars, liquor and other personal habits are answered freely by many people. However, "confidential" does not mean "anonymous." The receiver's name is often linked to a printed number on the questionnaire, or an ultraviolet invisible number, or special cuts on the paper or bar codes on the edge of the paper. According to *Privacy Journal* (December 1975), invisible code numbers have been used on literature sent out by *The National Observer, The Wall Street Journal, Barron's, Fortune, The Reader's Digest, Time, Saturday Review, Scientific American* and *New York* magazine. *U.S. News and World Report* and *Newsweek* stopped using invisible codes because of customer complaints.

In 1975 the federal government held approximately eighteen file records for every man, woman and child in the United States. How it used these files is largely unknown: their very existence was not known until the Privacy Act of 1974 required government agencies to publish the names of their files.

Citizens often feel that the government and other organizations know more about them than they know about themselves. People generally do not keep very accurate records on themselves. But others do. In 1975 the federal government held 6,723 files with 3.8 million records on identified persons in them. (See Appendix Tables A2.1 and A2.4.) The Commission on Individual Privacy in the State of Indiana published the results of its research recently. In 1977 there were 100 government agencies in Indiana, and 54 of them maintained file records with Social Security numbers or other personal identifiers. There are 199 state file systems in Indiana. The state is eleventh in population size, and its 5.1 million people are recorded in 82 million state records. Thus there are about sixteen records carried on every individual in Indiana, in addition to the federal government's eighteen records on each person.

Individuals have already lost their privacy in so many ways that the concept of privacy is largely a myth, a nostalgic remembrance.

In 1975 a questionnaire was presented to 4000 people employed in data-processing. The Data Processing Management Association sponsored the research. Of the twenty-nine hundred respondents, 14.8 percent selected privacy as the most critical issue facing their industry. This was the highest rating, indicating that people who work with this medium each day perceive its ability to amplify the gossip which formerly symbolized small town life but now crosses the nation at the speed of light.

What is the outlook for privacy in the presence of global satellite communication channels? It has already been compromised in so many areas of life that the quest for it is similar to that for the Holy Grail: a few good things may result from the quest, but the Grail itself is lost forever. Nothing will restore the privacy of the precomputer file cabinet era. It is too late; the new medium has already worked its magic.

Most applicants who apply for life insurance are required to sign a document which contains a lot of small print. As quoted by Lipson in *Privacy Journal* (June 1976), the small print says:

> I hereby authorize any licensed physician, medical practitioner, hospital, clinic or other medical or medically related facility, insurance company, the Medical Information Bureau, or other organization, institution or person, having any records or knowledge of me or my health, to give the insurance company any such information. A photocopy of this signed authorization shall be as valid as the original.

Lipson editorializes at length about the phenomenon that nearly all Americans have signed forms like these, often thoughtlessly, often not realizing that they have authorized the general publication and distribution of their personal health records. The editorial continues:

> Two hundred years ago, we fought a war and declared our independence from that kind of invasion of our personal rights. We then formed a government that was precluded from unreasonable search and seizure and from requiring us to incriminate ourselves. And today, in our proceedings against the CIA, we are demanding the re-affirmation of our rights of privacy. . . .
>
> What's worse, all those people with photocopies of your authorization are under no obligation to reveal to you their findings. They may be accurate—or they may not. You may never know. And may therefore never have the chance to challenge damaging inaccuracies. Neither will you know how many insurance companies—not to mention how many "other organizations, institutions or persons" may also know these truths about you. Our photocopy and computer technologies make it possible to accumulate and disseminate information with appalling efficiency.
>
> Legally, practically everybody can know practically everything about you—except you yourself. All because you were forced to sign that small print, if you wanted that company to insure you. (p. 4)

Privacy values in our exposed communities may be returning to the privacy modes common in the long houses of tribal villages where many families live and sleep together. They don't complain about the lack of privacy—they are adjusted to it and consider it normal.

Our government now considers it normal, too. In 1972 federal law required banks to begin to microfilm all checks and make them available on demand to the IRS or other federal agencies *without* informing the individual. The IRS is empowered to obtain from airlines the names of people who fly to Las Vegas. This data helps them to trace gambling winnings.

The government will probably link many of its computers together someday; government agencies continually request permission to do so. A National Data Center was proposed in 1972 but Congress did not approve it. Then FEDNET was proposed by the General Services Administration in 1974. It was a plan to link each federal agency's data systems with a message-switching system. Vice-President Ford led the Congressional vote against the plan. In 1976 AIDS (Automated Integrated Digital Services) was proposed. A message-switching system would link all government agencies with the existing Advanced Record System now operated by the General Services Administration. Now GSA plans to join forces with Western Union to accomplish the long-sought goal. The system is predicted to be able to include any and all federal agencies and their computer systems.

In this regard, *Privacy Journal* stated:

> There remains an insatiable desire to link all of the government's computers, whether or not they include sensitive personal data. The prototype is the Parent Locator Service, created by Congress to search the government's data banks for errant parents not supporting their children. The level of privacy sensitivity in the General Services Administration is evident from one part of the Western Union Systems Management proposal. The government would pay for computer components, and Western Union would own them until turning them over to the U. S. government—in 1984.

The FBI has requested bid proposals for a similar message-switching network. If you write to the FBI to see records about yourself, they search their central records system, which contains 20 million individual names. However, sixty-three additional record systems are carried, and these are *not* referenced by the central system. The *Federal Register* does not reveal what these sixty-three files contain (although required to do so by the Privacy Act).

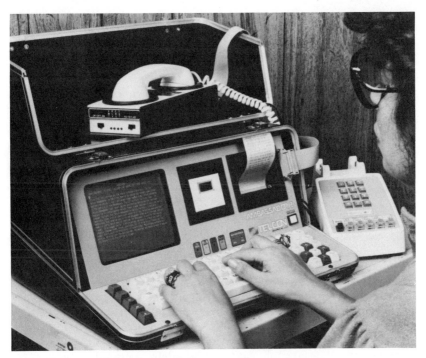

Travelers can easily carry this TELCON briefcase terminal anywhere in the world. Using toll-free numbers, they dial into various networks which then open to them their electronic mail boxes, word-processing services, sales reporting and limited fund transfer services. Anything on the screen can be printed on the paper tape by pressing the PRINT button. *(Photo courtesy TELCON.)*

The state of privacy awareness is reflected in the report of the Privacy Protection Study Commission (1977). Edited by D. F. Linowes, the volume encompasses 654 pages of tightly reasoned analysis. Extracts from this primary source help to underscore the state of lost privacy, to which the public is expected to adjust.

> The records of a hundred years ago tell little about the average American, except when he died, perhaps when and where he was born, and, if he owned land, how he got his title to it. Three-quarters of the adult population worked for themselves on farms or in small towns. . . . No military service was required, and few programs brought individuals into contact with the federal government.
>
> The most complete record was probably kept by churches, who recorded births, baptisms, marriages, and deaths. Town officials and county courts kept records of similar activities. Merchants and bankers maintained financial accounts for their customers, and when they extended credit, it was on the basis of personal knowl-

edge. . . . Few individuals had insurance of any kind, and a patient's medical record very likely existed in the doctor's memory. Records about individuals rarely circulated beyond the place they were made. (p. 3)

The substitution of records for face-to-face contact in these relationships is what makes the situation today dramatically different from the way it was even as recently as thirty years ago. It is now commonplace for an individual to be asked to divulge information about himself for use by unseen strangers who make decisions about him that directly affect his everyday life. Furthermore, because so many of the services offered by organizations are . . . necessities, an individual has little choice but to submit to whatever demands for information about him an organization may make. Organizations must have some substitute for personal evaluation in order to distinguish between one individual and the next in the endless stream of otherwise anonymous individuals they deal with, and most organizations have come to rely on records as that substitute.(p. 4)

It is important to note . . . that organizations increasingly desire information that will facilitate fine-grained decisions abut individuals. A credit card issuer wants to avoid people who do not pay their bills, but it also strives to identify slow payers and well-intentioned people who could easily get into debt beyond their ability to repay. Insurance companies seek to avoid people whose reputation or life style suggests that they may have more than the average number of accidents or other types of losses.

Often one also hears people assert that nobody minds organizational record-keeping practices "if you have nothing to hide," and many apparently like to think of themselves as having nothing to hide, not realizing that (it) can be a matter of opinion. . . . Few of us have the option of avoiding relationships with record-keeping organizations. To do so is to forego not only credit but also insurance, employment, medical care, education, and all forms of government services to individuals. (p. 5)

Such statements are measures of where we stand in this perplexing debate. Human beings often seek solitude for brief periods. Then, social creatures, people return to society again. Perhaps all of us are returning from an era of Gutenberg-induced privacy to an exposed, electronic, open culture. The Privacy Commission report gives shocking illustrations in this regard:

On April 21, 1976, a fateful day for personal privacy, the U. S. Supreme Court decided that Mitchell Miller had no legitimate "expectation of privacy" in his bank records and thus no protectable interest for the Court to consider. The Court reasoned that because checks are an independent record of an individual's participation in the flow of commerce, they cannot be considered confidential communications. The account record, moreover, is the property of the bank, not of the individual account holder. Thus, according to the Court, Miller's expectation of privacy was neither legitimate, warranted, nor enforceable. (p. 7)

It is ironic but true that in a society as dependent as ours on computer and telecommunications technology, an individual may still have to make a personal visit to a credit bureau if he wants access to the information the bureau maintains about him, or to get an erroneous record corrected. Although an error in a record can now be propagated all over the country at the speed of light, many organizations have made no provision to propagate corrections through the same channels, and existing law seldom requires them to do so. As a general proposition, system designers . . . have not fully used their knowledge . . . to make record-keeping systems serve individuals as well as organizational needs and interests. (p. 12)

. . . the Commission wants organizations to invest in improving their record-keeping practices; not to spend their money in costly litigation over past practices and honest mistakes. Hence the Commission's recommendation is to limit the liability of a record-keeper that responds to an individual's request for access to a record it maintains about him. (p. 28)

The commission wrote incisive chapters on The Consumer-Credit Relationship, Mailing Lists, Insurance, Employment, Medical Care, Investigators, Government Access to Personal Records, each of which reveals more about our lost privacy.

Personal labels—name, address, birthdate, telephone and Social Security numbers were the primary interest of the Privacy Commission. People can be identified by unique traits of hair, eyes, voiceprints, fingerprints, footprints, hand dimensions and handwriting. Carry-along identification can include keys, tags, passports or credit cards.

The commission observed that labeling procedures occur in all cultures. They may be systems of citizen registration or painted tribal identifiers. Such labeling systems serve groups of various sizes and are no different from a union number. But in the U. S., the Social Security number is a very imperfect identifier. The use of it can at times release the records of other people.

One reason is that until 1972, an applicant for an SSN was not asked if he had already been issued a number, nor was he asked to produce proof of identity. The result is that several million individuals now have more than one SSN—clearly a source of confusion. Another reason is that one SSN is sometimes used by more than one individual—as when a son, confused about how the system operates, uses his father's number when he goes to work. (p. 609)

The National Driver Register (NDR) contains about 5.7 million records. It receives 94,000 inquiries daily, produces 3,500 possible matches every day, and mails 900 probable matches to the states. Yet the SSN (or another unique identifier) is not the primary identifier used in this system. Instead, NDR first uses name and date of birth as primary identifiers and then uses sex, height, weight, and eye color to discriminate among records of people with similar or identical names and birth dates. The SSN is, in some cases, used to facilitate this discrimination process, but it is not available for all drivers listed in the system.

. . . the Commission is sensitive to the second point—the belief that being labeled with the SSN is dehumanizing. Clearly, a society in which each of us is called upon at every turn to state "name, rank, and serial number" is not pleasing to contemplate. The Commission fails to see, however, how drastically restricting the use of the Social Security number would make much difference in this respect, since any other widely used numerical label would . . . engender the same feeling. (p. 614)

The commission recommended that the use of the Social Security number be monitored but that no action be taken to develop or prohibit universal identifiers beyond the suggestions presented in the Privacy Act of 1974.

What if we lived as though every fact about our lives would be published? How different would life be from what it is now? Already many executives assume that their telephone conversations are being recorded. They should. Your local newspaper has for years published all of the private information about you or your neighbors that can be acquired, including arrests, divorces, complaints, lists of salaries of public officials, and sordid gossip about the romances and follies of prominent citizens. Senator Thomas Eagleton lost the Democratic vice-presidential nomination as a direct result of the media's revelation that he paid visits to a psychiatrist.

Most information about citizens is either already available or can be obtained for a few dollars from professional investigators. The *Privacy Journal* of December 1975 printed "The Snoopers Walking Tour" by Robert Ellis Smith. It featured a map of downtown Los Angeles showing where to walk in a six-block square area

Unto the satellites above we lift our fervent messages. We know they hear. And everyone else hears too.

to find twenty-four major sources of free or low cost information about California citizens.

Personal information is recorded in so many places that it can be retrieved one way or another from records or publications as shown in Table 12.1. Private detectives earn their livings doing this. This checklist of information sources reveals the amount of exposure to which we are all expected to adjust.

Public agencies are not the only culprits in the privacy dilemma. The writing teacher in elementary school may know the most about people. In a thousand words or less, children often artlessly confide clear details about family life. Follow-up essay assignments inquire about family ancestry, eating habits, religious beliefs and other intimacies (for instance, that mother is complaining again how father uses too much toilet paper!).

Scanning a classroom of kids' writing assignments isn't much harder than scanning the nation. Satellites can now track police

Table 12.1
Agencies or record systems that
commonly carry personal records

Abortion Records	Libraries
Adoption Records	Lie Detector Records
Affirmative Action Records	Loan Records
Alien Records	Mail Surveillance
Arrest Records	Mailing Lists
Automobile Registration	Marriage License Records
Bank Records	Medical Information Bureau
Bibliographies	Medical Records
Bicycle Registrations	Memo Files (company)
Biographies	Migrant Records
Blood Donation Records	Military Records
Blue Cross Records	Municipal Records
Book Club Records	National Crime Info Center
Building Permits	Neighbors
Business Permits	Newspapers
Census Records	Overseas Sources
Checkbook Records	Passports
Child Abuse Records	Patent Records
Church Records	Payroll Records
Citizens'-Band Licenses	Personnel Records
Congressional Records	Police Records
Court Houses	Prison Records
Credit Records	Print Shops
Criminal Justice Records	Race Relations Boards
Data Banks	Real Estate Records
Divorce Records	Satellite Data Monitoring
Driver's License Records	Public School Records
Drug Records	School Teachers; Principals
Educational Testing Service	Social Services Parent Locator
Employer Records	Social Security Number
Federal Trade Commission	State Tax Records
FBI	Sterilization Records
Fingerprint Records	Supreme Court
Fishing Licenses	Telephone Recordings
Guarantee Forms	Travel Records
Gun Permits	Vasectomy Records
Housing Records	Voice Printing
Hotel Records	Voting Records
Hunting Licenses	Warranty Receipts
Incorporation Records	Welfare Records
Internal Revenue Service	Wiretrap Surveillance

cars within 300 feet by spying on their radio transmitter signals.
The Aerospace Corporation of El Segundo, California, markets
an alarm system which can be worn as a wristwatch. When pressed,

it radios a signal to police headquarters telling them who you are, where you are and that you need help.

Is there any way to foil listening ears and watchful eyes? Gypsies are alleged to cope with the privacy issue in a realistic way. They are said to carry at least three social security cards and a wallet full of driver's licenses, and to rotate license plates from several states on the same vehicle. Such stories may unfairly categorize this little-understood minority group and may not be generally true; undoubtedly, such acts are criminal. But they would help a person to remain invisible in a hopelessly exposed society.

Marshall McLuhan summarizes the problem from the point of view of the media environment:

> We have reached a similar point of data gathering when each stick of chewing gum we reach for is acutely noted by some computer that translates our least gesture into a new probability curve or some parameter of social science. Our private and corporate lives have become information processes because we have put our central nervous systems outside us in electronic technology. (p. 60)

We praise privacy but at the same time require our agencies to interfere with it. We pay them to collect data about us, and to scout us out if we fail to provide it.

The desire for privacy came at the end of the Middle Ages after literacy and movable type changed medieval values. The new development, reading, was a private activity. Even if other people were in the room, the reader was alone—and wanted to be more alone. Castles housing many families (and their livestock) in very large rooms yielded to smaller structures with more rooms, giving opportunities for privacy. Readers wanted quietness; in the most extreme cases they became monks to obtain it.

The electronic media, it seems, may turn us back toward a more open society. Computer systems coupled with telecommunications and global satellite distribution systems seem to guarantee it. For everything about us to be available publicly is somewhat distasteful; however, the power of the media to bring about this outcome is far greater than any identifiable factors which could slow or prevent it. Our not liking this doesn't cause the media to interrupt their broadcasting of our personal data. Like Elull's "technique" which charts its own course toward efficiency in all things, the media relentlessly chart our course toward exposure and openness. That's their business.

We will probably adjust to it, maybe come to prefer it. People have always enjoyed being on TV. With the computer they'll be able to show off their minds and personal habits as well.

McLuhan states in *Understanding Media:*

> By putting our physical bodies inside our extended nervous systems, by means of electric media, we set up a dynamic by which all previous technologies that are mere extensions of hands and feet . . .—all such extensions of our bodies, including cities—will be translated into information systems. Electromagnetic technology requires utter human docility and quiescence of meditation such as befits an organism that now wears its brain outside its skull and its nerves outside its hide. Man must serve his electric technology with the same servo-mechanistic fidelity with which he served his coracle, his canoe, his typography, and all other extensions of his physical organs. But there is this difference, that previous technologies were partial and fragmentary, and the electric is total and inclusive. An external consensus or conscience is now as necessary as private consciousness. With the new media, however, it is also possible to store and to translate everything; and, as for speed, that is no problem. No further acceleration is possible this side of the light barrier.
> . . . Under electric technology the entire business of man becomes learning and knowing . . . and all forms of wealth result from the movement of information. (p. 64)

The question "Do Americans have privacy?" must be answered in the negative. Very little privacy remains for the individual. It has been traded for other things. The media negotiated the trade, secretly.

The airwaves, microwaves, radar waves, radio waves and infrared waves are full of personal data about us. The culture has become an information matrix, presenting to the interstellar spaces electromagnetic etchings of what we know about ourselves. There seems to be a human instinct to get information about us onto the media as soon as it is known—preferably the electronic media so that it can go further and faster.

We create agencies and institutions which have the express purpose of extracting data from us. Much of the data we give willingly, but, lest something should be accidentally hidden, we require the agencies to hassle us, quiz us, record us, call us, computerize our facts, analyze them for inconsistencies, and take periodic census rosters to determine the number of windows in each domicile.

Most agencies and companies routinely sell or exchange such data. Local telephone companies, American Express, Bank of America, Sears, Roebuck and Co. and other stores and companies provide information about customers' charge accounts to credit

We create agencies and institutions for the express purpose of extracting data from us. Further, we require them to quiz us, hassle us, record us, call us, computerize us and take periodic reviews lest we accidentally hide something.

reporting agencies, government agencies and attorneys. They do not inform their customers of this exchange. The Privacy Protection Study Commission brought this to light as early as 1976, after which some companies said that they would begin to notify their patrons before releasing data. None promised to stop doing it, more evidence that our attention to privacy comes only after the loss of it.

The transfer of data from company to company is often done on magnetic tape. Sears provides credit companies with tapes of outstanding balances on your credit card and mine.

When individuals apply for credit cards or bank loans, credit reporting agencies are notified by the banks. If the loan is approved, that information is also reported. Credit companies then can deduce which people failed to get loans, but they do not know the reason for the failure. The criteria on which banks refuse loans change over time. Thus the granting or not granting of a loan becomes a solid "fact" without any accompanying data.

William Canney, attorney for AT&T, is quoted in the March 1976 *Computerworld* as saying:

. . . although it is company policy to notify customers when records of their toll calls are subpoenaed by law enforcement agencies, customers are actually warned in less than 25 percent of cases. (p. 19)

Edward Pritchard, reservation director for the Sheraton Hotel chain, testified that room occupancy information—even the name of an individual who accompanied the data subject—is provided over the telephone to anyone who inquires, if the central computer has the information.

When the Privacy Act of 1974 was passed, the private sector was not included. Corporations were thought to have high standards and fair practice in these matters. Two years later, before the Privacy Protection Study Commission, company presidents, vice-presidents, directors and company administrators all told of sending monthly tapes to other companies, selling and buying personal data and trading it to advantage.

The State of Massachusetts openly advertises its master file of driver's license registration data to any organization wishing to buy it. The flow of information from agency to agency and from company to company should generally be presumed to occur if either party will benefit from it. The individual should have no expectation of privacy in his banking records (Supreme Court ruling) or in any other data collection system.

For $35 per month, merchants in California can lease a hand-held computer terminal linking the user with the seventeen million credit files of Telecredit Inc. of Los Angeles, Western States Bank Card Association and TRW's "Validata" system. Merchants can then learn quickly whether any resident of the state has a sufficient balance in the bank account.

Readers who would like to snoop on other people's personal confidential records will enjoy J. M. Carroll's book *Confidential Information Sources: Public and Private.*

The Federal Jury Service (a private company) will sell data on jurors to both sides in a lawsuit. This may include the jurors past voter registrations, public records, property records, past jury service, employment history, past addresses, family members and more.

Equifax Inc. has for some time been publicized as one of the largest brokers of personal information. It conducted (in 1977) more than 80 percent of the insurance investigations in the United States. The Federal Trade Commission claims that Equifax violated the Fair Credit Reporting Act with inaccurate files and unresponsiveness to consumer requests to check its records. The

4,700 field representatives were said to be pressured to complete certain quotas of work each day. Under pressure, unqualified sources, faked sources, hurried interviews, etc. can produce questionable data which are sometimes based on gossip. The $275 million conglomerate is based in Atlanta, Georgia, but owns credit bureaus all around the coastlines of the United States and Canada. (Robert Ellis Smith, January 1978, p. 1)

Privacy laws which vary from country to country create special loopholes for those people who wish to use personal data profitably outside the law. Data which passes across the borders of countries may be exempt from confining laws which would limit or impede the goals of private entrepreneurs.

Conversely, much business in the United States, as well as much government intelligence assumes that data can flow freely *into* the United States without limitation. This is not the case in other countries.

The French Senate started with a liberal privacy bill in 1975 but quickly modified it into a conservative protectionist bill which greatly limited the data which can flow out of the country. Such legislation does harm to United States business interests abroad because data must be kept within national boundaries.

Researchers of the privacy issue can be swept away by the deluge of source materials which originate in other countries. Sweden, for instance, requires everyone to obtain a license before keeping any personal files of information on other people. A governing board issues permits and directives covering file security, disclosure, correction, terminal access, etc.

Germany placed age limits on its data, preventing the use of any that are more than five years old. Of the eighteen countries which now have privacy laws, only West Germany has this data age limit. It applies to data received from foreign sources as well. We can see that a nation is like a grid of information channels between various social agencies and companies. Data flows from public to private agencies, and citizens must eventually adjust to this fact. No privacy laws will stop the traffic of information; the economy depends upon it and the media that handle it are already part of our lives.

The average citizen is not acquainted with the techniques of record-keeping or file searching, even manually. Automated databases can with electronic swiftness expose facts about a person's relationships to friends and to society in ways that the person has never considered.

There was a time (before 1970) when agency data were assumed to be confidential. Educational test scores, medical records, arrest records, and so on, were carried in trust by the agencies receiving them and were assumed to be safely kept.

In Minnesota this idea has been openly and legally negated. James Nobles's article in *Data Management* (April 1977) reports:

> In the 1975 and 1976 amendments the Legislature has reversed its original position that the Commissioner of Administration should limit distribution of data. . . . The law now contains the presumption that *all "data on individuals" is public unless the Legislature or Congress explicitly says otherwise.*
>
> In fact . . . (they) classified arrest information . . . as "not confidential" and said that after June 30, 1977, civil and criminal investigative information will also be "not confidential." (p. 24)

Similarly, the United States Supreme Court has ruled that citizens have "no legitimate expectation of privacy" in their bank or credit records. (D. F. Linowes, ed., *Personal Privacy in an Information Society*, p. 7) These two important decisions have to be related to the general thesis that privacy is a thing of the past.

The study of privacy is one that benefits greatly from the study of media theory. The communications revolution threatened to destroy privacy from its inception with Morse Code. The ability to communicate Morse signals at the speed of light across the globe guaranteed the transmission of data from person to person or institution to institution. As electronic media were developed greater bursts of data capsules in digital and analog codes were passed in ever increasing volumes through copper wires, microwaves, shortwaves, longwaves and laser beams.

Every check we write is microfilmed. For whom? Most insurance forms, when signed, give permissions for widespread distribution. To whom? For how long? Test answer sheets supplied to some test scoring companies must carry a Social Security number or else name and birthdate. Why? Who owns such data? Does someone make money when test scores are merged and compared?

Modern man has traded privacy for efficiency. The tradeoff was not conscious; our privacy just seemed to slip away. The media of computer communications (terminals attached to telephone lines) and computerized data-base management systems simply began to operate without anyone giving permission, denying permission or even seeming to talk about it. New media affect us subtly, turning us into new people with new values.

After privacy was lost, politicians began to see the need for laws designed to guarantee privacy. They help to perpetuate the idea that privacy still exists, and to foster the nostalgic myth of its existence despite the hundreds of privacy-negating forms signed throughout a citizen's lifetime.

Privacy laws apply only *after* the data have been contributed and privacy yielded. Most politicians and official commissions behave as though the privacy laws were going to restore privacy. Media scholars see in nearly all privacy laws a placebo strategy, making it easier for individuals to live with their already open, exposed selves. Such laws assist citizens in retaining equilibrium in a rapidly changing society and in feeling that someone cares, that something is being done. The courts have declared that citizens have no right to expect privacy in certain areas of life, and that the privacy laws have nothing to do with this reality. With eighteen files carried by the federal government on each individual and ten to sixteen carried by the state governments, the thesis of privacy lost is supported. Privacy laws will probably be counterproductive, because more agencies will have to collect their own data rather than relying on trading with others.

Bibliography

Brill, A., *The Right to Financial Privacy Act.* Englewood Cliffs, N. J.: Prentice-Hall, 1979.

Carroll, J. M., *Confidential Information Sources: Public and Private.* Los Angeles: Security World Press, 1975.

Creative Computing Survey. Morristown, N. J.: Creative Computing, 1975.

Dahl, N., and J. Wiesner, *World Change and World Security.* Cambridge, Ma.: MIT Press, 1979.

Davis, W. S., and A. McCormack, *The Information Age.* Reading, Ma.: Addison-Wesley, 1979.

Dertouzos, M., and J. Moses, eds., *The Computer Age: A Twenty Year View.* Cambridge, Ma.: MIT Press, 1979.

French, N., "Companies Admit to Privacy Commission They Share Data without Telling Subjects," *Computerworld* 7 (March 1976).

Hoffman, L. *Computers and Privacy in the Next Decade.* New York: Academic Press, 1980.

Linowes, D. F., ed., *Personal Privacy in an Information Society.* Washington, D. C.: U. S. Government Printing Office, 1977.

Lipson, B., "Search Warrants without Due Process," *Privacy Journal* 2, no. 8 (June 1976).

McLuhan, M., *Understanding Media: The Extensions of Man.* New York: McGraw-Hill, 1964.

Nobles, J. R., "Minnesota Privacy Experience Spotlights Complexity of Law," *Data Management* 15, no. 4 (April 1977).

Pipe, R., ed., "Australians Favor International Privacy Accord," *Computerworld* 11, no. 45 (November 1977).

Rosenberg, J., "Catch in the Information Act," *The Nation* (February 1978).

Smith, R. E., ed., *Compilation of State and Federal Laws on Privacy.* Washington, D. C.: *Privacy Journal,* 1976.

————. *Privacy Journal* 2, no. 2 (December 1975).

Smith, R. E., *Privacy: How to Protect What's Left of It.* New York: Doubleday, 1979.

Sorkin, M. D., "Data Bank Law Backfires, Secret Arrests Follow," *Computerworld* 8, no. 4 (October 1973).

Taylor, A., "Sale of State's Driver Master Tapes Causes Concern," *Computerworld,* (July 1977).

Chapter Thirteen

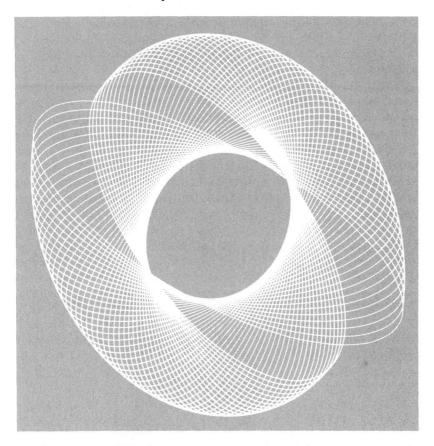

The Computer
as Stepchild:
Where Does It Fit?

☐ In organizational terms, there are about five places in a corporation where a computer can be placed. Each requires the organization chart to be redrawn.

☐ Distributed processing is an activity that reproduces computer centers throughout the branches of a company.

The impact of computers on organizations must be considered. How do they adjust to computer services? What changes in business organization can be projected as an outcome of our commitment to computers?

The evolution of data-base management systems has been traced from the manual records kept in file cabinets (1800 to 1950) to the automated data-base systems which became popular after 1970. In this chapter the evolution of distributed processing and the changing goals of computer-using institutions will be shown to be linked. Institutional goals often shift because of what is possible in the realm of record-keeping. And computerized record-keeping evolves because of what is required in the realm of institutional goals.

The effects of computers on organizational structure

Frederic Withington describes in *The Use of Computers in Business Organizations* the dilemma of where to put the computer. Its physical location within an organization profoundly affects the operation and internal relationships of the company.

Five locations were identified for a computer center within an organization, each having positive and negative effects for the company and its organizational structure. They are:

1. In a large company (insurance, for example) the computer center may be organized under one of the larger divisions or departments. The problem with this arrangement is that the computer center staff will be loyal to their department or division and more services may accrue to that division. Being better-informed and automated, that division may be more stable, cost-effective and growth-oriented. New applications will be written for those local administrators who control promotions and salaries, assisting the division in which they are employed.

2. The computer center may be organized as a wing or outside organization, providing computer power to all of the divisions and

departments, like a service bureau. An advisory or planning committee provides overall direction. The disadvantage with this arrangement is that the center will be profit-and-loss oriented rather than attuned to the information needs of the company. Each service will probably be billed. Difficult or doubtful projects will be viewed as money losers to the service bureau, even if they are greatly desired by the users. The internal communication channels of the larger company will remain unchanged. The computer will tend to mimic existing manual or paper procedures.

3. Computer centers may be placed under the comptroller's department. Payrolls and budgets are often the first functions to be automated and these offices often acquire early experience with computers. The comptroller is often an executive officer in the company and may provide system services to all departments. The disadvantage here is that financial applications may forever receive favored attention. Management decision reports are often outside the accounting field and will appear as foreign intruders. In this connection, students of media theorize that Japan had no history of card unit-record machines and therefore did not view computers as an extension of a previous medium. In the United States, since unit-record operations generally served the financial officer, the computer which replaced them came into the same department. The radical difference between the media of mechanical unit-record equipment and computers is only now being confronted or discerned in many U. S. firms.

4. Computer operations are sometimes placed under a staff vice-president. Thus each corporate division can be treated with equal service and respect. The requirements of each operating department can be given fair treatment. The trade-off here is one of accountability. While each department will have firm standards and procedures to induce line accountability, top officials are staff-oriented. The director of the center has no one to turn to for decisions requiring line-type action. Top staff awareness is broad and general, not detail-oriented, and therefore not very effective in computer administration.

5. Some companies create a separate computer division equal to the other divisions. It may be called the Information Services Department or the Administrative Services Department. The manager of the department can negotiate with other departments. The computer center will be accountable in line fashion for cost-effectiveness and deadline production accomplishments. Unfortunately the budget of this department will often be several million dollars higher each year than that of other departments. It will appear to

be a high cost center in the firm. Because its expenses are so visible in the profit-and-loss statements of the firm, the computer center may suffer cutbacks, never achieving corporate approval for the full automation of broad functions.

Today, online terminal-oriented systems have further heightened the quandary of where to place the computer center in the organization. With terminals, the former barriers of distance (as in widely spread branches or conglomerates) can all be united through terminals and common data-bases.

Withington states:

> If an organization is to employ an ambitious real-time system, then, it has no alternative but to establish the computer activity as an independent unit, probably as a new operating department of the company. With such a system, the total investment, personnel, and planning probably justify such organizational recognition. This is not to say, however, that such a setup is ideal. By the time an organization is fully utilizing a real-time system and has become completely dependent on it, all the old organizational lines will begin to crumble anyway; the distinctions between functional and geographic areas which existed in the decentralized organization will begin to seem obsolete. . . . The use of such systems is somewhat in conflict with the distinctions in the traditional organizational structure.*

This was written in 1966; a tribute to an author's incisive awareness of the new medium. If the computer is to be used boldly to company advantage, old styles of hierarchical organization will have to change; especially if every office has its own terminal and access to company data.

Functional organization groups such as research or marketing department management may be inconsistent with computer data-base metaphors. For in such data-bases, a company exists and is fully known as an information matrix. From this matrix a company can be guided, plotted, observed, modeled—even funded and stock-marketed. In order to make optimal use of its corporate data, the basic structure of the organization will change whether planned for or not. Like other media in the culture, the computer silently lures the corporation to new metaphors of organizational possibility.

---

* All Withington excerpts are taken from F. Withington, *The Use of Computers in Business Organizations.* © 1966, Addison-Wesley Publishing Company, Inc. Reprinted with permission.

Again, Withington states:

The use of the computer encourages centralization of decision making, and this, of course, implies change in the organizational structure itself. Centralization is encouraged in two ways. First, before the computer was available, centralized decision making was not feasible simply because there were too many data for centralized management to consider. Therefore, it was left to decentralized management to handle the relatively limited bodies of data connected with individual limited operations. With the aid of a computer, centralized management can give adequate consideration to all relevant data and, in doing so, can produce better decisions than were possible under the previous, fragmented system.

Second, the full power of a computer system is realized only when the system is provided with a comprehensive data base describing the environment of and conditions within the organization. Each operating department of an organization could, theoretically, develop its own data collection system to provide its own data base. But as these systems grow, they will become closer and closer duplicates of one another, and since such systems are expensive, it is not sensible to operate duplicates. It is therefore universally concluded that comprehensive data collection systems should be developed centrally. (p. 185)

Thus, each division, branch or department may feel some loss of identity as it begins to yield to centralized, uniform data standards. Since top management can analyze the performance of the branches at a detailed level, it may begin to make decisions which previously were made by branch managers.

As company planning becomes more computer based and centralized, the local branches and departments will not "know" evolving trends as quickly as top management knows them. Older, autonomous, departments and branches with their own chains of command and local feedback will falter in the presence of centralized daily profit-and-loss statements, production reports, sales reports and investors' reports. Top management will once again begin to govern by knowing more than the hierarchy below them—assuming that the terminals in the branches are limited in their inquiry ability.

Withington writes that

there is little doubt that the organization of the future will be different from the organization of today. Proof . . . is provided by the already abundant examples of organizations that are changing their structures to accommodate and make use of the powers of the computer.

The transition from the functionally oriented, qualitatively managed organization of today to the integrated, quantitatively managed organization of tomorrow is going to be immensely difficult and painful. (p. 200)

When the communications revolution began to affect company organizations, between 1950 and 1970, top management could not easily retain a pyramid organizational structure because the local branches and departments often possessed critical decision-making knowledge before top management knew it.

Copying machines, intercoms, office telephone systems, stock market online analyses, wireless telephones and radio links between various operations, etc. all contributed to *distributed* (less centralized) modes of company organization.

"Where shall we put the computer center in our organization?" This question has become the central battleground in many organizations. The struggle to get the computer physically located "in my branch, or my division, or my office" seems to be never-ending. The lure of the mini- and microcomputer hardware gives every office manager the hope of some efficient, snappy system which can run privately within the local office.

Data-base management systems gave management a new reason for owning and controlling large central computers. When such systems are placed centrally in the corporate office, top management believes that it will get its reports more dynamically and that the branches will see only those information details which are required to support their local activities.

Branch offices create tremendous pressure, however, to house computers at each branch site. All of the arguments sound familiar; "We will be more cost-effective, have more local accountability, more control, better profit-and-loss statements, better sales support," and so on. These arguments are presented as evidence that each branch should have its own computer center complete with system programmers, personalized programs, operators, supplies and air conditioning for the machine. The branches are really requesting local autonomy in the face of incessant centralization.

Only the high-profit companies could afford to grant this luxury prior to 1972. The high costs of central machines limited such installations quite naturally. Then minicomputers became available. They boasted memory which could jockey data up to four times faster than prior central machines, at least when the data was in main memory. The costs were lower—$50,000 to $300,000 purchase prices depending on the peripherals attached to them. And the salesmen offered "turnkey" promises, meaning that various applications would be able to run with ease almost immediately.

As the minicomputer gained acceptance and was applied to corporate problems, the concept of "distributed processing" was advertised as the solution for the branches or divisions which wanted local computing power. A general definition of distributed processing is: a system of minicomputers placed at various locations so as to provide local computing power that also conforms to centralized requirements for the periodic shipping of data to a larger central computer at the home office center. There it can be made part of the corporate data-base. The full corporate data-base is not shared with the branches in most cases.

The panacea of distributed processing was proclaimed as the cure-all for division blues. The rapid growth of minicomputer sales is perhaps half accounted for by the pent-up desire of company branches to confirm their autonomy in information handling. Reports which were provided after the fact by central machines were never good enough, fast enough nor adequately tailored to the problems which each branch claimed uniquely theirs.

Gerald Burnett and Richard Nolan assessed the situation in 1975:

> Most companies today are on a path toward centralization of computing. Some have already set up elaborate divisions that provide consolidated computer services for the entire organization, while others have centralized their electronic data processing (EDP) activities into regional facilities, commonly called data centers.
>
> But more recent evidence suggests that this path is not necessarily a good one. Regardless of the positive forces mentioned above, service levels seem to be deteriorating: users complain that data centers are lethargic and nonresponsive, and centralization of computer facilities all too often runs against the decentralized operations preferred by many companies.
>
> As a consequence of these administrative and organizational difficulties, a nagging question confronts management: Are the measurable economic benefits of centralized computing worth the side effects? Developments in minicomputer technology have dramatically changed the economic and organizational variables. Today minicomputers are available for a fraction of the cost of large computers and can be operated with less specialized support than the larger ones require.*

The statements above are characteristic of the distributed processing promotional era. Not until 1977 did the negative factors of distributed processing begin to receive equal press. Between 1974 and 1977 distributed processing was supposed to help everyone achieve their goals. It was said to be good for lower management to acquire some autonomy and it was said to be good for the corporate management goals as well. Data from company branches could be obtained with less resistance and more standardization. The hardware price was, by then, low enough to make the distributed processing option attractive and viable.

In the distributed processing literature between 1974 and 1977, dozens of advantages were set forth—most of them focusing on technique rather than on the medium and politics. Some advantages claimed for distributed processing were:

> Less data to be moved from the branches to the central site.
>
> Smaller central machines can be made possible due to the work now being done at the branches.
>
> Reduced job queueing requirements.
>
> Improved response time on terminals.
>
> Heightened computer awareness at local sites.
>
> Planned modularized programs and data-bases.
>
> Improved security and access checking.
>
> Improved adaptation of programs to local requirements.

The journal *Government Data Systems* presented the disadvantages of distributed processing in its January-February 1977 issue. In an editorial explanation, the advantages were countered by these points (p. 28):

> Loss of vendor support of operating systems and data-bases.
>
> Lack of computer-generated accounting information regarding who uses the machines for what.
>
> Poor systems may be designed locally due to smaller lower-paid staff.
>
> Short-staffing at the local center.
>
> Difficulty in rebuilding computer files which are damaged.
>
> Difficulty in retransmitting data to the central machine when faulty transmission occurs.

Lack of two- or five-year plans for data processing.

Indirect costs are greater than computer salesmen admit.

Decentralized minicomputers have much unused capacity.

Total data-processing costs are obscured.

The vulnerability of small staffs to high turnover.

Difficulty in maintaining corporate documentation.

Deviation from corporate guidelines.

Friction between local system analysts and corporate analysts.

Divisional tendency to solve data-processing problems which have been solved corporately in other ways.

The problem with the distributed processing medium is that it creates a new computer center wherever it is adopted. Corporate leaders were easily sold on the idea because it appeared to be low in cost. But the observable tip of a $30,000 iceberg gives little evidence of the added costs which may be incurred later as the minicomputer begs for attendants, management, communication hookups, operating systems, programs, data backup, documentation and permanent staffing.

Minicomputers do serve specific functions well. A branch office may have need for a flexible accounting system or inventory management programs or word-processing. But the computer which does any one of these functions is no sooner installed than the user wishes that it could perform one or two other functions as well. The minicomputer can do this, of course, if more memory is added, and more terminals and ports, more disk space and larger operating systems. Then it's not a mini any more. As the system becomes more complex, the salaries of the computer staff rise accordingly—if the staff can be found at all.

When the little branch office computer types a message on its console such as "DISK I/O READ ERROR" or "OPERATING SYSTEM PRODUCING DUMP," everything stops and the need for professional staff becomes clear at once. The vendor may be long gone, having left his turnkey wares and a booklet of directions. The common solution is to add more staff to ensure stable operation. And that is an annual cost. Distributed processing *does* create jobs for people—more jobs than can be filled.

In summary, the question of a centralized computer center versus distributed shops may come down to one of personal preference, and how much a company has to spend. We all have an innate desire to avoid the bureaucratic encumbrances which often characterize large centralized organizations. Low and middle management will always plead for local autonomy and control. However, most companies cannot afford to create five to fifty new computer centers complete with staff and insurance.

Citibank in New York spent $200 million in a three-year period in an effort to distribute its processing. It now has about 100 new computer centers and a professional staff tending the Interdata (and other) minicomputers. Meanwhile, the central shops still remain in operation. It is almost impossible to calculate whether the distributed system is more costly, or whether the capital investment could have been lower if data were processed through larger central systems.

Several conclusions are apparent for those who are heading toward distributed processing.

1. Significant capital and operational funding will be required—more than is apparent in the initial hardware list.

2. Salaries demand more dollars than the hardware—many more, and qualified staff are hard to find.

3. Distributed processing will radically alter the organization chart of those companies which adopt it.

Bibliography

Burnett, G., and R. Nolan, "At Last, Major Roles for Minicomputers," *Harvard Business Review* (May-June 1975).

Champine, G. A., *Computer Technology Impact on Management.* New York: Elsevier North-Holland, 1978.

Grosch, H. "Grosch's Law Revisited," *Computerworld* 16, no. 9 (April 1975).

Hoxie, G., and D. Shea, "Ten Hot Buttons Facing Management," *Infosystems* 24, no. 9 (September 1977).

Katzan, H., *Distributed Information Systems.* Princeton, N. J.: Petrocelli Books, 1979.

Kaufman, F., "Distributed Processing: A Discussion for Executives Travelling Over Difficult Terrain." *Data Base* 9 (summer 1978).

McLead, R., *Management Information Systems.* Palo Alto, Ca.: Science Research Associates, 1979.

Mowshowitz, A., *The Conquest of Will.* Reading, Ma.: Addison-Wesley, 1976.

Myers, C. A., ed., *The Impact of Computers on Management.* Cambridge, Ma.: MIT Press, 1967.

Naylor, T. H., *Simulation Models in Corporate Planning*. New York: Praeger, 1979.

Sherwood, H. F., "Citibank: 'All That Glitters,'" *Bulletin of the Information Technology Society*. San Jose, Ca.: SBS Publishers, 1977.

Surden, E., "Large Users Tending to Centralize Mini Policy," *Computerworld* 8 (October 1977).

Vandernoort T. J., and R. Bedford, "DP's Position in Corporate Structure," *Computerworld* 25 (November 1977).

Wagner, F. F., "Is Decentralization Inevitable?," *Datamation* 86 (November 1976).

Warren C., and M. Miller, *From the Counter to the Bottom Line*. Forest Grove, Or.: Dilithium Press, 1979.

Whistler, T. L., *The Impact of Computers on Organizations*. New York: Praeger, 1970.

Withington, F., *The Use of Computers in Business Organizations*. Reading, Ma.: Addison-Wesley, 1966.

Young, B., and B. Trainor, "Citiproof: New Policy Validates Net's Worth," *Data Communications* 7, no. 3 (March 1978).

Chapter Fourteen

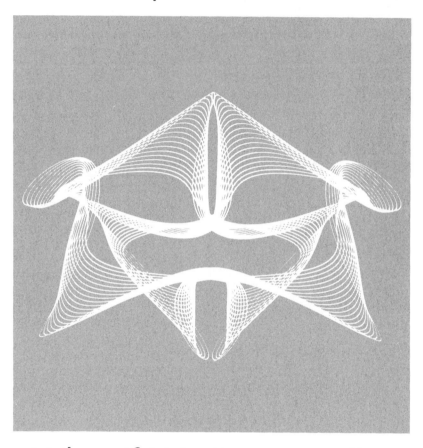

What If We Become Like Computers?

□ All media provide basic metaphors of life and culture.

□ The computer may add a third level of abstraction to our common reasoning powers.

□ We may wish to have all of our goods and services here, now, instantly, just like the computer which serves us instantly.

□ The computer may appeal to both sides of the mind; the rational and the gestalt.

□ The computer is the first electronic medium which depends on alphabets and writings as well as pictures and graphics.

Carl Jung wrote in 1928:

> Every Roman was surrounded by slaves. The slave and his psychology flooded ancient Italy, and every Roman became inwardly a slave. Because living constantly in the atmosphere of slaves, he became infected through the unconscious with their psychology. No one can shield himself from this unconscious influence.*

Media, also, have this subversive effect, remodeling the fundamental ways in which people relate to other people—both privately and organizationally. Media do this because they surround our minds; they are the environment of the mind. Missionaries who teach natives to read observe that after reading catches on, the tribe often dissolves, the readers drifting off to towns to work in factories. Reading instills a basic acceptance of sequentiality. People begin to act as though life is like a book. Activities can be broken into small events like pages in a book. Gradually assembly-line values begin to erode the tribal metaphors of wholeness, process and unity. Illiterate people who live in cities feel strangely displaced or out of place. Similarly, tribal dwellers have little desire for the city until they can read. Factories and structured city life make little sense to a tribal person until the metaphor "life is a book" takes hold.

What then of the super-medium, the computer? What metaphors will it lure us to adopt as foundations for living? Will we view life and work differently because of it? Will our discursive, rational skills be heightened or diminished? In what ways has the computer as a metaphor for human thought and behavior affected

* *The Collected Works of C. G. Jung,* translated by R. F. C. Hull, Bollingen Series XX, Vol. 10: *Civilization in Transition.* ©1964, 1970 by Princeton University Press. Reprinted by permission of Princeton University Press.

A floppy disk may someday contain the history of our personal transactions. We may pass it to our children as a keepsake.

our concepts of learning, problem-solving, goal identification and attainment? How has the computer affected our concepts of space, time and communication? Is the computer a neutral processor of messages? Does it impose any biases of its own?

We shall see that while some media reinforce the rational side of humanity's mind, other media reinforce the gestalt, stream of consciousness aspect of our minds. The computer will be seen to support and develop *both* of these attributes, in contrast to prior media which tended to develop one or the other.

The effect of computers on living habits

James Martin and Adrian Norman describe a likely outcome at the functional level twenty to thirty years hence. The reader should linger over these paragraphs, not to ask "What messages are passed on the medium?" but rather, "What is the medium doing to the people who use it?"

The rooms where he lives will initially have a telephone, then perhaps a computer terminal, then a multipurpose screen used for television, picturephone, and computer data. As the years go by the screen will become larger and more necessary. He will not be able

From this height in space, a satellite proposed by Bell Labs would sweep back and forth across the United States, picking up and dropping packets of data to each major city. Dual microwave beams would be steered simultaneously by the satellite.

to do without it any more than he can do without electricity now. Perhaps eventually the screen will occupy a whole wall of the room where he lives and works. . . .

Many of the (social) problems . . . will have been solved. Society will have new attitudes to help it survive in the new environment. The interim period will be chaotic because the machines are rapidly taking on their new functions before society is ready for them. The necessary changes in attitudes, ethics, laws, education, and employment will not have taken place in time.

Several decades in the future our ways will be different. Children will be brought up with the new machines. Perhaps they will learn to touch-type on terminals in kindergarten. Soon after they learn to speak to their parents they may learn to speak to computer terminals, in the precise, slow voice and limited vocabulary required.

They may grow up to regard the machines as obtuse, although entertaining and staggeringly fast and powerful. They will learn to program as soon as they have learned arithmetic. (*The Computerized Society,* p. 533)

New media alter our living habits. When pocket calculators appeared, some teachers were concerned that children would forget how to do arithmetic, or maybe never learn to do it. This did not prove to be the case. Similarly, just because computers can work out solutions to certain problems, it does not necessarily follow that people will stop thinking. The invention of fork-lifts did not cause man's back muscles to atrophy. Thus, while pocket calculators find the square roots of numbers, the users are freed to better direct the process of problem-solving. But this is not always apparent to the people caught up in the changing milieu.

The effect of computers on man's intellectual and conceptualizing abilities is predicted to be an expanding, not diminishing, one. Many generations of children grew up without erector sets, mechanical puzzles, cars, model airplanes, motor bikes and transistor radios. During the mechanical, industrial era these inventions became popular, permitting and developing more complex levels of thought, as compared to, say, the Middle Ages.

But the toys sold in 1981 are at least one magnitude more complex. They range from radio controlled cars to "Speak and Spell" computers for children. Such "toys" prepare children to welcome electronic terminals and computer procedures without hesitation or fear. Computers in the home are predicted to extend further the reasoning and abstracting powers of the people who use them. The act of writing even a simple computer program elicits significant concentration, analysis, definition of goals and conceptualization of the desired system results, and it even makes one think about how the media can be rearranged by formulas in the program. For those who use or program computers, this expansive effect on the rational mind is noticeable and exciting. Even if one's program is disorganized and barely readable, the development process stretches the mind.

Cultures which have pictographic alphabets probably operate at a low level of abstraction because a symbol on a page actually represents "tree" even if its shape has drifted away from the literal shape of the tree. Cultures with phonetic alphabets operate two levels of abstraction away from reality, however, because when they see the letters T-R-E-E on a page they must go through a mental process such as "these four symbols represent three speech sounds which, if someone uttered them, would sound like tree, and those sounds represent a wooden trunk and branches in my language."

A third level of abstraction is introduced when people begin to write simple computer programs. A line such as:

```
PRINT VARIABLES A, B, C, D
```

requires a mental process such as "if those four variables contain the letters T-R-E-E, then, at the time the program is run, the TV screen will display TREE which represents three speech sounds." This will surely expand the mind just as revolutionary changes resulting from phonetic alphabets did when they introduced the second level of abstraction to the rational mind.

Time magazine (February 20, 1978) addressed this issue and summarized the likely outcome of widespread computer access:

> Those who first used fire must have terrified their generation. Practically any break-through in knowledge carries with it the possibility that it will be used for evil. But with microcomputers, the optimists can argue an extremely persuasive case. The Industrial Revolution had the effect of standardizing and routinizing life. Microtechnology, with its nearly infinite capacities and adaptability, tends on the contrary toward individualization; with computers, people can design their lives far more in line with their own wishes. They can work at terminals at home instead of in offices, educate themselves in a variety of subjects at precisely the speed they wish, shop electronically with the widest possible discretion. . . .
>
> Some, like sociologist Seymour Martin Lipset, envision a "more egalitarian society" because of the computer. Transferring so much work to the machines, thinks Lipset, may produce something like Athenian democracy; Athenians could be equal because they had slaves to do their work for them. (p. 45)*

The effect of computers on certain values

One value change resulting from the general use of the computer medium may be that people will have less rigid, more accepting attitudes to social conventions and ways of doing things.

---

* Reprinted by permission from *TIME*, The Weekly Newsmagazine. Copyright Time Inc. 1978.

This mellowing of attitude would be predicted because of two features of the medium which may be adopted metaphorically.

Firstly, every letter or symbol carried in computer memory can be related to every other letter—equally, logically and by design. Everyone who runs a few programs on any computer, or who writes even the simplest four-line program, will quickly sense that all of the representations within it are equal in status and worth. Any symbol is capable of becoming the head of a chain of relationships. Living with that metaphor daily, it could reduce one's prejudices or beliefs that certain ways are the only ways.

A second feature of the medium is that there is no single correct way to write a program, accomplish a goal or solve a problem. Because of the flexibility of the program instructions with which users can state their plan of media processing, even in a simple language like BASIC, hundreds of different programs could be written, all of which might accomplish the same goal. This further instills the metaphor of equality and acceptable variance.

For social problems, then, no single solution would be thought of as an only solution. A population, adopting this metaphor, would seem to be more open-minded; more open to innovative ideas. Since there is no single right way to write a program or implement a plan, this metaphor, when extended to social relationships, could forecast a reduction in prejudice and bigotry. The social conventions of minority groups may be tolerated better because the metaphor implies that the other person is not doing something wrong, he is merely doing it differently. And just as any two symbols in the computer have equal status, so also contrasting social conventions, speech habits, eating habits, lifestyles, liturgical and territorial preferences may be more easily viewed as being equally as valid as one's own. The other fellow is seen to be "programmed" differently by his culture or genes. Such tolerance does not imply that one has fewer values or standards, but rather a more honest consideration and appreciation of other cultures and personalities. Such attitudes represent an extension of one basic attribute of the computer medium—its obedient willingness to accept any path toward a goal.

This feature of the computer medium also heightens one's feeling of creativity and individuality. The act of writing a simple program can be extremely satisfying, even to the novice, because of the sense that "I did it my way." It is a medium on which individuals really can create solutions for trivial tasks that are creatively unique, even elegant.

The medium is therefore more important than the messages it

carries. That is, the satisfaction of writing the program and of mastering the device which executes it may be more motivating, stimulating and growth-promoting than the problem which gets solved when the program runs. It is a new type of canvas on which to paint original landscapes of the universe, using any symbols the user desires.

Another prediction is that people may increasingly expect public decision-making to be based more on analysis and fact than on political ego and pronouncement. As more people sense what is going on in their home computer as the program of their choice executes some trivial goal, the metaphor "logical, rational planning always gets results" may be instilled, thus causing other social decisions regarding the distribution of wealth and goods to be similarly determined. The public may someday opt for a systems approach to social problems rather than one of political decision-making.

Just because a systems approach can be applied to social problems does not mean that it is good or should be done; merely that it is likely to happen. Weizenbaum *(Computer Power and Human Reason,* p. 226) suggests that this may *not* be a good or useful task for the computer.

A metaphor of instantaneity is presented subliminally by computers. All electronic media present this metaphor, of course, not just computers. Split TV screens between the earth and the moon, or between Japan and Finland, encourage a basic acceptance of all-at-onceness. Computers heighten this metaphor. As far as the human senses are concerned, the computer returns its solution to most problems instantly, causing the user to remark "How could it do it that fast?"

Users of such equipment will probably begin to desire instant results in other areas of life as well. Living in the presence of radios, computers, television recorders with instant replay, radio-controlled garage doors, point-of-sale terminals at department stores and satellite communications probably perpetuates the desire for instantaneity in general.

The home computer, when used for word-processing, can cast its inner eye over a 500-page document and report every occurrence of the letter "H" or the word "heart." (The text of this book was checked for spelling errors by a program on a mainframe computer. It reported that 9,287 lines of text and 78,427 words were checked for spelling. The entire process took 15 minutes, although 50 other people were using the computer concurrently for other tasks. It reported 142 wrong spellings.)

Fast food chains became popular after the electronic media had instilled the idea that speed in eating is possible and desirable. Do you remember when eating was a time for slowing down? Today our siestas are taken in jet airplanes, on the way to vacation packages crammed with planned activities. The metaphor of simultaneity created the need for the Concorde supersonic aircraft.

People subscribe to computerized dating services, for instant matchmaking. A chain of gasoline stations has a means for drivers to buy groceries while their tank is being filled. Reaching out of the car window, the customer pushes buttons representing the items desired for purchase. An attendant brings the goods (almost) instantly, and charges them on the credit card along with the gasoline.

Instead of factory foremen barking, "Let's not waste any time around here," the whole culture may demand its goods and services to be *here now immediately,* just like its information. Eventually institutions, bureaucracies and social relationships may also yield to this metaphor.

The effect of computers on rationality as a value

The question of interest is, will the logical mind of man be confirmed and developed by the computer medium, or in contrast, will the dream and gestalt processes of the mind be amplified? This question holds special significance because our heritage of rational thought could become less valued if a broad commitment to non-discursive media dominates the culture.

Christine Nystrom analyzes the precomputer effects of electronic media on human values in her article "Immediate Man" in *Et Cetera* (March 1977). These paragraphs provide an incisive review of what television and film (non-discursive media) have done to our rational and discursive skills.

> . . . Television evokes responses that are gestalt, non-analytic, immediate, present-oriented, non-reflective, and emotional. Television is not, in short, a medium suited for the communication of abstract ideas in logical arrangements. It is a medium which focuses attention primarily on the interpersonal and affective dimensions of the experiences it represents. (p. 26)

> Because of the physical form of television, viewers have virtually no control over the *sequence* in which they will experience represen-

tations, over the *pace* at which they will experience them, or over the selection of *angles* from which to view them. Given a book or letter, I may choose to read from the end if I like, or start from the middle and work backwards or forwards. Given a lecturer present in the flesh, I may ask for repetition or a different pace of delivery. Given an object literally before me, I may change its position—or my own—to see it in a different light. Not so with television. There, we are the manipulated, not the manipulators. And so, for all its excitement, television is intellectually passive. (p. 28)

Our culture has undergone a massive shift, in its symbolic environments, from discursive (rational, analytic, logical, reflective) to non-discursive (gestalt, appositional, emotional, presentational) forms of information and response. The symptoms . . . are to be seen everywhere, and not the least in our classrooms. . . . I have been made anxious by the increasing inability of my students— particularly the younger ones—to read and write. But I am more appalled by their seeming inability to talk—to articulate in an organized way either their ideas or their feelings. For it is talk, more directly than reading and writing, that symbolizes our processes of mind. . . . I am concerned that too early and too total an immersion in the non-discursive may eclipse our capacity to reason at all. It is not the non-discursive mode, but the near total preoccupation with that mode that is reshaping the intellectual character of our time and promoting the evolution of immediate man. (p. 30)

This analysis of the nondiscursive bias of the electronic media deserves thought. Between 1950 and 1970 there were very few indications that any new medium would be invented to challenge or complement the nondiscursive electronic media (movies, TV, radio). Even the invention of the computer provided no relief because it too was an electronic medium. And between 1954 and 1973 it showed no signs of becoming a medium suited for popular or widespread use.

Then, in 1971, the invention of the microcomputer changed all of the prices when Ted Hoff, working for Intel Corporation unveiled his computer on a chip. It was one-sixth of an inch long and one-eighth of an inch wide, containing 2,250 transistors. With peripheral gadgets attached to it, it could manipulate data better than 1960 computers costing $30,000. It was so small and cheap ($15) that it could be considered for use anywhere. Today, millions of microcomputers have been reliably installed in typewriters, elevators, weighing scales, music synthesizers, carburetors, ovens, toys, dashboards, and other household appliances.

Now the microcomputer is coming to our homes with small

styled keyboards, and they may offer a counterforce to the non-discursive nature of previous electronic media. None of the electronic media which induced the gestalt awareness point of view relied on alphabets, print or logic for their use. Illiterate people could buy and use tape recorders, television, radio, LP records, and CB radios. Literacy was clearly unessential to the process.

But the microcomputer terminal, newly engineered for home and public use, is the first electronic medium which *does* rely on alphabets and logical, rational intervention before it performs its service for the user. Anyone who runs a program on these little computers will usually come back to do it again. Almost any type of encounter with a computer terminal causes the user to ponder what is occurring in the process (a discursive activity). Anyone who has written the simplest five-line BASIC program with its immediate feedback and execution will find his or her mind opened to the pleasures of rational, discursive, logical thought.

Unlike the passive, visual television medium, computers accept their directions through letters and words. For the most part, their output is a printed line of phonetic text—English, French or any other language. Thus the sequentiality of the print culture is not lost with this medium.

As a likely outcome, it can be predicted that the large-scale use of home and small-business computers will provide the missing link needed to restore status to the old rational, discursive ways of looking at the world. *The primary symbol set of the computer is letters.* Even if one writes a program to draw random artwork on the screen, the program is written logically with English verbs. Users of the medium deal constantly with the precise meanings of words. The poor arrangement of two lines within a program can be immediately rearranged and executed again to see if improved results are obtained—a discursive or reasoning process.

The basic metaphor which supported discursive thought was momentarily overshadowed by the early electronic media like radio and television, but the widespread acceptance of microcomputers will surely restrain or moderate that influence.

The computer does not undermine the nondiscursive values of the visually-oriented TV generation. Being an electronic medium, it is clearly in a class with the instant, all-at-once media.

Like an ultimate constant in the universe, computers couple the wholeness, the gestalt, the all-at-onceness, with the sequential, the lineal and rational. If the best of humanity is contained in its reasoned thoughts and printed documents, the computer will eventually give these resources the status they deserve, sweeping them up in a unified awareness of both the mystical and the rational, both wholeness and linearity, simultaneity and history. Table 14.1 places these two value systems side by side. This table does not imply that the two value systems cancel each other, but rather that both value systems are promoted metaphorically by the computer medium.

Thus we see that human behavior is modified by the addition of each new medium in the social environment. The computer is a medium more universal than any other and is therefore likely to alter the values, organization and relationships of life more than any other invention in history.

If the dominant metaphors of the computer are adopted, then several new values might prevail. 1) A more accepting attitude about varying social conventions. 2) A systems approach to governace and planning. 3) A desire for goods and services to be

Table 14.1
Two opposing value systems that
the computer promotes metaphorically

Rational, logical, and sequential	Simultaneous, gestalt, and process awareness
The world should be viewed as regular, sequential and capable of being analyzed mathematically because all aspects of the world, when presented to the computer in symbolic form, seem to yield to formulas and rules which are predictable and sequential. The world is a long sentence.	The world should be viewed as a gestalt process. All of it does occur concurrently with itself, just as when a process is presented to the computer and is instantly blended into a whole. Just as the computer blends many things together concurrently, the world itself is a cloud of interacting phenomena.
The world's problems should be analyzed with a systems approach because problems which are presented to computers get solved quickly when this approach is used.	The world would have no problems if we flowed with nature. People should be linked to the universal unconscious and flow with the world, not attempting to structure it so rigidly with systematic precision. Electronic and computer messages all merge together to flow through the airwaves, and we should all merge with the universe in the same way.

Table 14.1 *(continued)*

Rational, logical, and sequential	*Simultaneous, gestalt, and process awareness*
The world's important knowledge resides in the pages of books (not films) and these writings should be available in various logical arrangements without heavy research requirements. The computer easily sorts things into order by Zip code or alphabetically. It should sort out the world's knowledge as well, assisting the research process. It should communicate the holdings of all libraries to my information terminal. The best of humanity is held in its rational recorded history.	The world's knowledge resides in many media and they should all be available to everyone instantly, just like the computer which retrieves all types of information (audio, graphic, print) from its disk storage without any delays. Visual media like television or movies are best. Most important ideas have been recorded on film and films provide a closer view of reality than books.
Certain values and standards are better than others, just as certain computer verbs have priority over others. Computer verbs hold specific meanings which are precise and reliable. The precise meaning of instructions in computer programs makes them consistent and reliable. Social relationships should also be based on precise definitions of tasks, organizational flow charts and hierarchies of relationships.	No single set of mores is right or wrong. Clothing and cultural standards are appositional issues, just as there is no single right way to write a program or solve a computer problem. Other people who behave differently from me are simply doing something differently, not wrong. We are all equal. Corporate organization charts should be horizontal, not hierarchical.
Personal life styles should be guided by creeds and formal statements of belief. Logical systems of truth should support every personal decision and action just as rational flow charts give foundation to computer programs. All things should be systematized including matters of faith, religious belief and strict laws. Daily decisions should not result from default stream-of-consciousness accidents, but from regularized formulas and belief systems.	Personal life-styles should be guided by meditation, spiritual discovery and transcendental linkage, for the universe is full of speed-of-light communications, some of them coming from my computer. Prayer lets me tune in to other ways of knowing, quite apart from ordinary consciousness. My rational mind can only get in the way of "real" communication. Let my mind communicate where the wisdom really is—on the speed-of-light, spiritual wavelengths.

Table 14.1 *(continued)*

Rational, logical, and sequential	Simultaneous, gestalt, and process awareness
It is good to be alone. When I read books I am either alone or unavailable to those around me. When I use my rational mind to work arithmetic, solve problems, write books, write programs or use my computer terminal, I am essentially alone with my mind. Good ideas sometimes lead to dialogue with other people, but the dialogue is always lost unless I withdraw to write it down. The computer terminal requires many hours of pleasant concentration. Social pleasantries only interrupt what is most unique about humanity—its logical rational thought processes.	It is good to be with people. The electronic media arouse emotional responses and deep feelings. There is no need for talk, words, or reason. We should touch each other more, live together in harmony and respect the sights we see as holding reality. Time spent alone does not lead to personal development or self awareness. Only with other people do the unique capabilities of people develop—love, caring, being. The computer terminal links me to other people and brings me the world's best films, TV tapes and art.

instantaneous. For a while it seemed that the electronic media were diminishing the rich history of human heritage contained in archives and libraries. But after fifty years of electronic evolution, the computer medium embraces the earlier media, both print and electronic, giving each of them a place in the media halls of fame. This leads us to consider the computer as the ultimate medium of communication. For just as photographs became the content of movies, and radio became the content of television, so also all of the world's media have become the content of the computer—it subsumes and manipulates them all, print and television, speech and film, Morse code and abacus.

Bibliography

Dorf, R. C., *Computers and Man.* San Francisco: Boyd and Fraser, 1978.

Johansen, R., et al., *Electronic Meetings: Technical Alternatives.* Reading, Ma.: Addison-Wesley, 1979.

Martin, J., and A. Norman, *The Computerized Society.* Englewood Cliffs, N. J.: Prentice-Hall, 1970.

McGuire, W., and R. F. Hull, eds., *C. G. Jung Speaking: Interviews and Encounters.* Princeton, N. J.: Princeton University Press, 1977.

Nystrom, C. L., "Immediate Man: The Symbolic Environment of Fanaticism," *Et Cetera* (March 1977).

Raben, J., ed., *Computers and the Humanities.* New York: Elsevier North-Holland, 1980.

Weizenbaum, J., *Computer Power and Human Reason.* San Francisco: W. H. Freeman, 1976.

Chapter Fifteen

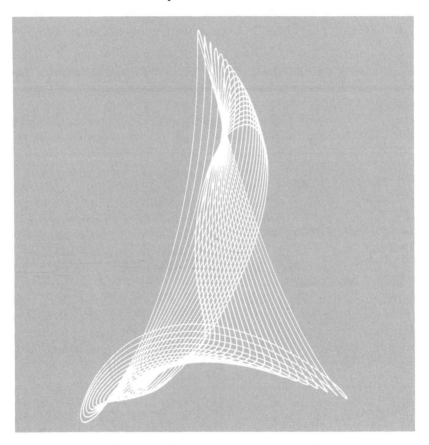

Computers and
the Centralization
of Power

□ Electronic media enable central authorities to monitor global events as they happen, and to control some of these events.

□ As electronic media proliferate, they will someday broadcast so many facts that anyone will be able to intercept almost anything.

□ The Department of Defense was a decentralized organization until electronic media and computers enabled centralized decision-making.

□ Corporations follow the same reorganization pattern as the Defense Department when they adopt computers and electronic media.

A centralized society is one in which many people who could participate in minor decisions are denied that privilege. For instance, in days gone by, when mail could not cross the ocean any faster than the speed of wind-driven ships, or travel faster overland than the speed of the fastest horse, war and battle decisions had to be made by the officers present at the scene of conflict. Such organizations (armies, navies) were decentralized; local decisions were final and generally undisputed. Orders to advance or retreat, kill or take prisoner were judgments to be made by the commander closest to the action.

In an era of radio, television, radar and satellite networks, top generals, sitting in a war-room remote from the combat, make decisions about the way it should be fought. Hot lines, spy planes, satellite mapping and simulation computers give new centralized power to the generals. Officers present at the actual battle are permitted to make only minor decisions.

Will our culture become more centralized or decentralized in a computerized society? Will individuals have more opportunities to participate in decision-making, or less? Will power return to the individual or will it accrue to the bureaucracies and corporations? These questions can be addressed from the vantage point of media theory. Enough data have been presented in the preceding chapters to make possible an assessment based not only on theory but on the collected observations of various scholars. A two-phase effect is predicted:

1. Computers, when provided to any society in the world, will significantly assist the centralization of power and decision-making during the first twenty to forty years of their use.

2. After forty years of use, so much data will be so widely available to so many individuals from so many sources that most secret files will either be published or obtainable from other sources. In such an open society, with all things known to everyone, power may return to the individual.

Initial centralization

The reasons for predicting centralization of power after computerization are found in the constraints of the medium itself. The home microcomputer is no match for the bureaucratic data-base computers. Corporations and governments can navigate through data-bases because 1) they have collected the data; 2) they have large data-base programs available; 3) they have adequate machine memory and power to manage large data-bases; and 4) they are organized to perpetuate the system.

The home microcomputer fails on all four scores. Where would average citizens find a government data-base to scan or interrogate? Would we want to? What would we do with the results? Citizens can obtain obsolete data-bases to analyze, but such hobbies do not return much power to the people.

The home microcomputer owner may get a home information system program with his or her computer. With it one can manage household insurance records, tax records, bills due, recipe lists. The complexity of giant data-base navigation is several levels of difficulty away from the home tinkerer.

The average citizen would not care to browse through a data-base, of course. As citizens, we sometimes wonder why governments want to do it at all. The presence of powerful computers which *can* do it helps to create the need to do it.

The contrasting uses of home computers and corporate computers are shown in Table 15.1. Without doubt the microcomputer will revolutionize the lifestyle of Americans. Like other popular media, it will probably alter the base-line assumptions on which home life and private life rest. Hundreds of thousands of Americans will learn to write simple programs in BASIC and will spend countless leisure hours smiling (and complaining) into the glassy screens of their home computer terminals, finding pleasure in the shifting characters, numbers and games which they invent, buy or trade.

But the microcomputer is no match for the big central data-base systems which manage the closely held files of governments

Table 15.1
The uses of home computers
contrasted with corporate uses

Home uses	Corporate, bureaucratic uses
Balance checkbooks	Merge information from credit and loan sources with income tax data and banking data, reporting inconsistencies
Play games: chess, backgammon, tic-tac-toe, star-trek	Collate profiles of neighborhoods and their buying habits, assisting political and marketing efforts.
Calculate income tax, perform bookkeeping, desk calculations	Report all people who contribute over $4000 per year to churches and who also order books from witchcraft societies
Sort recipes, wine lists, diets, calorie tables	Tag all people in a computer file who have parking or speeding violations, making the data available nationwide keyed on license number
Provide word-processing and text editing services	Scan a personnel file to find all teachers who are tenured and whose highest degree is a Master's Degree
Graphics experimentation, design drawing, computer art	Deliver portions or summaries of data files to other government or corporate agencies
Computer-aided instruction, simulations, tutorial programs	Provide 100 ports into which credit bureaus may connect their terminals to view portions of bank or Social Security records

and corporations. Such files and systems work *against* decentralized power alternatives. The home terminals will be able to plug into data banks of various types for browsing in medical, legal or other encyclopedic resources. But such users will not affect the data nor be able to analyze it in the creative manner available to governments and corporations.

The data-base management services which assist the centralization of power have their foundations in: 1) the giant machines with their expensive data channels; 2) in economics—DBMS is too costly for most citizens to operate or run; and 3) in politics—top management will use its resources to confirm and expand its power.

These factors have not been balanced by any factors which distribute power back to small groups or individuals. One example of the overwhelming power of a corporation to collect data is illustrated by the system at Citibank in New York.

In 1976 Citibank, with 40,000 employees, processing three million checks every day, encountered the limits of paper-based systems. In its New York City banks alone, 100,000 stock certificates, 2 million checks, 10,000 fund transfers and dozens of other types of transactions led to the installation of a computer-based microfilm file-retrieval system. Citibank already had computer processing, but the paper printouts averaged 3 tons per day. The new microfilm system, fully indexed and computerized, contained 625 million checks in 1977 and it was growing at the rate of 3 million each day. It was probably the largest random film file in the world. Any one of those 625 million images can be located and displayed within a few moments. Such a system can make a positive contribution to the lowering of costs and the efficient use of information.

Efficiency is the primary attraction which the computer carries when it is used for records management. Citibank can use its 400,000 cubic foot warehouse of paper records for other purposes now. The clerks who previously sorted through them looking for pieces of paper can now do other things.

This example reveals positive things about a company which is willing to invest so much money in automation and the quest for efficiency. But if an individual is looking for a share of power (decentralization) he cannot match corporate capitalism, whose magnificent electronic systems capture every gesture as a new fact to be microfilmed and indexed.

Business and government do not capture centralized power without our assistance, however. We create the centralized agencies and give them their data-collection powers. Until their data-bases were built, they were helpless—and they got the data from us. It took years for some agencies to establish their files with our data, but we assisted them and now the files are nearly complete. When we have a choice between obtaining insurance or not giving permission for data distribution, we take the insurance. The same is true with driver's licenses, credit cards, loans and medical care.

The predicted negative outcome is that so-called privacy laws will actually encourage broader data capture because they usually hinder agencies from sharing data freely with each other. Hence each agency must collect its data from original sources (us) repeatedly. There is no law against requiring citizens to give information, and there are penalties for citizens who refuse to give it. Thus, power becomes more centralized.

Although the computer could be used to assist the decentralization of power, few if any opposing forces are likely to appear on the social or political scene prior to the year 1990. Power will be significantly centralized, assisted by computer technology.

Eventual decentralization

One other fact of media remains to be considered, however: the bias of the medium will have its way. Over the long term, it is the opinion of this writer that the computerized media will reverse the trend, between 1990 and 2000, into a rapid decentralization of power.

So much data will be collected by so many agencies, institutions, states, municipalities, credit houses, newspapers, banks, and bureaus that it will be essentially available to everyone who wants to get it. A progression of publication is predicted:

1. No government files are shared with the public. (1776 to 1973)

2. The names of government files are published. (1974)

3. The data elements within government files will be published. (About 1984)

4. The actual contents of certain government files will be made available to researchers. (About 1990)

5. Agencies will not be funded or licensed to collect information unless they are willing to make that information available in published and computer-readable form. (About 2000 and beyond)

Citizens will argue that if they pay the state and federal agencies to collect all that data (a costly task), then they deserve to see it, scrutinize it and sort it. "After all, it's our data."

This concept of open data files appears to be inherent in the future of multimedia satellite computer-assisted communications. There was a time when there were very few communication channels and many messages to pass on them. Today there is more nearly a communication channel for every message. We offer unto our satellites above our fervent messages. We know they hear. And everyone else hears too.

A society in which we are so exposed may seem undesirable, partly because we have only recently emerged from the era of manual record-keeping, where secrecy and confidentiality was possible because of the vaults in which records yellowed.

What would it be like to live with such open exposure? What if every check we wrote was microfilmed, as they are now, and then became available to everyone? What if all tax records were revealed? (Politicians began to publish theirs about 1974.) Medical records? (Call any hospital.) Credit records? And everything else about you?

Someday, when government files are published or made available on computer tape, it is possible that a new profession may arise. It may be called professional file analysis, or data bounty hunting. These people or organizations would perform hound-dog functions for the open data culture and may assist in returning power to the people. They may not be known as well as columnist Jack Anderson, but they could multiply his function through their minicomputer detectors. Day and night these sleuths will set their little computers to scanning their copies of government files, bank files, credit files, corporate files, wiretap information and any other data they can get. Poking through the files they will relate this to that, check on consistencies, probe inconsistencies and try to make a case against every embezzler, evader, cheat, trickster and public offender they find—just like the government would like to do but doesn't. In such an open society, this surveillance could be of the people, by the people and for the people, assisting the return of power to the people. If it happens, at the very least, it might be more difficult for politicians to accept payoffs.

Computers are likely to be used by management and government as a tool for promoting the centralization of power. The leaders who allocate funds for the purchase of computers will use them to further secure their management roles. Later, however, the widespread availability of data and the proliferation of data channels is likely to have a neutralilzing influence.

Nearly all authors agree that computerization aids the trend toward centrality of power—even when the distributed processing mode is used. This is not because of anything inherent in computers, but because of the persons who direct the medium toward their goal of centralization. As a fact of the medium itself, however, dictatorship cannot be considered inevitable, because the medium could be used equally well to aid the cause of decentralization.

Just as radio did not displace Morse code and just as television did not eliminate radio, minicomputers are not likely to displace central computing facilities. Most companies cannot afford to set up thirty-five additional computer centers with million-byte minicomputers held back by the primitive data channels which come with the minicomputers. Even when each employee possesses a desktop microcomputer, it will probably support the particular functions of the job and may, as a by-product, supply data to the corporate information system as well.

When the divisions of a company implement their local computer systems, they can actually run the division like a separate company with its own profit-and-loss statements. If that helps each division to remain profitable, it helps the larger corporation too.

But the scattered division heads may never see the MIS reports which headquarters produces on the central computer. The powerful MIS reports are now fed by the distributing computers which have fuller data than ever before. With these reports, corporate centralized control over the details of each division can be exercised daily and hourly. The division has autonomy in name only. Even board members and stock holders will be able to study the MIS reports and dictate actions which the branches must execute. Eventually the profit-and-loss reports will force the issue.

The computer provides a new model of organization to business enterprises and governments. As a medium it causes us to view an organization as an information matrix. The powerful persons who referee the information-matrix-game control the company. The facts of the business can be made available dynamically—daily, hourly, on video screens in a vice-president's office. This activity heightens the metaphor of unity of command. Intuitive guesses will be less valued than decisions based on "facts."

When control is centralized, the common worker, the foreman, even the local manager becomes isolated from the decision-making process. Action is achieved with less responsibility, innovation or thought. Responsibilities are formally defined and the goals of the authorities are executed blindly by the paid followers.

In this regard, Withington (*The Use of Computers in Business Organizations,* p. 186) uses the changing organization of the Department of Defense as an example. Computers were made available to the Defense Department earlier than to corporations. The reorganization which resulted in 1947 is a primary example of media-forced organizational change. It is a good example because much of the corporate world followed the same pattern of change between 1965 and 1977.

To paraphrase Withington, there was no Department of Defense when World War II began. Figure 15.1 shows the pyramidal

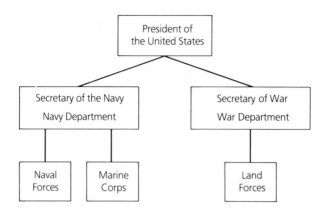

Figure 15.1
Armed forces organization before World War II
Source: F. Withington. *The Use of Computers in Business Organizations.* © 1966, Addison-Wesley Publishing Company, Inc. Reprinted with permission.

relationship of the divisions as illustrated by Withington. Each service group received general instructions from Washington and these were passed down the line to command groups, each of whom filled in more details, field commanders finally carrying them through to execution. Washington rarely gave details or directed the execution of events. Its radio and telegraph messages were simple, short and broad, providing summaries of desired goals and actions. The army and navy operated separately. When joint operations were required, they were viewed as special projects and commanders would consult together as required to complete a project.

Given the requirements of that era, the organization, though simple, functioned adequately. But new communications media and weapons required Washington to become more detail-conscious and have closer control over the armed forces. Missiles, satellites, nuclear weapons, nuclear submarines, aircraft carriers, supersonic jets, early warning systems and radar required and also promoted more centralized control. Local events anywhere in the world could precipitate chain reactions, and the handling of these crises might be essential to world peace.

The new Defense Department was created in 1947, replacing the earlier Armed Forces Organization. Three media-related factors caused this reorganization. Withington identifies them as:

1. Communication of substantial volumes of data from the tactical zone to Washington in a matter of minutes;

2. Immediate evaluation of the information received and consideration of possible courses of action, on the basis of data describing the state of the forces of the United States, its allies, and its potential enemies;

3. Transmission, also in minutes, of detailed commands back to the tactical zone, to major commands in all parts of the world, and to widely dispersed strategic weapons bases.

Obviously, the old organization, with its chains of command and its assumption that local commanders will handle local operations independently of one another, was no longer satisfactory. (p. 189)

After its creation in 1947, it stabilized into the organization shown in Figure 15.2.

Centrality of command is the most obvious feature of the current organization; a mode of operation made possible or perhaps required by electronic media and computers. The army and navy do not conduct or direct military activities on their own design or initiative. Instead, under guidance from above, they supply resources to the various geographical fields of action.

One virtue of this arrangement is that quick, decisive centralized reactions are possible with the unity of operation coordinated on a worldwide scale. In order to maintain this central control, however, a tremendous complex of communications gear and computer power is required. Thousands of pages of data are transmitted each hour from Washington to all parts of the world. Computer systems are on standby to assess every gunshot and battle.

Jet airplanes fly daily reconnaissance missions in routine operations. One unexplained radar blip triggers instant alerts in the communication networks and a highly efficient, automated analysis of the event becomes available to the president and the joint chiefs of staff, wherever they may be.

Similarly, central control can be exercised by the central offices of any company when computers are mediating the transactions of the business. The goals of business have always been to gain profit through an understanding of the marketplace, the controlling of competition and of the company resources. Businesses are rarely operated democratically, because votes cannot be taken on the dynamic issues of competition or changing resources. Corporate leaders cannot be expected to relax their control of their company's resources, nor to accept dollar losses for the sake of more democratic, decentralized decision-making. Electronic me-

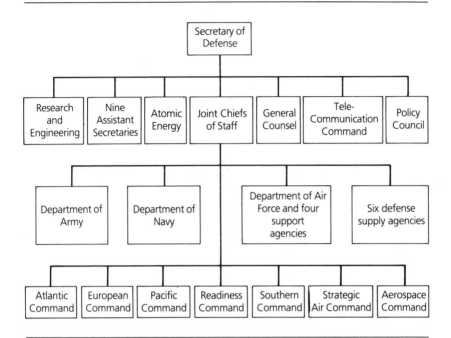

Figure 15.2
Department of Defense reporting to the President of the United States, 1977

Source: Summarized from the *Government Manual.* Washington, D.C.: U. S. Government Printing Office, p. 161.

dia, with surprising subtlety, gave more autonomy and power to the branches and divisions for a while, but the computer redirects that power back to the "joint chiefs" whoever they may be; not surprisingly, since it is they who determine how the computer systems will be designed. The propensity of computers for directing power back to the chief executives does not always appear to be consistent with the democratic ideals of most Americans.

Mowshowitz states:

> Concentration of decision-making in the upper echelons of management may possibly promote increased efficiency of production, but at the same time it poses a threat to democratic institutions. There is little difference between consolidation of power by a small group of political managers, and centralization of control in the large corporations which dominate our economic life. In either case,

the average individual with limited resources has virtually no voice shaping the course of events. (*The Conquest of Will*, p. 81)

Bibliography

"Electronic Funds Transfer," *Communications of the ACM* 22, no. 12 (December 1979).

McCarter, P., *The EFT Act is Law.* Pennsauken, N. J.: Auerbach, 1979.

Mowshowitz, A., *The Conquest of Will.* Reading, Ma.: Addison-Wesley, 1976.

Pawley, M., *The Private Future.* New York: Simon and Schuster, 1977.

Ramsgard, W. C., *Making Systems Work.* New York: Wiley, 1977.

Sanders, D. H., *Computers and Management.* New York: McGraw-Hill, 1980.

————. *Computers in Society.* New York: McGraw-Hill, 1977.

Whisler, T. L., *The Impact of Computers on Organizations.* New York: Praeger, 1970.

Withington, F., *The Use of Computers in Business Organizations.* Reading, Ma.: Addison-Wesley, 1966.

Chapter Sixteen

Computer Fraud
and Other Forces

□ Computer embezzlement occurs much less frequently than other forms, but it involves much greater losses when it does occur.

□ Computers work so well with their digital symbol sets that other electronic media are adopting the digital standard as well.

□ Paper-based systems have their own momentum, but it is costing more and more to maintain and service them.

In 1928 the Benz Company of Germany hired a consulting firm to analyze the marketplace for its proposed new automobile. How many cars would they be able to sell during the next forty years? They wanted to be sure before putting it into production. The consulting firm responded that as many as 40,000 cars might be sold, the only limiting factor being the number of chauffeurs that could be trained to drive them.

From the perspective of 1928, the act of driving was so complex that no common person—banker, clergyman, housewife—would ever want to learn the disciplines of cranking, adjusting choke levers, timing levers, gear shifting, clutch pushing, lantern lighting, or hood raising.

The consulting firm failed to consider three things:

1. Technology might someday simplify the motoring experience.
2. People might enjoy being responsible for their own driving.
3. The access of people to automobile transportation could not forever depend upon the profession of chauffeur.

The question of how to make people feel at ease with cars is replaced by the question of how ordinary people can be made comfortable with computers. Consulting firms are hired today to predict how many minicomputers will be sold during the next thirty years. And the same sort of mistakes as were made in 1928 can be repeated when the analyst is too close to the environment being evaluated.

The Mercedes Benz incident appears to be so striking in retrospect that it seems like a parable. In 1954 when the first computers were installed by government, similar oversights were made. So-called experts predicted that five or ten computers would satisfy the total requirements of the nation.

James Martin writes:

"Only ten or a dozen very large corporations will be able to take profitable advantage of the computer" was a view expressed in 1948. Sometime later IBM (International Business Machines Corporation) made an historic decision not to market the computer because it would never be profitable. The problem was that people failed to see how the machine would be used; they lacked imagination to think of suitable applications. They thought of the machine as doing only scientific calculations and could only visualize a small number of calculations that were big enough. (*Future Developments in Telecommunications*, p. 11)

Other instances of shortsightedness are listed by Martin, such as that disk storage is just an American gimmick; that real-time systems are *only* good for airlines and banks; that data transmission will never be cheaper than mail; and that broadcasting would only be useful for Sunday sermons.

By 1960 we were wiser, but still believed that there was a limit to the number of computers likely to be installed, the limitation being the number of operators, system analysts, programmers and control clerks that could be trained to "drive" them.

We may still fail to take into account the same three variables as the German consulting firm:

1. The possibility that computer access can be greatly simplified.
2. The possibility that ordinary people might enjoy tinkering with small computers at home.
3. Public access to computer services cannot forever be dependent on chauffeur-like software systems.

Look at the computing environment today. We are surrounded by millions of microcomputers in the U. S., many costing less than $500.

Here we identify some factors which are likely to affect future computer use. Each factor could have its effect either by delaying or promoting computer use. Viewing the computer as a medium may sharpen our prophetic vision.

Computer fraud

The U. S. Chamber of Commerce stated that the fraudulent use of computers costs Americans more than $100 million each year. The chief crimes are embezzlement and blackmail.

As with any technology, unscrupulous people can use computers for selfish or illegal purposes. Most such crimes fall under four headings:

1. *Theft of money.*   As when a programmer fixes the payroll program to round all cents to the correct hundredths decimal place, but places all of the leftover mills in a private account for personal use. Or, when dummy stock accounts are set up in the computer with complex credits and debits which benefit the criminal.

2. *Changes of data to favor one's personal records.*   As when students get into computer records and change their grades.

3. *Inventory theft.*   As when a criminal causes the computer to give blind orders to ship (say) perfume bottles to distant loading docks—one of which belongs to the criminal.

4. *Sabotage.*   As when irate users take their revenge by disrupting a computer. Iron filings dropped into the top of the processor cause havoc. Coffee, spilled into the processor, will do it too.

The problem with computer fraud is that the crimes, though less frequent than other types of embezzlement, do involve large sums of money. And the person who knows the most about what is happening is the criminal. Prosecutors rarely know enough about computers to prosecute the crimes intelligently. Police often don't know how to investigate—the criminal's "fingerprints" are symbolic and encoded. Network criminals who dial cross-country to get into a computer do not appear as criminals to the police. The police may ask what the policy is on locking the door to the computer room.

One classic case reveals the reality of the problem. A programmer stole *all* of the operational programs (on computer tape) from a computer center, erased all copies, and tried to collect a $100,000 ransom. He was caught, and the programs were held in the sheriff's vault as evidence. The company was brought to a complete standstill because the prosecuting attorney refused to release its computer tapes. Finally, in desperation, the president of the company broke into the sheriff's office and "stole" back the programs and tapes. That confused everyone. The police didn't know what programs were, and the prosecuting attorney couldn't understand why a business would stop functioning just because he held its programs in his vault for a few weeks, so he dismissed the case.

Universities give courses such as computer operations, the design of operating systems and system architecture. But computer ethics and law have not been adequately emphasized as part of the computer curriculum. Many universities have no penalty for students who gain free computer time by using identification numbers other than their own to gain access. An attitude of "boys will be boys" dominates many faculty and student environments. The Association of Computing Machinery and other professional societies do not have an enforcement policy associated with their codes of ethics.

Sometimes corporations are the criminals. Fifty-six insurance companies were indicted in Denver in 1976 for illegally obtaining individuals' medical records. The crime included conspiracy, impersonation and theft of trade secrets as determined by the grand jury after eight months of investigation.

Don Parker, whose primary occupation has become that of analyst of computer crimes, states that $10 million to $15 million are lost each year—not counting the $2 billion equity funding fraud. The top five areas in which fraud occur are banking (19 percent), education (18 percent), government (16 percent), manufacturing (12 percent), and insurance (8 percent).

There are far more cases of fraud and embezzlement in manual, paper-based systems than in systems which use computers. For example, there were 10,000 cases of fraud (all types) in the U. S. in 1975, but only 250 cases *in the world* involving computers. The number of dollars lost in each computer case, however, was high, averaging $450,000. Don Parker predicts that the number of cases of computer embezzlement is likely to go down but that the loss per case is likely to go up. In his address "The Future of Computer Abuse" he stated:

> It doesn't matter whether you steal $2,000 or $2,000,000. It's just another couple of zeros, and it makes little difference in the technical methods we find people using. And, of course, you also know that your probability of going to jail is much lower if you steal $2,000,000. . . . So why not go for broke? It's all there; just run your crime for another couple of milliseconds, and you're on your way. A programmer once told me, "I don't understand why people think I did something so wrong. I only changed two numbers in that system for three ten-thousands of a second. Now surely doing some-

thing for so short a time could not be very wrong and would have been even less wrong if it was only one millisecond." (p. 67)

As a factor in the development of computers, the fear of fraud is not likely to slow the use of computer applications any more than the existence of criminals prevents banks from operating. Hardware scientists will develop devices to encrypt the material on data lines. Software scientists might develop operating system monitors which secretly observe each activity, watching by some formula for signs of likely fraud. Criminals will still find ways to cheat, just as they do in manual systems. As an actual example, the Mafia in Chicago attempted to get programmers in debt to them and then to demand information, such as passwords, names of key programs, procedures used, etc.

Files or monies which are kept in drawers are more likely to be violated than records kept on computer disks or tapes. Fewer people work with the computer files and a much higher level of competence is required to access the records. Computerized records represent a safer method of handling than does manual filing and the public will gradually come to see this.

The convergence of digitized communication channels

In 1967 the telephone networks began to convert telephone voice signals into rapid digital pulses before sending the signals through long-distance phone lines. Prior to that year, most telephone conversations were transmitted as simple voltage variations on the copper lines. With this new digital technique, the voice is represented by a series of on-off pulses passing down the line. The telephone companies were motivated to make the change because: 1) hundreds of voice conversations could be mixed together on the same wires; 2) computer signals were tying up dedicated lines between cities and voice signals could not easily be mixed with them on the same wire; and 3) incompatibility between various carriers pointed toward the digital form as the standard for everyone.

Nearly all long-distance voice or computer signal transmission is now standardized in this way. Signals from many varied sources are all reduced to on-off pulses, transmitted together, then separated at the other end for conversion back to their original forms. Such signals keep their fidelity over long distances and eavesdropping from telephone wires is greatly handicapped with so many signals mixed together. The companies now freely intermix any type of data on these channels—voice, facsimile, computer terminals or any other signals, all can be intermixed, then separated at the receiving end.

The equipment which converts the analog voltages to digital on-off pulses is known as a modem, and is dropping in price. Some creative businesses are broadcasting their data over FM side-band channels, as well as over short-wave and microwave channels.

Satellite communication channels numbered 240 circuits when the Intelsat service began in 1964. The circuits have doubled every two years until today there are 30,000 circuits capable of carrying two-way voice or digital data. Over 400,000 circuits are planned by the year 2000. This growth rate applies to only one of the dozens of such satellite networks now operating. Bell scientists project that by the year 2000 more than one million two-way circuits will be provided by the satellite channels.

Like the rings of Saturn, satellites are placed in orbits in a band far out in space, where their speed keeps them stationary above a certain spot on earth. There is a limit to the number of satellites which can be accommodated above the United States. They must be spaced at least three or four degrees apart which means that only six or eight of them can be used for fifty-state coverage. The space shuttle makes bigger satellites possible, the complexity of the ground stations thus being reduced. (Interested readers will enjoy the writings of W. White and M. Holmes, who design and manage these systems.)

This decision to "go digital" closes the communications loop. Federal Communications Commission (FCC) regulations—which have been very slow in evolution—cannot hinder the growth of the proliferating communication channels. There are simply too many ways to communicate the data. If FCC regulations hinder the use of one channel, others will be used.

The momentum of paper-based systems

The Commission on Federal Paperwork reported (after two years of study) that each American pays $500 per year for the paperwork generated by the federal government. We pay more, on top of this, for the paperwork at every other level—state, local, company, union and more. Drug companies, for instance, gave evidence that they add fifty cents to the cost of every prescription drug because of the 27,000 forms and reports which they fill out for the government annually.

Breakdowns of the annual costs for paper based systems were: federal government $43 billion; private industry $25 billion to $32 billion; state and local government $5 billion to $9 billion; individuals $8.7 billion; farmers $350 million; labor organizations $75 million.

As a parody on paperwork, the commission generated its share:

> Despite the fact that a privacy commission was created at about the same time, the paperwork commission first paid for a 72-page private study on how federal agencies were implementing the Privacy Act and Freedom of Information Act. And then a staff researcher presented the commission with a 152-page study on much the same subject. He then lost his job. Less than a month after the privacy commission issued its 654-page report, the paperwork commission issued its own staff report on privacy and confidentiality in federal record keeping. The staff (cleverly) did not number its pages, but veteran paperwork watchers will discover that this version has 295 pages. It incorporates some, but not all, of the original private study. The staff report provides good references on federal government information policies and recommends codifying them under a new Fair Information Practice Act. All of the recommendations, naturally, would require a huge increase in paperwork, including one for "a new organization with broad responsibilities for standard-setting, monitoring agency compliance with privacy and confidentiality laws. . . ." The greatest contribution of the report is a footnote listing the eight other federal commissions that have been created to study aspects of the same problem in the past two years. The commission stresses that this is a staff report, which can only mean that a multi-page *commission* report is still to come. In still another report, the commission staff devoted only 75 pages to the job for which the organization was established. That report reaches the conclusion that the paperwork burden can be reduced by simplifying federal government procedures. No kidding. (R. E. Smith, *Computerworld,* January 1978, p. 2)

A piece of paper does not weigh very much, but the shipment of a book costs much more than the transmission of its contents over any of the existing communication channels. For instance, banks that attempt to retain paper-based transactions into 1990 may find that other banks are operating at half the cost of the paper-based systems. The same is true in government and corporate business. Thus the high cost of moving paper can be seen as a significant factor in speeding the acceptance of electronic transmission and manipulation of every type of data.

The federal government is frequently criticized on this point. R. A. McLaughlin reports that:

> Each year 300 billion pieces of information are reported to the Federal government by states, local governments and individuals. Between $100 and $140 billion, approximately $500 for every person in the United States, is spent annually collecting, reviewing and storing this information. Six federal agencies use over 200 forms requiring 3.5 million responses annually and 11 million work-hours to complete.
>
> In spite of these stark facts, there is no central policy dealing with the collection and flow of information, no standard method for managing this vital national resource. . . . We firmly believe that ADP (automated data processing) is the single, most important key to coping with today's knowledge industry and the complex, overlapping, interrelated policies and programs of the federal government . . . (*Datamation,* July 1978, p. 147)

Three factors have been pinpointed as being likely to affect the further acceptance of the computer as a primary medium in our culture. Digitization of all types of information assists the intermixing of widely diverse office equipment such as xerography, word-processing and graphics. The high cost of moving paper gives economic impetus to computerization. The problem of computer fraud is judged to be a nuisance factor, unlikely to slow the trend toward total reliance on computers. Few factors seem likely to slow or impede the trend toward fuller computer dependency.

The individual services of typewriting, data transmission, facsimile copying and telegram passing are likely to be combined into a unique service known as electronic mail. The computer is predicted to become equal to television as a primary medium during the years 1985 to 1995. Its ascendancy within a thirty-five year period is a phenomenon unequalled anywhere in history. Television became a primary medium during a ten-year period of growth, 1950 to 1960. Computerization requires a much greater concentration of money, professional staff, organization, training and readjustment. The shift from mechanical automation to computer automation has occurred without any affirmative action laws requiring it. No promotional campaigns or pressure groups have prompted its acceptance. With little conscious awareness of the revolution, we have obediently carried out the urging of our cells to communicate by every means possible—and with the greatest speed.

Bibliography

Ayres, R. V., *Technological Forecasting*. New York: McGraw-Hill, 1969.

Bigelow, R., and S. Nycum, *Your Computer and the Law*. Englewood Cliffs, N. J.: Prentice-Hall, 1975.

Clarke, A. C., *Profiles of the Future*. London: Gollancz, 1962.

Couger, J., ed., *Computing Newsletter* 2 (March 1976).

Davidson, R. P., "Letter from the Publisher," *Time* (February 1978).

EDP Industry Report. Waltham, Ma.: International Data Corporation, 1978.

French, N., "Insurance Companies Indicted for Data Theft," *Computerworld* 10, no. 26 (June 1976).

"FAX Pace Quickens," *Data Communications* 7, no. 3 (March 1978).

Keller, A. E., "The Costly Role of Paperwork," *Infosystems* 24, no. 12 (December 1977).

Krauss, L. I., and A. MacGahar, *Computer Fraud and Countermeasures*. Englewood Cliffs, N. J.: Prentice-Hall, 1979.

Martin, J., *Future Developments in Telecommunications* 2nd ed. Englewood Cliffs, N. J.: Prentice-Hall, 1977.

McLaughlin, R. A., "The (Mis) Use of DP in Government Agencies," *Datamation* 24, no. 7 (July 1978).

Miller, F., ed., "Electronic Mail Comes of Age," *Infosystems* 24, no. 11 (November 1977).

Occhiogrosso, B., "Digitized Voice Comes of Age," *Data Communications* 7, no. 3 (March 1978).

Parker, D. B., "The Future of Computer Abuse," in *Computers and Public Policy: Proceedings of the Symposium Man and the Computer,* Teresa Oden and Christine Thompson, eds. Hanover, N. H.: Dartmouth Printing Co., 1977.

Petersohn, H. H., *Computer Failure and Energy Shortages: Effects of Power Problems on Computer Operations*. Fairfax Station, Va.: Technology Press, 1979.

Problems Associated with Computer Technology in Federal Programs and Private Industry. Washington, D. C.: U. S. Government Printing Office, 1975.

Smith, R. E., ed., "The 1000-page Misunderstanding," *Computerworld* 11, no. 45 (January 1978).

White W., and M. Holmes, "The Future of Commercial Satellite Telecommunications," *Datamation* 24, no. 7 (July 1978).

Word Processing Report. Waltham, Ma.: International Data Corporation, 1978.

Chapter Seventeen

Giving the Public
What It Wants

□ Five fast-selling computer services are word-processing, phototypesetting, electronic mail, teletext almanacs and games.

□ These computer services change the way we write, the way we print literature, and the way we communicate, the way we obtain information and the way we entertain ourselves.

Gutenberg's mechanical printing press was not accepted as a valid method of reproducing books for many years after its invention. Rondthaler writes:

> Gutenberg's brilliance, however, was not welcomed by the scribes of his day. Like many inventors he was a threat to the status quo, and cautiously carried on his work behind closed doors. To keep the enterprise solvent he found it necessary to imitate manuscript letters so perfectly that buyers rarely suspected his books of being printed from type. It has been suggested, tongue in cheek, that Gutenberg was our first counterfeiter. A more worthy appraisal is to credit him with a keen awareness of public prejudice against novelty in so highly regarded an art as the making of books.
>
> When finally the idea of printing from type was accepted, then and only then could type be less imitative of the scribes' letterforms. Shapes became more legible, more compatible with metal casting, and the elimination of most ligatures (two letters linked together on the same block) drastically reduced the number of different characters required. (*Life with Letters*, p. 5.)

In this decade we face a similar departure from the status quo. Some 72 billion paragraphs, new pieces of information, arrive each year and typewriters, copiers, offset presses and readers cannot keep up with it. Professionals can rarely read all the journals of their discipline.

People want to sort these data, edit them, store them and retrieve them. Paper, however, cannot be filed that fast—nor even manufactured that fast. New departures are required, and this chapter examines five areas in which new departures are occurring.

Apparently we are adjusting to change much more rapidly than the medieval reader who judged the printing press as an impostor. After about ten years of evolution, the computer has been welcomed to our homes and Christmas stockings. The five popular uses of the computer give it a million permanent homes in which to dwell. Even if the only popular domestic use for computers was in toys and games, its hold on our culture would be evident. Taken together, the five uses demonstrate our firm embrace of this new medium. Most homes have two or three microcomputers hidden somewhere—in the oven, sewing machine, automobile or electronic games. With children in the home, there are probably five to eight microcomputers around the house. The average home now has eleven electric motors. There will probably be a higher count of computers than motors by 1986.

Word-processing

Word-processing provides a service to offices by automating the preparation of documents and memos. Some sysems even check the spelling of words. The original draft of a document is typed on a typewriter keyboard attached to a viewing screen. Lines of any length can be typed in without regard for their final appearance. The letters are converted to digital form, however, and are stored on disk devices for instant retrieval and replay. Any letter or word in the document can be revised, deleted or added anywhere throughout the document, after which many copies can be printed for distribution. This service is available on almost all general purpose computers—micros, minis and mainframes.

Using these services, busy executives can revise their report a dozen times in one day, new copies being furnished to them between each revision. On each new printout, the computer resupplies page numbers, footnotes, justifies the text on the right side and checks for spelling errors.

Publishers often bypass the typesetting phase entirely by coupling the editing power of the word-processor with high-speed photographic typesetting. *Time* carried feature stories on the computer in its February 20, 1978 issue. On page 2 of the magazine, the publishers revealed some of their technical secrets:

> . . . using an electronic "dictionary" which it scans in a fraction of a second, the system can figure out how to break almost any word up to and including the 14 syllable (words). It can set type in any one of Time Inc's own 127 fonts, tailor-fit copy to a layout, and draw in boxes and assorted lines. Finally, at the rate of a page every 15 seconds, the system can whisk the whole magazine to our printers in Chicago via telephone wires. . . .
>
> But for all their ingenuity, *Time's* electronic machines still lack the human touch—the skills of writing, editing and analyzing that are really responsible for this week's look at the computer society.*

---

* Reprinted by permission from *TIME,* The Weekly Newsmagazine. Copyright Time Inc. 1978.

In 1981 several microcomputer vendors began to offer systems to small businesses which competed directly with the minicomputer market. Priced between $2,000 and $4,000, this Commodore Business Machine CBM 8032 features dual floppy disks, 45-character-per-second printer and memory in the computer capable of holding programs of 32,000 character length. Dozens of software systems such as word-processing, office accounting or inventory control were available, ranging in price from $50 to $700. 5.2 million desktop computers will be installed by 1985. *(Photo courtesy Commodore Business Machines.)*

In 1981 there were ninety-five companies supplying word-processing equipment. The early systems encouraged centralized rooms with many terminals and a pool of secretaries who were managed as a group. Later, systems were developed which allowed distributed typewriter terminals to be placed in each using office, a strategy which allowed more local and individualized use of the systems. Each desk-top unit costs between $3,000 and $10,000. Today, the count of word-processing terminals installed is over two million and climbing.

The spelling checker is the innovative part of the system. This service program checks each word in a word-processing file to determine if any are misspelled. Some systems have access to 50,000 correctly spelled words. Words that the machine considers misspelled are listed on the user's terminal or on the printing device. If a word-processing file contains any words which are not in the master list, the program displays them to the operator. It also states the number of the line where the error occurred. The user can then correct those words which turn out to be truly misspelled. The entire sentence does not require retyping; only the isolated word. Figures 17.1 and 17.2 show an actual use of the spelling program.

Photo and digital typesetting of text

Between 1950 and 1960 the world of print was revolutionized after centuries of little changed manual typesetting. Instead of having alphabets engraved in steel and duplicates made in lead, the alphabets were carried on photographic negatives and then

Figure 17.1
Sample word-processing output

The universality of the computer symbol set

Science fiction writers fanticise how organisms on other planets evolve. The creatures learn to refine metal, communicate through media and create machines on which they then become dependent.

With each invention, a race evolves less because of the genes, and more because of the symbiotic attachment to the inventions. The group evolves: the group being machines and creatures.

For the human race, an inventn more basic than any other has emerged; a channel whose method of encoding is more universal than any other, and whose function is to playfully manipulate these codes. The digital notation of the computer is a kind of universal language. As each medium acquires the digital recording standard, the information can be sorted, rearranged, communicated at the speed of light and transformed into any other medium for playback or storage.

Thus, any feature of the universe which can be represented symbolically in any medium, can

Figure 17.1
(continued)

---

be brought into the computer's universal coding
system for luxurious rearrangement.

The word "machine," cluttered with its images of
mechanical motions, is a false analogy which hinders
people from perceiving the wholly new environment
which computers create. Computers do not really
depend on any moving parts. They are speed of light
blenders of fragments into unforeseen unities. They
are media coordinators. They are electronic file
cabinet navigators. They are data transformers.
They are process accelerators, assisting the
evolution and change of anything presented to them.
They are extensions of the human nervous system.
They are models of the thought process, speeded up
under formula control.

We have no single word like "machine" to convey these
features of the new medium. There is a new medium in
the culture and we don't know what to call it.

Certain words are deliberately misspelled. Note that the word-processor justifies each
line and changes line widths on command.

Figure 17.2
Sample use of spelling checker

EXEC SPELL

Spelling Checker. Proceed? YES
List misspelled words on terminal or printer?: P
Wish to monitor the progress on this terminal?: YES
Enter name of Source Text file to be checked: D.WPSAMPLE
Pausing to scan the file.

    4.0 FANTACISE (FANTASIZE)
    15.0 INVENTN

File D.ANNUAL completed.
46 lines checked.
291 words checked.
Misspelled words sent to printer.
2 words may be misspelled.

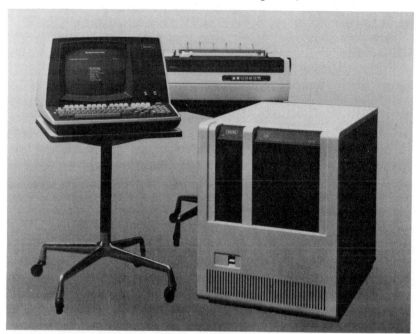

The Wang 2200 Word-Processing system is integrated with other small-business office functions to provide a low-cost text and document-processing system. Approximately eighty companies provided word-processing equipment in 1981. *(Photo courtesy Wang Laboratories.)*

reproduced quickly and cheaply for every type of printing need. Photolettering Inc. of New York pioneered this reform. New styles of alphabets were designed and carried on photographic negatives, and today there are thousands of styles of alphabets available in film form.

Photolettering was an improved, but still manual process for getting words into print.

Then came the computer. It could be used to quickly change one photographic font to another, to manage the enlargement or reduction of any letter or line and to automate the whole process. With the computer, the photoprocess is speeded to produce up to eighty lines of final print per minute.

Then terminals were added to the photolettering computer. A word-processing system, when attached to a phototypesetting system, can generate immediate top-quality offset-ready text, quickly and in any of several hundred font styles. Eighty thousand such units were installed by 1980.

A few companies now market computerized digital typesetters which do not carry photographic negatives of type. Instead, the computer generates (draws) each letter from its memory of one hundred styles, so that each letter is formed anew each time it occurs. Even pictures can be digitally represented and retained in the memory of the computer, so that in the composition of pages both print and pictures are generated afresh by the laser beam each time it is called up. By 1980, the old hot metal typesetting was something for the history books.

Electronic mail and facsimile transmission

Electronic mail might seem to be a trivial use of computers, but it is more likely to affect the daily lives of most Americans than any other application. Like a 1-2-3 punch, first will come low-cost home computers, then national communication networks for banks and libraries, then electronic mail. The act of typing a message on a terminal and having it appear seconds later on another screen or typewriter across the country may seem cumbersome compared to our conditioned telephone habits. But there is a place for it, and Western Union has been doing it for years.

High-speed facsimile attachments can transmit any page of information or drawings. Word-processing typewriters and their storage media can also communicate their digital versions of books or articles across the same network lines and large companies are doing it.

The Wharton School of Business in Philadelphia, for example, has 110 terminals located in faculty homes and student areas. The system has become a popular and enjoyable medium of communication. Message output can be on screens or paper or both as the user desires.

The United States Postal Service has outlined a blueprint for adding electronic mail service as a post office function. The proposed system would place terminals in every post office, and the network would accept facsimile material for transmission, as well as magnetic tapes, optical character reading and terminal typewriting with instant readouts on printers in other cities. Satellite transmission will provide the basis for the network. Several types of delivery could be purchased including guaranteed one-hour service. Also, the same message could be delivered to many addresses. The primary motivation for this service is to reduce the post office debt, incurred by the costs of physically handling so many items, and to be first in the race to provide electronic mail service, which could seriously hurt the post office if provided by a competitor. The electronic mail services will be coupled with facsimile transmission, a business that has boomed from nothing in 1972. Revenues approaching $300 million are anticipated in 1981 from these services.

The biggest demand is for $300 desk-top units which can transmit one page of text or graphics across a phone line in less than thirty seconds. The speed keeps rising and the price dropping as digital transmission techniques become standardized.

The Alaska State University Network provides electronic mail services to 9,000 subscribers on its various campuses. A dozen letters may arrive in a user's mailbox coming in from any location in the network for a total cost of about 14 cents. It is one of the most-liked services on the system and the firm which installed it (Systems and Computer Technology) has received much publicity for its early and effective implementation. The map of Alaska (Figure 17.3) shows the scope of the network, which is linked by satellite across 7,000 miles of tundra.

Electronic almanacs

Most people in the U. S. already own two-thirds of the equipment which is necessary to bring the world's information directly into the bedroom or den. The color TV set can display almost anything and the home telephone can connect it into a distant computer which guides the user in browsing through the data-banks of the world's knowledge. The only missing item is a keyboard or set of buttons by which the user can direct the process.

These systems were launched in the year 1980. England and France preceded the U.S. by about two years but their systems were stage-setters. In France the system is called "Intelmatique". The terminal will be given free of charge to accompany or replace every telephone in France. The cost savings resulting from not printing address files (different from America's white pages) and other directories makes this possible: such information comes up on the screen, along with any other information the consumer wants.

In England the system is called "Viewdata" or "Prestel." By 1982

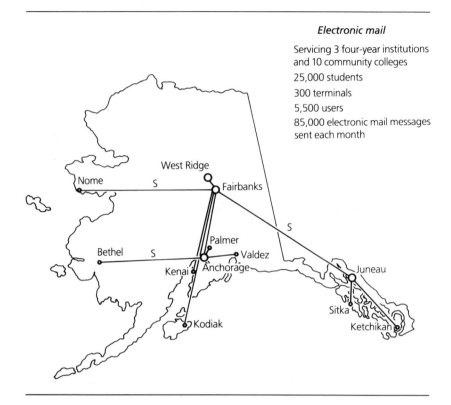

Electronic mail

Servicing 3 four-year institutions
and 10 community colleges
25,000 students
300 terminals
5,500 users
85,000 electronic mail messages
sent each month

Figure 17.3
University of Alaska Computer Network (UACN)

about 200,000 homes will have the keyboard device which directs
the encyclopedic search. When first turned on, the TV set presents
a menu such as this:

```
ENTER CHOICE:
1. WEATHER
2. LIBRARY INFORMATION
3. AIRLINES SCHEDULES
4. WINE SALES
5. NEWS HEADLINES
6. SHOPPING SPECIALS
7. THEATRE LISTINGS
8. EMPLOYMENT ADS
```

Using a hand-held calculator keyboard, the user can press 7 and the screen comes up with the theatre menu, giving a choice of cities such as 1) London, 2) Paris, 3) New York, 4) Other. With each display, the operator can run through outlines of encyclopedic information until the desired data is reached. Some paths may display the message "50 cent charge. OK?" If the user presses the "YES" button, the telephone bill will reflect the choice.

In the U.S., several communities have already received trial systems. Austin, Texas, called its system EIS for Electronic Information System. EIS will display the local telephone book information plus personal lists of data such as recipes, phone numbers of friends and personal schedules. About 700 subscribers used the system in 1981, with one million names and phone numbers on file plus about 100,000 TV displays of up-to-date schedules, theatre lists, and the like.

This style of computer access is likely to become a major service attraction, and only computers can provide it. Whereas libraries preserve the world's knowledge, protecting it from theft and loss, electronic home systems will broadcast the world's knowledge, getting it out and off the shelf for everyone to see. Dormant research instincts may be awakened in thousands of amateur browsers who switch from the late-night movies to the data-banks of facts and lists.

In Chapter 19 the criteria by which we judge new media will be presented. This medium of electronic encyclopedias will pass every test as a likely hit. It will be embraced as a popular service by 1986, with distribution to nearly every home, rich and poor, by 1995. Also, by 1990 specialized data-banks will be licensed for hobby groups (such as those for archery, cars, stamps, model airplanes, coins, bird watchers) and every other interest center, and will be available to those who pay the extra charge.

Who will prepare these specialized data-banks? Universities have in the past functioned as the special guardians and dispensers of information. But universities have not been bold in reorchestrating knowledge into the forms required for electronic broadcasting; a major activity which should have been underway between 1970 and 1985. Other agencies have been employed in this process, and they may steal the university's traditional business as they begin to offer courses which interact with users in their homes day or night. Language lessons and all other learning materials will gradually become available through the electronic networks. The competing agencies are newspapers, journals, cable TV companies,

The Kurzweil reading machine for the blind. The machine reads aloud from the magazine or book which is placed upon it. Regardless of the line spacing or the type font, the text is interpreted into speech. The keyboard allows the user to back up, repeat sentences, and do other things sighted readers do.

news agencies, Western Union, banks and government agencies, including the post office.

In 1980 we got our information from magazines, books, newspapers, leaflets, television, libraries and lectures. In 1990 we will rely more on electronic sources—hologram-based video disks, specialized computer data-banks and automated files of microfiche. Such stored information will be personally requested, electronically formatted, instantly transmitted and unhurriedly reviewed, either in private or on a big five- by seven-foot screen with a group of colleagues.

The world's data is one thing, our personal data and history are another. The Xerox Corporation's Learning Research Group in Palo Alto is attempting to perfect its "Dynabook." This device will solve math problems, translate languages, store personal information, edit pages of text, create drawings, receive the user's sketches and store them, animate the drawings, generate music or receive the user's new music ideas. Who would want to use such a device? Musicians, architects, students, teachers, writers, researchers, doctors, artists—probably everyone. It could become our personal electronic almanac, containing documentation of our personal histories. Like an heirloom, its floppy disk could be passed on to our children (copies for everyone) with ritual and pleasure; the twenty-first century's rite of passage.

Businessmen and writers often wish that they could talk into a microphone while a typewriter immediately types out the text of what they said. The reverse of this process exists and can be seen in many public libraries throughout the U.S. The Kurzweil reading machine for the blind converts the printed pages of magazines and books into speech. The book or journal is laid out on the top of the reading machine and it scans the lines, reads the letters and converts them into speech. It sounds like a computer talking—but is perfectly understandable. The amazing feature of this invention is that it can read any type of printed page, whether the lines are far apart or close together, whatever the type style. It will even go back and repeat a sentence or word—or even spell a word. About ninety machines were available to the blind in 1980, each costing about $28,000. If blind people wish to use a computer terminal, Kurzweil has a $4,000 device which attaches to any terminal, letting it speak aloud the letters or words which are on the screen.

Meanwhile, we cannot at present satisfactorily convert speech to print, although the process is being researched by many laboratories, including Bell Labs, Texas Instruments, IBM and others. It may be generally available between 1987 and 1991.

Games and toys

By now almost everyone has held in hand one of the computerized games, and probably sensed the potential they offer for mental and physical exercise. Some of them teach words to children. Others duplicate common games such as chess, Mastermind, or Othello. Some of them attach to the home TV set. Others can be bought that convert the home computer terminal into a simulated space war, backgammon board or football field.

The price is affordable and the sophistication is remarkable. Most games allow individual gaming—you against the computer, or two-person contests in which the computer referees the rules of the game. Some can even offer instruction to the gamer. BORIS, an electronic chess game, in one of its modes will ask the player "Are you sure you want to make that move?" and then presents the move which it would judge to be best. Unlike most chess critics, this one can be silenced at any time.

Computerized games are a significant medium—especially influential for the children who play with them. The differences between the erector-set–generation babies, the television-generation babies and the computer-generation babies may be measurable in 1990. Most children can play the computerized memory games "Simon Says" or "Match Me" significantly longer than their parents. Children are noticeably more bold in toying with computer terminals, programs, joy sticks and keyboards.

One ninth-grader showed her parents the chess program which she had written at school. The parents called her an expert and told everyone how well it worked. She got no points at school however: her friends noticed that it used a playing board that was only six squares by six. It had no bishops or knights. And the kings often drifted into check. At school, everyone said it was a very stupid program.

These, then, are the five areas of life which are significantly altered by our acceptance of miniature computers.

The way we write and author text—word-processing.

The way we print and style our literature—computer photolettering.

The way we communicate with each other—electronic mail.

The way we obtain information and skills—electronic almanacs and videotext.

The way we entertain ourselves—computerized games and toys.

In the future the microcomputer will probably alter the way we drive, the way we cook, the way we learn, the way we worship, the way we make war, the way we make peace, and the way we organize.

Table 17.1 lists the various communication devices which, when computer-assisted, can link different parts of the world. We do not yet know which path the evolving medium will take through this maze. We may secretly wish that all of these devices were available in a single box. Perhaps someday they *will* be. A pocket-

Table 17.1
Routing the information
(All electronic media should be able to
communicate with any other medium
elsewhere in the world)

These local devices	Can transmit worldwide through these channels	To any of these remote receivers
Microcomputer terminals	Telephone lines	Microcomputer terminals
World-processing screens or intelligent typewriters	Microwave channels	Newspaper printers
	Satellite land-based networks	Facsimile printers
Intelligent copiers	Rooftop antenna to satellite	Videotext devices
Facsimile transmitters	Fiber optic cables	TV or cathode-ray screens
Drafting devices	FM sideband	Telephones
Telephones	Infrared transmission channels	Computer disk or tape storage
Electronic mail terminals	Cable TV sideband	Cassette tape recorders
Stored word-processing documents	TV sideband (airwaves)	Online plotter devices
Electronic funds transfer terminals		Online library terminals
Online library terminals		
Files in data-banks		

sized display/control/printout unit will be our window on the heritage of mankind.

Bibliography

Bergerud, M., and J. Gonzalez, *Word Processing Concepts and Careers.* New York: Wiley, 1978.

Boutmy, E. J., and A. Danthine, "Teleinformatics '79," in *IFIPS Conference Proceedings.* New York: Elsevier North-Holland, 1979.

Gottschall, E. M., ed., *U & l c. Vision '80s* 7, no. 2 (June 1980).

Kleinschrod, W., *Management's Guide to Word Processing*. Chicago: Dartnell Corporation, 1975.

McCabe, H. M., and E. L. Popham, *Word Processing: A Systems Approach to the Office*. New York: Harcourt Brace Jovanovich, 1977.

Rondthaler, E., *Life with Letters*. New York: Hastings House, 1981.

Uhlig, R. P., et al., *The Office of the Future*. New York: Elsevier North-Holland, 1979.

Chapter Eighteen

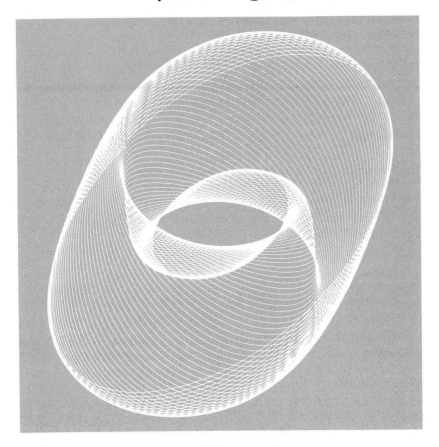

The
Ultimate Medium

- ☐ Computers assist all of the older electronic media, giving them new power and making them more flexible.
- ☐ Computers have spawned at least six wholly new media which are already in use.
- ☐ Computers are not machines. This is a false metaphor.
- ☐ Computers are not giant brains. This is another metaphor which serves us poorly.
- ☐ Computers are universal media manipulators.
- ☐ The world's knowledge will gradually be reorchestrated for easy delivery by computer to our homes and offices.

The computer is not only a new medium in our culture; it is a supermedium, a kind of ultimate medium in the same way that light is the culminating factor in many science equations.

This statement is supported by the fact that the computer can imitate most other media, can convert any electronic medium to any other medium, and when hybridized with certain other media creates wholly new media.

Imitation of other media

The mimeograph machine. Word-processing commonly runs off multiple original copies at half a cent per page with easy editing.

The typewriter. Computer hardcopy terminals provide typewritten copies of computer input and output.

The desk calculator. Calculators are available for immedaite use on most timeshared terminals complete with all logarithmic and trigonometric functions, plus several memories. Also, most hand-held calculators contain digital computers.

Learning environments. Computer Aided Instruction provides interactive and personalized learning modules for students at all grade levels.

Morse code. Pulsed coded tones (digital bits) are sent through telephone lines enabling terminals to communicate with computers.

Speech. Computers convert digitized phonemes into analog voltages for loudspeakers and telephones. "Speak and spell" toys use such computerized speech.

Mail. Electronic mail passes telegraph-like messages point-to-point by reproducing the printed page on remote typewriters. Western Union is a major supplier of message-switching services for the public.

Xerography. When stored digitally, pictures or pages can be manipulated, revised and transmitted cross-country for replay on the facisimile machine in another city.

Microfilm. Computer output on microfilm is commonly used to save paper. Also, computer retrieval of microfilmed documents is common.

Typesetting. Computerized typesetting in hundreds of type fonts enables most newspapers to bypass moveable and lead type.

Conversion of one medium to another medium

Radio signals from Mars are converted into photographs.

TV signals are "matrixed" so that one image can dance inside the silhouette of another image.

Radio signals from the moon are converted into color television pictures.

Speech sounds are converted into voiceprint pictures.

Punched card data is converted to magnetic tape media.

Punched card data is converted into a printed page.

Bar codes are converted into numbers and letters.

Magnetic stripe ledger cards are converted into account numbers.

Typewriting on a terminal is converted into a sports arena scoreboard display.

Cartoon drawings are converted into animated movies.

Hybrid new media

The computer, when joined with record-keeping media, produces data-base management systems, making obsolete manual file and search media.

The computer, when joined with point-of-sale terminals in stores and with bank files produces electronic funds transfer systems, obsoleting paper-based financial transactions.

The computer, when joined with library archives, produces on-line libraries which have no card catalog or books.

The computer, when joined with typewriting and editing, results in word-processing.

The computer, when joined with typesetting and photography, results in phototypesetting.

The computer, when joined with message distribution systems, results in electronic mail.

The public image of computers has rested on mechanical analogies, which gives us a cloudy, if comforting metaphor. This will be slow to change since the "content" of any medium usually attracts our primary attention. Thus, the book-club bills, bank statements, credit card invoices and airline reservation systems appear to the average person as older benign technologies speeded up a bit.

A tremendous social power is contained within the printed circuitry of the computer medium. This power is part of all media, unobserved by most people and rarely measured in its ability to reshape culture. But in the future, the computer may be regarded as the culmination of humanity's media inventions.

The universality of the computer symbol set

Science fiction writers have fantasized about the evolution of organisms on other planets. Each race reaches a point at which it can refine metals, communicate through the media which it invents and eventually tool machines on which it becomes dependent. With successive inventions, a race no longer evolves according to the program of the physical genes, but progresses in symbiotic attachment to the inventions. The group evolves; the group being machines and creatures.

For our race, the time is ripe to invent a medium more basic than any other; a medium whose method of encoding is more universal than any other coding system and whose function is to manipulate these codes. Every known coding system can be converted into the binary (on-off pulse) notation of the computer—it is a kind of universal language. Once it is reduced to this pulse format, speech or photograph can be manipulated by the computer, and then converted back to any lesser coding system. While in pulsed form the information can be communicated at the speed of light to any point in the world. There is no more basic form for encoding information than this binary on-off form. Like saying yes or no, plus or minus, something or nothing, this binary system is as simple and elementary as the logical mind can conceive.

The lesser coding systems include the speech, print, photographic, arithmetic, alphabetic and others. All media (except for mathematical logic) are "lesser" than their binary representations in the sense that in their normal representations, each is mechanically slow, not easily rearranged and not capable of representing all the features of the universe.

Computers, by virtue of their speed and basic on-off coding systems can do these things quite easily. Any feature of the universe which can be symbolically described in another medium can be brought into the computer's universal coding system for rearrangement:

By converting other symbol systems (music, art, print) to this binary system we can analyze voiceprints, or triple the speed of a speech without tripling the frequency of the speaker's voice, or enhance old photographs, or clean up old Caruso recordings. Music is now being recorded digitally, with the microphone signals converted to on-off pulses. Digital recordings offer pristine aural fidelity. Eventually our record players will be altered to play these pristine recordings that have no grooves. Until then, we can enjoy digital recordings on grooved records, although they cost more.

But more important than the messages it carries or the things it does are the implications of such a medium in our lives. Our evolution henceforth will be as symbiotic partners of this universal medium.

Computers do not yet operate at the speed of light, but they are getting closer to it. Battery-powered computers using fiber-optic switching could, in theory, outperform the present giant computers which peak at 800 million additions per second. The microcomputer in our homes might as well be operating at the speed of light, however, because it performs its tasks instantly as far as human senses can register.

Computers cannot be understood as adding machines speeded up or factories put into a higher gear. It is totally different when a word, letter or concept is held in the memory of a computer *not* by the angle of a mechanical gear, nor by the turning of a clumsy motor, but in pure electrical flip-flop energy which can relate it instantly to every other word in its memory. And the words can be elements from any other medium. The formulas for manipulating them can be changed a dozen times a minute by loading new programs.

This phenomenon is unique. It does not exist anywhere in nature, except perhaps in cells, where miraculous communication between dozens of individual cell parts allows each cell to be influenced by the well-being of every other cell.

False metaphors for the computer cloud its uniqueness

The subtlety with which all popular media modify our personal values would be better understood if the media were observed for what they are rather than as analogies of the past. Trains are more than iron horses. Cars are more than horseless carriages. Phonographs are more than talking machines. Light bulbs were measured in candlepower for many years. Engines are still measured in horsepower. The users of these media are not served well by such outdated analogies. It is difficult to walk forward while looking backward.

Computers are not machines. The word "machine," with its image of mechanical motions, is a false analogy which hinders people from perceiving the wholly new environment which computers create. Computers should not be called machines. They do not really depend on any moving parts. They are speed-of-light blenders of electronic fragments into unforeseen unities. They are media coordinators. They are electronic file-cabinet navigators. They are data transformers whether the data is alphabetic, numeric, kinesthetic or motor. They are process accelerators, assisting the evolution and change of anything presented to them. They are extensions of the human nervous system. They are models of the rational thought process, speeded up under formula control. We have no single word like "machine" to convey these features of the new medium.

Media scholars suggest that the introduction of print, printed books and movable type eventually prompted the industrial revolution with its assembly lines, bureaucracies and view of life as a sequential process. Sequentiality is the basic metaphor of type, printing presses, alphabets and of all machines with moving parts. The metaphor of sequentiality has been obediently adopted into the behavior of every society which submitted to the print medium.

The electronic processing of our writings and our TV pictures, our films and our factories may restore us to more tribelike styles of organization which might reestablish speech and touch as more equal in status to print and writing. Until then, business administrators will continue to follow up phone calls with a memo.

Another false metaphor should be observed: *computers are not giant brains.* The word "brain," cluttered with its image of being the center of humanity's uniqueness, hinders people from perceiving the differences between computers and people. This is perhaps the worst effect that computers have on society—they cause us to imagine that since one or two features of the mind have been extended electronically, people are therefore very similar to computers.

The pervasiveness of this false metaphor deserves attention. As a syllogism it would read: People have brains; computers are giant brains; therefore people may be thought of as having little computers. Another variation of this metaphor is: People are like information processors in certain respects; information processors are like people in certain respects; people are merely information processors. The "in certain respects" is usually dropped from the conclusion. Weizenbaum writes in *Computer Power and Human Reason:*

> . . . we come to know and understand not only by way of the mechanisms of the conscious. We are capable of listening with the third ear, of sensing living truth that is truth beyond any standards of provability. It is *that* kind of understanding . . . which I claim is beyond the abilities of computers to simulate. (p. 222)

> What could be more obvious than the fact that, whatever intelligence a computer can muster, . . . it must always and necessarily be absolutely alien to any and all authentic human concerns? The very asking of the question, "What does a judge (or a psychiatrist) know that we cannot tell a computer?" is a monstrous obscenity. That it has to be put into print at all, even for the purpose of exposing its morbidity, is a sign of the madness of our times. . . . What emerges as the most elementary insight is that, since we do not now have any ways of making computers wise, we ought not now to give computers tasks that demand wisdom. (p. 226)

> . . . The computer is a powerful new metaphor for helping us to understand many aspects of the world, but . . . it enslaves the mind that has no other metaphors and few resources to call on. The world is many things and no single framework is large enough to contain them all, neither that of man's science, nor that of his poetry, neither that of calculating reason nor that of pure intuition. (p. 277)

The most annoying and destructive result of living with computers from day to day is that we take the dominant characteristics of them—rational, mathematical, logical-calculator—and then transfer these characteristics onto fellow humans. This causes us too often to disregard the intuitive, emotional, dreaming, worshipping, inventing, moralizing, laughing and playing aspects of people. Rationality and efficiency are valued ever more highly—at the expense of human warmth and humanitarian values.

There seem to be very few counterforces to this unfortunate metaphor. In fact, it may be extended broadly to all areas of life. The outcome would be that home life would be more efficient, better scheduled and budgeted. Places of worship would be more efficient (illustrated by drive-in churches). Sports would be played faster. Business decisions would be based only on facts, computer facts. Education would be more efficient (as illustrated by speed reading, pretesting and post-testing). Social relationships would be tangibly profitable, or else avoided. Hobbies would be operated like businesses and should be profitable.

This outcome is clearly negative and its sad consequences can be seen already, between the computerized courtrooms and the computerized war rooms in the Pentagon. The irresistible force which brings the computer to our homes and offices is the drive for improved efficiency.

Biases imposed by the computer

Like most electronic media, computers bias their messages with an added message of instantaneousness. Whatever information is manipulated, it is done at nearly the speed of light.

This bias has a practical outcome which is interpreted as efficiency. Our drive toward efficiency is promoted and perpetuated by the biased messages passed by the computer. If the messages are financial, then electronic funds transfer will be embraced because of the competitive edge it gives to those banks that use it. If the messages are about personal facts or credit records, then data-base management systems are expected to lift record-keeping out of the file cabinet to become the cockpit of the highly efficient navigator-manager. All of the earlier media (each of which carried its own bias), when touched by the computer, are empowered and granted an added bias—"use me and you will be more efficient."

Thus the computer offers seeming speed-of-light transformations of material which in its native media could not or should not be manipulated so speedily. Computers commonly predict election results so early that some citizens are discouraged from voting; they know the results before they cast their votes. When 15 percent of the votes are in, computers are sometimes able to fill in the rest of the blanks algebraically. Perhaps the election process does not need computer efficiency. Or the electronic networks could perhaps apply their efficiency in a different way—a push-button in every telephone with which each citizen could cast a vote on any issue—or candidate. A true popular vote is entirely feasible with existing technology.

Another bias was observed in our earlier discussions, namely that the computer places everything into categories whose descriptions only fit theoretical, not real, cases. Even "blind data files" in which no actual people are identified can cause insurance rates on one side of a street to be significantly higher than on the other side. The bias here is one of placing everything into boxes, labels or categories without discriminating when the process is unfair or undiscerning. Here the bias is, "Whatever data you give me, they can be categorized according to the statistical formulas which the programmer gave me." Unfortunately, special cases which were not thought of by the designer will be lumped together with averaged populations of data. Such pigeonhole treatment can be a negative bias.

Redeeming services
promised by the computer

On the positive side, the public may develop an appreciation for scholarship and historic thought through the computer. Tremendous resources of information can be accessed and analyzed by computers. Some social commentators feel that the evolving services to the public for dialing into specialized library resources and requesting specialized entertainment on cable channels may be the greatest asset to come from computer-assisted media. This new form of entertainment may present any of the world's knowledge— some of it in interactive form, arranged for engaging pleasure and personalized presentation.

The mathematician John G. Kemeny, President of Dartmouth College, gave the keynote address at a symposium titled "Computers and Public Policy" in 1977. He stated:

I look forward to a new kind of human evolution where, with the means of computers, one can have all of human knowledge shared almost simultaneously.

The marriage of computers and libraries will open the world's knowledge to individuals in ways that nonelectronic media cannot provide. Books tend to hide information by being kept on shelves in libraries. The effort required to unearth even simple chains of reference or source material is an unavoidable hindrance produced by the print media. Film and TV archives are even harder to research.

But when the world's knowledge is ready for playback to home and university terminals, the computer will be able to trace the research chains in minutes or seconds, using simple directions from the user. One could narrow a subject search down to 100 interesting titles, then eliminate those which were written before a certain date unless written by a certain author. Upon evaluation, selected articles and books could be flashed to the screen for browsing or reading. The original may exist nowhere except as magnetic spots on disk drives or laser storage media somewhere in the world.

Such services are in preparation. With the reduced price of home terminals and rooftop antenna links to satellite relays, low-cost bibliographic networks will be part of college and home life from about 1985 onwards. Copper wire channels can no longer meet the demand either for bandwidth or for traffic demands. But satellites and fiber optic cables can meet these demands. *Popular Science*'s special issue of March 1978 on this subject stated:

> Already if you live in Florida you can pick up today's copy of the *Wall Street Journal*—hot off the satellite. The paper is transmitted, page by page, from the *Journal's* own earth station at a Massachusetts typesetting plant, via the WESTAR satellite to a printing plant in Orlando. . . . It's cheaper . . . a hop up and back costs the same whether the data is being sent 100 or 3000 miles. (p. 69)*

On evolving media such as the video-disk many trillions of bits of information can be recorded, such as important books, journals, speeches, films and historic documentaries, in readiness for public retrieval. Such services will distribute the best of humanity's work—its reasoned and remembered experiences, its science, music, literature and poetry. New bases for decision-making will arise which include our past experiences and our best projections.

Some of the evolving TV disk recorder systems record the visual information digitally. While there is a great demand for sorting

---

*Reprinted from Popular Science with permission. © 1978 Times Mirror Magazines, Inc.

and rearranging the alphabetic information we work with, there has been little reason to sort out TV or movie frames in any information sense. Online facsimile transmission (sending xeroxtype pictures through the phone line) represents the most current commercial reason for converting visual data into digital form.

Eventually, selected films, books, art work and music will be stored digitally so that users can perform computer-assisted research. Tables 18.1 and 18.2 display the remarkable strategies of sorting and searching which will someday be available to hobby enthusiasts and scholars.

About five hundred data-bases are available for home users to access during the working day. The subscribers to Source Telecomputing Corporation based in McLean, Virginia, number about nine thousand. Service and data-bank lists are offered to anyone who owns a computer terminal. Other services are available from Micronet's Compuserve in Columbus, Ohio, and from EIES at New Jersey Institute of Technology in Newark. The *New York Times* data-bank has been online since 1975, all of its articles available by keyword request.

The two false metaphors will be very slow to die. Computers as "machines" or "giant brains" are rear-view metaphors which may assist people in retaining stability in rapidly changing times, but they also cloud the many ways in which computers are *not* machines or giant brains. In the future, with no unique words to describe the uniqueness of computers, the old metaphors are likely to remain with us as paleolithic handicaps.

The primary redeeming service of the computer may be its international lookup and retrieval options for the home user. Between 1985 and 1990 competing home services should begin to provide interactive and entertaining reorchestrations of the world's knowledge, suited to every special interest group as the demand requires. Computer channels will develop for lawyers, photographers, bird watchers, hunters, travellers, artists, musicians, politicians, wine makers and every other hobby interest group.

The retrieval of much of world knowledge on home computer terminals is not unrealistic. Three computer systems now provide such services in England through the cable TV system. TV magazines can be requested by viewers using a calculator-like device as the link to the system. With it they can request information in any of the following areas:

News headlines.
News abstracts and expansions.

Table 18.1
A survey of selected media that, when digitized, can be stored, transmitted, sorted, or manipulated

Written text	Books, articles, monographs, paperbacks, magazines, encyclopedias, reference works, almanacs, journals.
Television program tapes	Network specials, educational programs, documentary programs, college TV productions, cable TV specials, historic recordings, corporate news releases, world news archives.
Movie film	8 mm, 16 mm, color, black-and-white, university film libraries, science films, documentaries, historic recordings of events, Broadway shows.
Pictures	Graphs, charts, art work, famous paintings, architecture analysis, sculpture, slides, photographs, drawings, sketches, technical drawings.
Microfilm	Microfilmed books, magazines, photographs, technical drawings and most others above.
Courses of instruction	Computer-assisted instruction using interactive learning modules. Incorporates TV recordings, slides, and other media excerpts as above. Language skills, typewriting skills, mathematics skills, science laboratory simulation, etc.
Audio tapes	Famous speeches, debates, conferences, lectures, news events, radio programs, language lab instruction tapes, etc.
Long-playing records	Music, famous speeches, historic events, etc.
Access to the files of other computers	Medical libraries, NASA network, EDUCOM network, INTREX network, legal networks, other specialized library holdings.

Stock market prices.
Football scores.
Theatre listings.
Racing results.
Weather forecasts.
Business research reports.
Railroad timetables.
Airline schedules.
Public announcements.
Cooking, recipe instructions.
Gardening hints.
Job vacancies.
Yellow page directories.
Educational courses.
Popular quizzes.
Games (two-way interaction).

Users view these systems as pleasant to use and much more accessible than books or encyclopedias. The currency of the information and the personal interaction cause it to be extremely popular. At any time the user can switch back to normal TV channel viewing.

The BBC provides one version called CEEFAX ("See Facts"). The IBA Network provides ORACLE. The British Post Office has "Viewdata."

Beyond the information services thus provided, users can send messages to any other user in the network—electronic mail via TV. About 80,000 pages of information are stored in the computer. As the data are displayed on the screen, they can also be recorded on cassette tapes for later (free) replay.

The trend toward broad uses of microcomputers in our homes is well attested. The executive editor of *Popular Science* quotes Alan Kaplan in the March 1978 issue:

> The computer is a tool. It's a mind expander. It's as basic as the wheel and the lever. . . . Twenty years from now, historians will look back at this time and see something they will label the intellectual revolution. It will make the industrial revolution look pale by comparison.
>
> When the automobile came along, we though it would just get us around a little more efficiently than the horse. It did that, but it also changed the way we work, play, and build cities. It changed our lives in fundamental ways we could not predict at the time.
>
> I think the same thing will happen with the personal computer.

Table 18.2
Potential strategies for searching and comparing the world's knowledge as recorded in various media

Title searches	Given the title *A Tale of Two Cities*, in how many media is it available? What book editions? What films? Any TV tapes? LP records? Microfilmed? Audio tapes? Any programmed instruction courses? Any famous paintings? What other computerized libraries have resources related to it? If fewer than 3 TV tapes, schedule them to be shown on this terminal at 7 PM tonight.
Media searches	Locate all TV tapes and 8 mm or 16 mm movie films involving Bishop Pike. Only those holdings created after 1955. Do not retrieve if psychic phenomena is included. In how many of Paul Cezanne's paintings do landscapes occur? Compare those paintings with bright skies to those with dark skies. Which occurred most often? Display one by one all those movie frames which contain more than 10% blue in all of Bergman's films before 1973.
Subject searches	Retrieve a bibliography of books (not articles) related to archaeology in China written after 1971. (Here the computer automates the card catalogue.) Search for significant chapters on this topic regardless of book subject. Display pertinent paragraphs related to the above subject. How many sentences relate to this theme? Display 40 random sentences.

Author searches	In what paragraphs of C. S. Lewis's writings before 1956 does he mention "pain"? In what media can one obtain biographical information about him? Schedule a TV documentary on his life to be shown next Friday at 7 PM.
Date searches	In all media produced in 1967, what holdings relate to the subject of "hippies" and "communes"?
A about B searches	Retrieve and display all those sentences in which President Nixon spoke about Leon Jaworski. Flag those which come from newspapers as opposed to TV statements.
Comparison searches	Comparisons between media: Find statements on TV tapes which relate to nuclear power plants and compare them to film statements on this subject.
	Comparisons between authors: Display the statements of Barry Goldwater and J. F. Kennedy on war.
	Comparisons between subjects: Were more sentences in 1978 related to communication or to transportation?
	Comparisons between dates: How many journal articles in 1955 and 1975 related to "organ transplants"?

July 1980 marked the beginning of the trend toward popular home information access systems. As they spread to the general public, they may become the most common medium for receiving instruction, researching information and for shopping. They will eventually include electronic home banking, electronic mail and entertainment routing. *(Photo courtesy NYT Pictures.)*

Today, we think of it in terms of taking over jobs we now do by hand. Sure, it will balance our check-books, do our income tax, play checkers or chess, keep recipes filed, look up telephone numbers, and perform hundreds of other chores we now do in a more laborious way. But the real impact, I believe, will be in ways we can't even guess now. When everyone has what amounts to unlimited computing power, human ingenuity will find hundreds, thousands, millions of ways to use it. I bet the changes brought about by the intellectual revolution will make the industrial revolution look pale.*

Just as the compulsive urge of the sixties was to "get on the

*Reprinted from Popular Science with permission. © 1978 Times Mirror Magazines, Inc.

media," especially the electronic ones, the urge of the eighties will be to "get your data into digital form." Whenever data are translated into digital form they can be intermixed with other data for transmission on any communication channel and can be stored most compactly for future reference or revision. This is true of all types of data including telephone, music, alphabetic, graphic or photographic data.

Willis Ware of the Rand Corporation has stated:

Information is a universal commodity. It makes organizations run; it makes processes run; it makes each of us as a biological organism run. Computers deal with information in very general ways. Therefore computer technology is becoming and will increasingly become all pervasive—a point that very few managements seem to understand. What has occurred in the last twenty-five years is minimal compared to what we have yet to see. (*Computers and Public Policy*, p. 2)

Bibliography

Gilmor, C. P., "Computers for Everyone," *Popular Science* 65 (March 1978).

Gottschall, E. M., ed., *U & l c. Vision '80s* 7, no.2 (June 1980).

Graham, N., *Artifical Intelligence*. Blue Ridge Summit, Pa.: TAB Books, 1979.

———, *The Mind Tool: Computers and Their Impact*. Mineola, N. Y.: West Publishing, 1977.

Kemeny, J. G., "The New Symbiosis," in *Computers and Public Policy: Proceedings of the Symposium Man and the Computer,* eds. Teresa Oden and Christine Thompson. Hanover, N. H.: Dartmouth Printing Co., 1977.

Renner-Smith, S., "Satellite to Your TV is Only One of COMSAT Wonders," *Popular Science*, 212, no. 3 (March 1978).

Ware, W., "Public Policy Aspects for an Information Age," *Computers and Public Policy* 2 (1976).

Weizenbaum, J., *Computer Power and Human Reason*. San Francisco: W. H. Freeman, 1976.

Chapter Nineteen

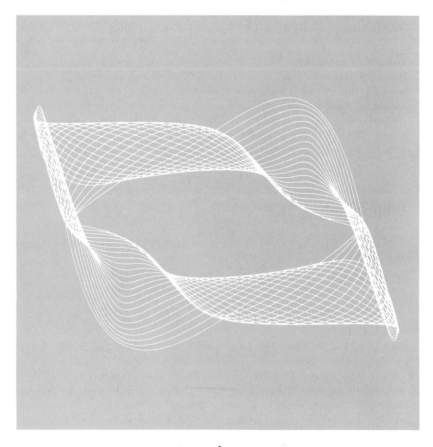

Judge
and Jury

- The human nervous system casts the ultimate vote on whether to extend itself through this or that medium.

- Seven criteria can be isolated which we unconsciously use to rate new media.

- These criteria may be biologically based and independent of culture or race.

- The future mind of man is formed as we rush toward more ideal media.

The view of electronic media and of computer use in the United States is like an X-ray of the central nervous system. The human mind is totally surrounded by the media of the culture, in the same way that the brain is surrounded by the media of the senses. As we have seen, the mind is so totally dependent on media for communication and thought that these media remain quite invisible, their messages and services taking the spotlight. We have only just begun to notice that media are the environment of the mind.

When we add new media to a culture the psychological and social effects are appreciated only in retrospect. Why does one medium become popular while others never do? Why were telephones welcomed into nearly every office and home when there was "a plentiful supply of messenger boys?" Why was the widely advertised system for showing 35 mm slides on the home TV set not installed in every home? Why has the video telephone been so slow to spread throughout the business world and the suburbs? Why has the computer been accepted so widely despite its difficulty of access and high cost?

The seven criteria which follow are not principles of media but are rather intuitive social reactions to media. They are seemingly built-in responses; the attitude of the unconscious toward media. These criteria do not have to be taught or learned although considerable effort is required to identify them or bring them to conscious attention. These judgmental criteria may actually be part of the human heritage, independent of race or time. When a medium meets the standards of these criteria, it wins favor and foothold in the society to which it becomes available. We shall evaluate the computer in the light of these criteria and will use them to project to the future. No single criteria makes or breaks a medium—we score them separately on these seven tests.

Criterion One:
New media are judged by their
apparent omniscience

Ideally, people would like all of the world's recorded knowledge—its libraries, journals, films, encyclopedias, almanacs and blueprints—to be available to them on request. If all-wise servants could research the answer to every question we raise (about jobs, about bargain hunting, about illness, about anything) demand for their services would be insatiable.

Our media are these servants. That is their role—the passage of information to and fro on request, within their diverse coding and transmission systems. Though each medium falls short of being all-wise we can grade it on a scale from excellent to poor.

To judge a medium by its omniscience assumes that it has a method for recording and retrieving stored information. Using alphabets, words can be stored on paper or stone. Using electronics, sounds can be recorded on magnetic surfaces. Using chemistry, sights can be recorded on photographic paper or film. Most media utlitize one of these recording techniques. Speech and music, of course, had no direct recording mechanism until the phonograph and electronic recording were invented. Generally speech was rated lower after alphabets provided a method of recording the phonemes uttered by people. The business memo embodies this judgment. Verbal instructions are viewed as "nonprofessional" in the corporate value-judgment of media. The pattern of media evolution has been to provide a recording system for each medium so that its messages or information would not be lost. The pleasure of replay and retrieval, of being able to read a memo today and again tomorrow, to hear a cassette tape repeatedly, illustrates this criteria in action. Early copying machines made copies which faded and could not be read two years later. Such machines are judged now to be second-rate.

Faced with a choice of being deprived of all books, or of all photographs, the omniscience factor makes a clear choice for us. Abstract ideas can be expressed in words much more reliably than in photographs or pictures.

The computer scores highly on the omniscience scoreboard. Already home-based terminals can use the phone to call into databanks in all fields. And data-base management systems also amplify the omniscience factor, for they make the computer appear to know more facts.

Looking to the future, several converging circumstances combine to give the computer ever more access to information. (1) Many publications are now typed onto magnetic disks for editing prior to typesetting. Thus the contents of the latest book and newspaper can be loaded directly into computer storage for later retrieval. (2) Word-processing means that editors and secretaries type their reports, articles and dissertations into computer memory for editing. (3) Digital recording techniques render speech, music, film and TV tapes equally accessible by computer.

Since none of the three primary recording techniques are denied to the computer and since it is used ever more widely to store and retrieve data for local purposes, at some point a unified approach to the long-sought omniscience which earlier media gave hints of, but could not execute, may be precipitated. Whatever knowledge lies encoded in the various media systems of the world, it will someday be retrievable on the new universal media player, the computer. Tables in Chapter 20 attempt to foretell the varieties of questions which we should be able to ask without embarrassment after we pass the Omega Point.

Criterion Two:
New media are judged by their
degree of omnipresence

Those media are best which work instantly anywhere, any time. Here portability, speed and universal acceptance are the primary features desired. Most people wish at some time in their lives that they had a wrist or wallet device that could instantly perform their bidding. Pocket calculators were quickly accepted and were sold to nearly every family in the U.S. within a five year period. People might wish that the data on their entire personal histories could be retrieved or sorted out on demand on a small device which constantly records all things. Similarly corporations wish to retrieve their company history and decisions. Instant retrievability and continuous recording would characterize the ultimate medium. It would be present everywhere, always recording and always ready to transmit, standardized across country boundaries.

We realize instinctively that a single world language, present everywhere, would be valuable. Morse code operated so much faster than carrier pigeons, it appeared to possess this trait of omnipresence to a greater degree and therefore, even though its messages could not be directly understood and although its apparatus required skilled operators, it survived as a medium by being more nearly everywhere at once.

Radio, TV, FM and all of the electronic media became instant favorites because of this trait. Shortwave radio still startles with its instant global blanketing of messages.

The computer's speed and efficiency mean that ten person-years of "work" may be accomplished by it in a few seconds or minutes. Couple this processing speed with the global satellite networks which now carry the digital data from place to place and the computer can become omnipresent. Salesmen call their home-based computer (often in another country) and, using the push-buttons of the phone, present to the computer their daily sales data and expense lists. Nearly all large computers can be accessed by telephone from anywhere in the world.

Computers score high on the omnipresence score sheet. From Mars and the moon, computers pass information to other computers regularly and routinely.

It is difficult to see how this feature can evolve any further than it is now. Processor speeds increase each year, but they are already so much faster than the human sense of time that further increases mean little to the lay person. Fiber optic cables and other communication channels will continue to pass data faster and more accurately, and at costs within the range of smaller businesses and homes. Its effect is difficult to foresee. We already live in the presence of prolific global communications and take it for granted that we can pass our ideas around the world at the speed of light.

Criterion Three:
New media are judged by the breadth of the universe they encode or communicate

Here the *richness* of the medium is isolated. Can an idea be encoded and transmitted with ease or difficulty in a given medium? Philosophical ideas cannot be easily stated in the language of semaphore. We choose our media in part because of the richness of vocabulary, the ease of its encoding, the ability to present both graphics and words, sounds and letters, for this enables aspects of the world to be communicated with specific and detailed intent.

In the story about prairie dwellers who used smoke signals to tell distant neighbors what television channel to watch, one of the two media is preferred because of this value-judgment. Silent movies yielded to talkies for this reason.

But the computer can encompass and amplify the usefulness of all the other electronic media. Because of this we welcome it, for the richness of its vocabulary includes all previous symbol sets; its encoding method is more basic than any other, and subsumes them all. Most of the special effects in movies are now created or controlled by microcomputers. We spend vacations watching computerized characters on stage at Disney World.

Electronic mail is a service which, by its generality of message-forwarding, illustrates our reach for a medium which encodes diverse messages with ease. Electronic funds transfer similarly exploits this feature. Computers are judged to be rich because they carry the words and ideas of our lives with great speed and accuracy.

The computer has not yet been graded on the criteria of richness. We have embraced it for other reasons than this. The public contact with the computer has not yet allowed it to fully reveal its superiority on the scale of richness. When the score comes in, it will further confirm that the computer is our ultimate medium.

Criterion Four:
New media are judged
by their flexibility

The perfect medium would have equal facility with all types of data. How does a new medium fare in manipulating or storing alphabetic information, numeric data, phonetic data, musical data, visual data, kinesthetic data? On this criteria we judge quite sternly. People wish that they could talk into a microphone and a machine would print what they said. Most people can't understand why this hasn't been done yet. Full color Xerox machines were desired for years before they were perfected.

What the tape-recorder did for the manipulation of audio data, computers provide for all recorded media. Consider that printed pages are easily edited or revised by the computer (word-processing). TV signals are easily manipulated by the computer (image-processing). Drafting and plotting are easily automated by the computer (graphics programs). Movie films are manipulated by computers to produce special effects. *Star Wars* showed the potential dexterity of the computer in its specialized robots and droids.

These parts of the movie were more fact than fiction. Computers are the only devices that possess this complete flexibility. In the future the public will become more aware of this flexibility and will like it.

Criterion Five:
New media are judged by their accessibility and availability

Some media are simply too costly to use. By their scarcity they may be bypassed. A remote village in India held a three-day celebration in 1978 when a foot-treadle sewing machine arrived. After three years of pooling village money, the villagers were rightfully pleased; it was a community resource. Even though satellites may be beaming educational programs to that village, the medium of TV will not be used until their standard of living allows them access to a community TV set.

The obvious criterion of availability of the medium suggests that a new medium must be plentiful, and cheap. Color TV presented a cost barrier during its early years. Full-color copying machines are desirable, but their high cost limits their use.

The rising numbers of computers and the decreasing dollars required to obtain them tells a lot about our access to them. A $1 million computer in 1970 could typically support twenty-five timeshared users. In 1977 a $1 million computer easily supported 100 concurrent users. Today, $1 million machines can support 500 concurrent users.

Looking to the future, we can anticipate media abundance, with high percentages of government agencies, schools, business offices and homes having access to computer power at low cost. Specialized terminals (like specialized calculators) with flairs for certain types of media manipulation will be developed. Terminals for stockbrokers, small-store owners, real estate agencies, and so on, will be available as low-cost turnkey systems. General computer services became available at a time when the average home possessed about a hundred transistors (1965). In 1985 the average home will probably possess about twenty microcomputers. One hundred channels of fiber optic or satellite TV should be available. Connections to world-wide computerized libraries should be low in cost. On the criteria of accessibility, the computer will score higher as the years go by.

When mechanical advances allowed printing presses to produce large amounts of printed material, a stamp tax was imposed. In a democracy, life would be quite different if only the wealthy could afford the daily news.

Criterion Six:
New media are judged by their simplicity or complexity of operation

Some media are simply too complex to be widely adopted. Some may be unforgiving of mistakes; not sufficiently idiot-proof. The ideal medium would have one knob, on/off, and would be as portable as a wristwatch.

This criterion suggests that a medium should be capable of being used by almost anyone. It should permit ideas to be encoded with ease, with few rules governing the process. Users should not feel any loss of identity when using the device; no humbling of oneself to the rules of the machine or medium. Cameras with automatic focus, automatic light setting and automatic flash, find a warm welcome on this principle.

During the period 1954 to 1965, computer access was so complex that its current popularity could not be envisioned. Only large government agencies or corporations could hire the skilled staff which was required. Only trained specialists could use them. Large central facilities provided batch services and two- or three-day turnaround.

Changes in computer access point toward more personalized, immediate access, with ever-fewer rules or restrictions. Today home computers costing a few hundred dollars offer simple, forgiving procedures to lay users. Their availability at a local store for inspection, trial use and training makes them an ideal gift for the person who doesn't have everything.

Two factors lure the public to learn to use computers. 1) Home computer users can purchase "canned" programs which they can exchange with their neighbors and through computer clubs and journals. They can use them without having written them. 2) The act of programming, once mastered, is usually viewed as pleasant, challenging, exhilarating and addictive.

Looking to the future, children may learn to touch-type in kindergarten. They may be drilled in speaking selected words into the terminal earpiece. The screens which display their work will become accepted as furniture and necessary household furnishing. Every office employee will require a terminal, desk and computer link as standard office equipment. The computer scores high on the criterion of access.

Criterion Seven:
New media are judged by the
fidelity they maintain

How accurately can a medium encode some portion of the universe? Does its message store easily? Does it deteriorate with time? Does the medium encode several levels of sensory data or only a few?

The common sense of this criterion is seen when color movies are preferred to wallet snapshots, or stereo FM is preferred to shortwave radio. Fidelity makes a difference and the judging party does not have to be skilled in the disciplines of bandwidth or distortion measurement to make the judgment. People ruled against viewing 35 mm slides through the color TV set for this reason. The slides looked so much sharper on the wall than on the TV screen. Manufacturers bet (wrongly) that people would enjoy "getting on TV" through this device, but the criteria of fidelity, of picture reproduction, ruled against it ever becoming a popular device.

Fidelity is not merely a luxury in a medium. Two major social activities make it of primary value. Firstly, decision-makers at all levels rely on the records of various media; sometimes they place their lives in jeopardy trusting the media records to be accurate (for example, airplane radar in cloudy weather, instructions for assembling a bicycle, property records at the courthouse, a satellite photograph of foreign missile bases, etc). Decision-making demands accuracy in media.

Secondly, we require media fidelity in our documentation and research. Scholars browse through the libraries of media records and archives in an effort to associate fact with fact creatively, to link cause with effect. They look for patterns, relationships, new theories to explain current events. Researchers hope that defects in the fidelity of their media do not lead them falsely astray.

Payrolls were the earliest business applications to be computerized. If you trust your money to it, it must be trustworthy. If you trust your mail to it, it must be trustworthy. Electronic mail represents the most popular service on many networks. If you trust your personal records to it, it must be trustworthy. Electronic funds transfer represented a pioneer use of the medium: if it takes your credit card it must be trustworthy. Or is it? The questionnaires are obediently returned by people who imagine that the computer systems at the other end would never betray them. But personal privacy has already been largely sacrificed on the altar of media. The media are in the broadcasting business and our personal data are radioed everywhere, with computer assistance. A good mirror shows skin blemishes more clearly than a cracked one, and the fidelity of the computer works against personal privacy.

The digital encoding system of the computer—its on-off switches, eight of which can represent any of 256 letters, numbers or other symbols—is more basic than the coding system of any other medium. It therefore provides the most tightly woven canvas on which coarse grained media can be painted or manipulated. Its fidelity is superior and is generally recognized by the public as such—notwithstanding the wrong billings and missing magazine issues which seem to represent computer mailing systems in the public mind.

Television disks which previously recorded their data in analog form are now moving to digital on-off pulses or holograms for recording. They will then be compatible with computer storage and computer data transmission standards. The telephone networks are in the process of converting to digital standards. Satellite networks were mostly digital from the start. All media will move toward this standard and by 1990 digital encoding standards will probably be uniformly accepted for all media in the U.S. Globally, it will take a little longer—until the year 2000.

These seven criteria operate quite unconsciously and automatically. Society does not take a formal vote on each medium. We simply buy it or we don't; we embrace a new medium or we don't. When we do, new psychological boundaries are established for communication and human relationships, steering us perpetually into our future mind.

Bibliography

Graham, N., *Mind Tool: Computers and their Impact on Society*. Mineola, N. Y.: West Publications, 1976.

Lenk, J. D., *Handbook of Micros and Minis*. Englewood Cliffs, N. J.: Prentice-Hall, 1979.

Martin, J., *The Wired Society*. Englewood Cliffs, N. J.: Prentice-Hall, 1978.

Rondthaler, E., *Life with Letters*. New York: Hastings House, 1981.

Chapter Twenty

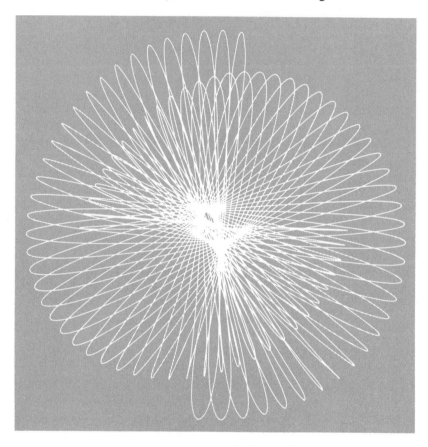

Future Mind:
Toward the Year 2040

Five information instincts probably reside in all the nerve cells of the human species. Through the millenia, dormant, these instincts stirred only every century or two. The invention of alphabets gave them quite a nudge. With the invention of radio and other speed-of-light channels, these instincts got out of bed, itching. The following list is a view of these central nervous system innards.

1. All data assembled in my lifetime should be available instantly. In my business, all company history should be available instantly.

2. All information in all libraries of the world should be available instantly upon request.

3. Information should be effortlessly rearrangeable, whether alphabetic, numeric, phonetic-oral, visual-graphic, kinetic or whatever.

4. I want to manipulate data free of charge. I live in an information age with incessant demands for facts and reports. Therefore, this is necessary as a freedom or birthright. Do not provide this service on the basis of wealth or class. Everyone deserves it.

5. Few rules, if any, should govern the use of information systems. Like television or the telephone, don't explain to me how it works.

Driven by these information instincts government agencies began in 1953 to utilize computers for statistical and accounting purposes. Then in 1955 manufacturing companies began to use them, followed by education in about 1960, business in about 1970, then toy and game manufacturers in about 1978. The 1980 model Lincoln and Cadillac featured fully digitized dashboards, plus digital radio and fuel computers. The computers come with the car.

The number of computers has risen each year since 1954 to the current level of about 800,000 of the mainframe class. The dollar expenditures have also risen each year even though the price-performance ratio has improved by approximately one-half every eight years since 1955.

A pattern of movement away from early, complex centralized access methods can be seen. Our information instincts led us to grope toward simplified, personalized, distributed access methods. Today the public encounters computers through home computers, through time-shared networks and through toys, games and calculators. Ninety-five percent of all schools and businesses will have computerized 95 percent of their business functions by the year 2000.

The software reveals the dynamic growth of the various applications of computers to life and work. The data carried in computer files is shown in Appendix 1 to have increased from year to year because of the reporting requirements of government and the increased capabilities of the machines. Data-base operating systems enable entire computers to be devoted to record management. These programs have become widespread systems in business and government.

As a problem-solving tool, the computer is often used to solve lengthy calculations, to simulate learning environments as in computer aided instruction, to assist researchers in proving the feasibility or truth of their theories, to analyze large census or blind data files, and to manage large inventory or warehouse files. The popular problem-solving uses are enjoyed by the users and are likely to grow.

Computer technology has been applied to records management, giving us the new medium of data-base management systems. More than 8,000 such systems had been installed in 1977, provided by 141 vendors. In 1981 more than 16,000 business installations were estimated to exist. The growth-rate of data-base systems is phenomenal, considering its introduction in 1970. Data-base systems promote the centralization and control of decision-making in its early years, but will someday reverse the process when data are carried in so many files that they might be considered public property, available to nearly anyone who wants them.

Computer technology has been applied to banking, giving us the new medium known as electronic funds transfer. In 1977 nine such systems were operational but many more came into existence as the legislation and communication channels permitted. When using these systems, people yield their personal financial facts to the banks, credit companies, government and merchants. In return the public obtains great flexibility in managing wealth and credit anywhere in the country. It is predicted to grow slowly with broad acceptance after the year 2000.

Electronic mail and word-processing represent two new services which are already popular. The demand for these two services points toward a rapid acceptance; humanity's central nervous system is showing its hidden agenda, no longer ashamed.

The establishment of new digital communication channels is a significant shift away from the earlier analog channels. This rapid shift began in 1975 and has become the standard for all satellite and long-distance networks. Most media will adopt digital techniques for recording and transmitting. With it, each medium will have a new, common set of symbols which, being digital can pass through any satellite, computer or cable.

The high cost of paper-based systems is a factor which encourages computer use. Banks and corporations pay heavily for warehouses and clerks to maintain paper records which are quite difficult to recover when needed. At some point, such systems break down and the computer is the likely alternative. In the future, as computer costs drop further, the break-even point becomes attractive earlier for each company facing the problem.

Our urge for faster and cheaper media is greater than our urge for privacy. Most legislation about privacy is politically beneficial but has little to do with the reduction of data collection. Projections indicate that so-called privacy laws will actually work against individual privacy because they hinder agencies from sharing their data with other agencies. Thus, each agency will ask (us) for the data repeatedly and will store it in many computers, redundantly. Eventually, personal data will be available from so many sources that the public will realize that privacy is not possible in an electronic age. We will probably adjust to living in an open, exposed society. It is the business of electronic media to broadcast our data between agencies and individuals.

Instinctively we wish to be like the media we love. People often adopt values which are metaphors of the dominant media available to them. Certain computer-induced metaphors have been considered; their outcome, if adopted, would be: (1) a more accepting attitude about diverse social conventions; (2) a systems approach to governance and planning; and (3) a desire for goods and services to be provided instantaneously—just like the electronic information media.

Some media seem to support the left (logical) side of the brain; others support the right (emotional) side. The computer appears to support both the rational and the gestalt sides of the mind. It is the first electronic medium to operate on the command of words and letters. Its support of rationality and of the gestalt was contrasted in Table 14.1.

Based upon the findings, Chapter 15 suggested that computers have aided the centralization of power and will continue this pattern for some time. About 1990 to 2000, a rapid decentralizing effect may occur because the data files collected by every agency will expose most secrets, and because the computer terminals in every home and office will have access through one channel or another to these facts. Thus centralized power relying on secret knowledge or the censoring of news releases may be reversed through the ease of access to knowledge.

Since the computer subsumes and includes all prior electronic media, it represents a culminating point in the evolution of media.

It can store data from any medium, can translate it to any other medium and can imitate most other media. Six new media were observed as direct outcomes of computer use: data-base records management, electronic funds transfer, online libraries, word-processing and phototypesetting. Electronic mail should become broadly available by 1985.

Two false metaphors were isolated, one suggesting that computers are machines, the second that computers are giant brains. The dominant bias which the computer imposes on its messages is one of instantaneousness. It offers seeming speed-of-light transformations of data which in their native media could not be manipulated so speedily.

The most useful computer service may be the public information utilities which will arise as the microcomputer permits individuals in their homes to access international libraries for reasons of research, entertainment or learning.

Until the discovery of the transistor and integrated circuit, there would have been no value in searching for a medium which would satisfy all of the five information instincts. Even in 1975 the list would have appeared pretentious and unrealistic. But today the quarter-inch square computers on a chip and the speed-of-light communication channels thrill the central nervous system, and these devices are certain to be widespread by the year 1985. Social and political approval is already evident in the public enjoyment of calculators, citizens'-band radios, microcomputer TV games, space age movies and the burgeoning information commerce. The public demand for information services, while unconscious, is frantic. The trend is too well established to imagine a major deviation from the instinct drives listed. Moreover, we have a medium which fulfills them all.

The evolutionary pattern can now be seen as a social process of instinctive groping toward the five ideals above. The age of factory automation (1950 and following) was the result of society's ability to manipulate sensory and mechanical data. The automation of assembly lines and other motion control was a forerunner of the electronic computer which can now control any type of data and transmit it through telephone, infrared, fiber optic or satellite digital channels.

By 1965 the information instincts caused society to reach toward other ideals. Information retrieval strategies were invented for government agencies that faltered under their paper-based manual filing systems. Data-banks began to form for government agencies, law, medicine, library networks, international corporate networks and others. At the same time the existing telephone networks began to be used to distribute computer power and alphabetic data. By 1968 powerful timesharing languages developed and individuals could access large computers through simple dial-up connections. Capital was not required, and the costs were within the reach of schools and smaller organizations. Timeshared computers may expect a five- or ten-year span of business services, probably yielding in 1990 to the home and office devices which offer a wide range of specialized services for a few thousand dollars and which will access national or state data-banks.

As the ultimate medium in the media processing picture, computers are predicted to follow these trends into the future:

Present to 1985. Providing enhanced information-processing at the personal level for people or groups who previously could not afford it or who were unable to cope with its complexity. The public desires simple, user-oriented services. Computers in cars, home furnaces, stores and game rooms will surprise people with their simplicity and usefulness. In addition 5.2 million desktop computers will be installed and virtually every office will use them.

1985 to 1990. Certain data-files will be licensed for replay to specialized audiences, both from video-disk and from digital disk. Information will be popularized in nearly all subject areas, beginning about 1985. The materials will be available in our homes on low-cost videotext systems, reorchestrated for easy public access. The Telidon standard will be adopted by other countries as a teletext transmission method.

1990 to 2000. The standards for data storage, data transmission and data collection will be stabilized so that both individuals and businesses will be able more easily to have access to the specialized banks of data which will be developed by various special interest groups. The price of microcomputer terminals will drop below $150 purchase price. Various data services will be advertised in the popular journals, attracting the user to data-banks for a small fee, with toll-free numbers for dial up. Competitive TV cable services will offer interactive almanac and library services to the home. The mission of the college and university will be to train students in the skill of exploiting the global data banks associated with each discipline. Research will be conducted online in the classroom using live ad hoc access to specialized data banks. Basic skills such as typewriting, shorthand, and languages will be learned in the home through interactive computer materials.

2000 to 2010.   Demand for public educational materials in the home will cause training organizations and a few schools to offer interactive computer aided instruction and other interactive encyclopedias in the home. Hidden computers will handle the switching requirements of the cable networks. People will be able to request special documentary entertainment to be shown at a certain hour and date on a six- by eight-foot screen in a room where guests with common interests meet. Informational resources will be requested with ease from anywhere in the world and displayed through the computer terminal and wall TV screen in the home or office. Satellites will scan the United States each one-hundreth of a second, picking up and dropping large packets of information in each city.

2010 to 2030.   Newer strategies for distributing indexed portions of very large information blocks will be perfected. They are likely to utilize dozens of microcomputers, broadband communication channels and unique divisions of processing split between the distributors and the local receivers. Bursts of high-speed transmission may drop large blocks of data into the local computer memory, after which local microcomputers in the terminal will manipulate it according to the user's purpose. Twenty-five percent of the population will be communicating electronically with each other or with information resources at any given time of the working day. By 2010 most computers large and small will be able to be programmed with English statements which the hardware will directly execute without any conversion to machine code or secondary language. This will simplify further the creative use of the equipment and will be welcomed by all lay users.

In the media perspective, there is only one more world to conquer. All of the media now imitate the rational side of the mind in some way—the languaging, counting, viewing, perceiving, reasoning, sorting, comparing, declaring side of the mind.

There is another side to the mind and a whole universe of media may be waiting for discovery to assist that other side—the dramatizing, dreaming, disassociative, misremembering, playing, intuitive, creative, moralizing side of the mind. It may be possible for the computer to model that side of the mind as well, but it has not been done yet. When we think about the processes which occur when we dream or daydream, our logical thinking brings us back to a rational process and we lose that which was unique.

Someone may devise a computer which stores a billion holograms and which merges ten or twenty of them in chains of relationships to see what new images result; the computer-assisted dream machine. But the choice of image would have to obey some blend of randomness and purpose.

Human history, of course plays out the drama of this uncharted side of the mind—the unbelievable inventions and the unbelievable wars, the Saturn probes and the nuclear bombs, antibiotics and laser death rays.

It is probably best that we modeled the rational side of the mind first. The computer enables us to stand back from our rational processes and see them more clearly. In general we like them and consider them worthy of preservation and development. Our books hold our rational heritage, clumsily but adequately, awaiting the computer for final support and global, instant distribution.

Information specialists are going to provide the most demanded services ever to arise in human history. Their activities will eventually reorchestrate the world's knowledge into indexed electronic pulses which can be flashed to and fro between people, institutions and nations. The nervous system of every person could begin to link to any other nervous system, the world culture pulsating its ideas throughout the global cell. This needs no development. It arises from deep within the central nervous system. We are programmed to want it and therefore, in our technological playfulness, we have made it possible.

Sitting with delight across from the information wall screen, we will glimpse the familiar GLOBELIST. Smiling, we will touch in for several of them.

GLOBELIST

☐ Inform me		☐ Riddle me	
☐ Tutor me		☐ Lecture me	
☐ Quiz me		☐ Entertain me	
☐ Drill and practice me		☐ Compare for me	
☐ Game me		☐ Condense and summarize for me	
☐ Comic book me		☐ Simulate for me	
☐ Conference me		☐ Diagram for me	
☐ Movie me		☐ Surprise me	

Bibliography

Dertouzos, M. L., and J. Moses, eds., *Computer Age: A Twenty-Year View.* Cambridge, Ma.: MIT Press, 1979.

Feigenbaum, E., and J. Feldman, *Computer and Thought.* New York: McGraw-Hill, 1963.

Gottschall, E. M., ed., *U & l c. Vision '80s* 7, no. 2 (June 1980).

Lucas, G., *Star Wars.* New York: Ballantine, 1976.

McLuhan, M., and O. Fiore, *The Medium is the Message.* New York: Bantam, 1967.

Mowshowitz, A., "Human Choice and Computers," in *IFIPS Conference Proceedings.* New York: Elsevier North-Holland, 1979.

Newborn, M., and B. Mittman, *The Eleventh ACM's North American Chess Championship.* New York: ACM Publications, 1980.

Weizenbaum, J., *Computer Power and Human Reason.* San Francisco: W. H. Freeman, 1976.

Zampino, M. P., "Microimage Technology and Practice," *Datamation* 77, no. 10 (October 1977).

Appendix One

Media Case Study: What Data Elements Comprise a Typical Computer File?

In order to illustrate the classes of data elements which are sometimes collected by companies in their business systems, the area of payroll-personnel will be used. Although the functionality of a payroll system appears obvious when you get your paycheck, a business manager must satisfy many other requirements besides merely issuing checks. Reports are required by the federal government, state government, insurance companies, labor unions, affirmative action officers, veterans coordinators, credit-loan plans, banks and retirement-pension plans, and these authorities force employers to carry ever more data on each employee.

As an example we will compare the data elements carried by a payroll-personnel system in 1966, 1972 and 1980. The example is drawn from a payroll system which ran on an IBM 1401 in 1965, an RCA 70/46 in 1972 and a UNIVAC 9080 in 1980.

The evolving computer hardware made it easier and less costly to carry the data online so that, in its latest version, the payroll data are fully available to the personnel and payroll offices through two video-screen terminals for instant viewing and updating. Paychecks are issued from the system almost as a byproduct. Most of the data elements would be demanded for other reasons even if paychecks were not required.

Table A1.1 compares the three data-element dictionaries as used

Table A1.1
Comparison of three payroll systems as used in one institution

Data element name	Character size in 1966	Character size in 1972	Character size in 1980
INSTITUTIONAL DEPT. NUMBER	2	4	6
CLASSIFICATION CODE	—	1	1
SOCIAL SECURITY NUMBER	9	9	9
PENSION NUMBER	—	4	6
FULL NAME	20	25	30
BIRTH DATE	6	6	6
SEX	1	1	1
MARITAL STATUS	1	1	1
EXEMPTION ALLOWANCES	2	2	2
ACTUAL EXEMPTIONS	2	2	2
STREET ADDRESS	20	30	30
CITY	15	15	15
STATE	2	2	2
ZIP CODE	—	5	5
PAYROLL STATUS	2	2	2
EXTRA FWT	—	5	5
CREDIT UNION YTD	—	5	7
SAVINGS FUND	—	5	5
CURRENT MO. DEDUCTIONS	5	5	5
BLUE SHIELD CODE	1	1	1
EMPLOYER SHARE BLUE SHIELD	5	5	5
AMT DUE FOR MONTH	5	5	5
AMT DEDUCTED THIS MONTH	5	5	5
MAJOR MEDICAL CODE	—	1	1
EMPLOYER SHARE M.M.	—	5	5
AMOUNT DUE FOR MONTH	—	5	5
AMT DEDUCTED THIS MONTH	—	5	5
MISC. INSURANCE CODE	—	1	1
AMT DUE FOR MONTH	—	5	5
AMT DEDUCTED THIS MONTH	—	5	5
CURRENT PAY CODE	1	1	1
STEP NUMBER	1	1	1
JOB TITLE CODE	2	2	4
SECOND JOB TITLE CODE	—	2	4
CURRENT RATE OF PAY	7	7	7
YEARLY SALARY	7	7	7
QTR PENSION BASE	—	5	5

Table A1.1
(continued)

Data element name	Character size in 1966	Character size in 1972	Character size in 1980
PENSION CODE	1	1	1
PENSION RATE (FULL)	–	5	5
PENSION DEDUCTION THIS MO.	–	5	5
PENSION DEDUCTION QTR	–	5	5
EMPLOYER SHARE PENSION	–	7	7
PENSION ADJUSTMENT THIS PAY	–	5	5
PENSION LOAN DUE	–	5	5
PENSION LOAN DEDUCTION CURR.	–	5	5
PENSION LOAN DEDUCTION QTD	–	5	5
PENSION LOAN ADJ THIS PAY	–	5	5
PENSION ARREARS DUE MO.	–	5	5
PENSION ARREARS DED QTD	–	5	5
PENSION ARREARS QTD	–	5	5
PENSION ARREARS ADJ THIS PAY	–	5	5
CONTRIBUTORY INSURANCE CODE	1	1	1
CONT INS DED CURR MONTH	–	5	5
CONT INS DED QTD	–	5	5
CONT INS ADJ THIS PAY	–	5	5
SACT PERCENT	3	3	3
SACT DED CURR MONTH	5	5	5
SACT DED QTD	5	5	5
SACT ADJUSTMENT THIS PAY	5	5	5
CURRENT TSA ADJUSTMENT	3	3	3
TSA DED CURR MONTH	5	5	5
TSA DED QTD	5	5	5
TSA PERCENT	5	5	5
CREDIT UNION ACCT NUMBER	3	3	3
CREDIT UNION PER PAY	5	5	5
CREDIT UNION DED CURR MO	5	5	5
DEPT ADDITIONAL EARNINGS 1	–	4	6
ADDITIONAL EARNINGS AMT 1	–	7	7
DEPT ADDITIONAL EARNINGS 2	–	4	6
ADDITIONAL EARNINGS AMT 2	–	7	7
DEPT ADDITIONAL EARNINGS 3	–	4	6
ADDITIONAL EARNINGS AMT 3	–	7	7
BOND AMT PER PAY	–	5	5
BOND BALANCE	–	5	5
BOND TYPE CODE	–	1	1
BOND OWNERS NAME	–	20	30
BOND OWNERS ADDRESS	–	30	30
BANK CODE FOR DEPOSIT	–	2	2
BANK ACCOUNT NUMBER	–	8	8
STATE UNEMPLOYMENT INS MTD	–	5	5
STATE UNEMPLOYMENT INS QTD	–	5	5

Table A1.1
(continued)

Data element name	Character size in 1966	Character size in 1972	Character size in 1980
STATE UNEMPLOYMENT INS YTD	–	5	5
IRS LEVY CODE	1	1	1
COURT ATTACHMENT EACH PAY	5	5	5
COURT ATTACHMENT BALANCE	7	7	7
COURT ATTACHMENT PAYEE	30	30	30
UNITED COMMUNITY FUND	–	5	5
COMMUNITY FUND YTD	–	7	7
FOURTEEN YEAR-TO-DATE AMT	7	7	7
FOURTEEN DECLINING BAL	5	5	5
NINE GROSS FIELDS	7	7	7
SIX STATE AND FEDERAL TAX	7	7	7
VACATION CURRENT	–	3	3
VACATION USED	–	3	3
PREVIOUS SICK	–	5	5
CURRENT SICK	–	3	3
SICK USED CURRENT PAY	–	3	3
COMPENSATORY TIME	–	5	5
COMP TIME USED	–	3	3
STATE TAX CODE	–	1	1
PERMANENT SERVICE DATE	6	6	6
TERMINATION DATE	6	6	6
LAST CHANGE DATE	6	6	6
HOLD PAY STATUS	–	1	1
DATE HIRED	6	6	6
LEAVE OF ABSENCE DATE	6	6	6
ACCOUNT NUMBER	9	9	9
SUMMER RESERVE BALANCE	–	7	7
GROSS PAID MTD	–	7	7
FWT MTD	–	7	7
FICA MTD	–	7	7
SWT MTD	–	7	7
FISCAL YTD	–	7	7
ADDITIONAL STATE TAX	–	5	5
STATE TAX ADJ	–	5	5
PAY ENDING DATE	6	6	6
PAY DATE	6	6	6
PAY NUMBER YTD	–	2	2
PAY NUMBER QTD	–	2	2
REGULAR UNITS WORKED	–	5	5
VACATION UNITS	–	3	3
SICK UNITS	–	3	3
BASE PAY	7	7	7
GROSS ADJUSTMENT	7	7	7
SIX PAY BY DEPT FIELDS	–	7	7

Table A1.1
(continued)

Data element name	Character size in 1966	Character size in 1972	Character size in 1980
OVERTIME PAY	7	7	7
TOTAL GROSS	7	7	7
FWT PER PAY	7	7	7
FICA PER PAY	5	5	5
STATE TAX	–	5	5
REGULAR PENSION	5	5	5
PENSION ARREARS	5	5	5
PENSION LOAN	5	5	5
CONTRIBUTORY INSURANCE	5	5	5
SACT	5	5	5
TSA	5	5	5
DUES	5	5	5
BONDS	5	5	5
SPLIT HOURS ON CALC	7	7	7
CREDIT UNION	5	5	5
IRS LEVY	7	7	7
ATTACHMENT ONE	5	5	5
UNITED COMMUNITY FUND	5	5	5
MISC ONE	5	5	5
MISC TWO	5	5	5
TOTAL DEDUCTIONS	7	7	7
NET PAY	7	7	7
CHECK NUMBER	6	6	6
NET PAY ADJUSTMENT	5	5	5
OLD RATE FOR SPLIT ADJ	–	5	5
OVERTIME HOURS	5	5	5
STATE UNEMPLOYMENT INS	–	5	5
QUARTER AREAS FOR 7 PAYS	–	1106	1106
CITIZENSHIP	–	3	5
CIVIL RIGHTS RACIAL CATEGORY	–	–	1
EMPLOYEE'S OFFICE BUILDING CODE	–	–	1
EMPLOYEE'S BUILDING NAME	–	–	20
EMPLOYEE'S ROOM NUMBER	–	–	4
EMPLOYEE'S OFFICE TELEPHONE NUMBER	–	–	7
PHYSICAL HANDICAP STATUS	–	–	1
PROFESSIONAL AFFILIATION 1	–	–	15
PROFESSIONAL AFFILIATION 2	–	–	15
PROFESSIONAL AFFILIATION 3	–	–	15
PROFESSIONAL AFFILIATION 4	–	–	15
LICENSES, CERTIFICATES, REGISTRATIONS 1	–	–	15
LICENSES, CERTIFICATES, REGISTRATIONS, 2	–	–	15
SPECIAL COMPETENCIES 1	–	–	15

Table A1.1
(continued)

Data element name	Character size in 1966	Character size in 1972	Character size in 1980
SPECIAL COMPETENCIES 2	–	–	15
SPECIAL COMPETENCIES 3	–	–	15
TYPE OF PREVIOUS EMPLOYMENT	–	–	10
TYPE OF PREVIOUS EMPLOYMENT	–	–	10
TYPE OF PREVIOUS EMPLOYMENT	–	–	10
LOCATION PREVIOUS EMPLOYMENT	–	–	18
LOCATION PREVIOUS EMPLOYMENT	–	–	18
LOCATION PREVIOUS EMPLOYMENT	–	–	18
HIGHEST DEGREE EARNED	–	–	5
AUTOMOBILE REGISTRATION NUMBER	–	–	9
AUTOMOBILE REGISTRATION NUMBER	–	–	9
DEPENDENT BIRTH DATE 1	–	–	6
DEPENDENT BIRTH DATE 1	–	–	6
DEPENDENT BIRTH DATE 2	–	–	6
DEPENDENT BIRTH DATE 3	–	–	6
DEPENDENT BIRTH DATE 4	–	–	6
DEPENDENT BIRTH DATE 5	–	–	6
DEPENDENT BIRTH DATE 6	–	–	6
FACULTY RANK	–	–	11
1ST INSTITUTION ATTENDED	–	–	20
INSTITUTIONAL CODE	–	–	2
2ND INSTITUTION ATTENDED	–	–	20
INSTITUTIONAL CODE	–	–	2
3RD INSTITUTION ATTENDED	–	–	20
INSTITUTIONAL CODE	–	–	2
4TH INSTITUTION ATTENDED	–	–	20
INSTITUTIONAL CODE	–	–	2
5TH INSTITUTION ATTENDED	–	–	20
INSTITUTIONAL CODE	–	–	2
1ST DEGREE OR DIPLOMA	–	–	5
DATE OF DEGREE	–	–	6
2ND DEGREE OR DIPLOMA	–	–	5
DATE OF DEGREE	–	–	6
3RD DEGREE OR DIPLOMA	–	–	5
DATE OF DEGREE	–	–	6
4TH DEGREE OR DIPLOMA	–	–	5
DATE OF DEGREE	–	–	6
STUDENT MAJOR 1	–	–	10
STUDENT MAJOR 2	–	–	10
STUDENT MAJOR 3	–	–	10
STUDENT MAJOR 4	–	–	10
CREDITS BEYOND HIGHEST DEGREE	–	–	2
APPOINTMENT TITLE	–	–	12
APPOINTMENT TITLE	–	–	12

Table A1.1
(continued)

Data element name	Character size in 1966	Character size in 1972	Character size in 1980
APPOINTMENT IDENTIFIER	–	–	2
APPOINTMENT IDENTIFIER	–	–	2
APPOINTMENT ORGANIZATION UNIT	–	–	4
APPOINTMENT ORGANIZATION UNIT	–	–	4
PAYROLL ACCOUNT NUMBER	–	–	6
APPOINTMENT FULL-TIME EQUIVALENT	–	–	4
APPOINTMENT PERIOD	–	–	4
APPOINTMENT EFFECTIVE DATE	–	–	6
APPOINTMENT EXPIRATION DATE	–	–	6
LEAVE STATUS	–	–	1
TENURE STATUS	–	–	1
CURRENT JOB CLASS	–	–	1
FRINGE BENEFITS	–	–	6
EMPLOYEE TYPE	–	–	2
SPECIAL ASSIGNMENT	–	–	12
NO. SEMESTERS TAUGHT	–	–	2
CONSECUTIVE SEMESTER CODE	–	–	2
YEARS TEACHING EXPERIENCE	–	–	2
ACTIVITY FULL-TIME EQUIVALENT	–	–	2
ACTIVITY FULL-TIME EQUIVALENT	–	–	2
PROGRAM IDENTIFIER	–	–	4
PROGRAM IDENTIFIER 2	–	–	4
PROGRAM SECTOR IDENTIFIER	–	–	2
ACTIVITY OUTCOME CATEGORY	–	–	2
COURSE IDENTIFIER	–	–	8
SECTION IDENTIFIER	–	–	2
COURSE IDENTIFIER 2	–	–	8
SECTION IDENTIFIER 2	–	–	2
COURSE IDENTIFIER 3	–	–	8
SECTION IDENTIFIER 3	–	–	2
COURSE IDENTIFIER 4	–	–	8
SECTION IDENTIFIER 4	–	–	2
COURSE IDENTIFIER 5	–	–	8
SECTION IDENTIFIER 5	–	–	2
COURSE IDENTIFIER 6	–	–	8
SECTION IDENTIFIER 6	–	–	2
ACTIVITY BEGINNING DATE	–	–	6
ACTIVITY BEGINNING DATE	–	–	6
ACTIVITY ENDING DATE	–	–	6
ACTIVITY ENDING DATE	–	–	6
NUMBER OF SEMESTERS TAUGHT	–	–	2
TOTALS	441 (1966)	1955 (1972)	2716 (1978)

Table A1.2
Typical records as carried in computer files

S.S. number	Last name	First name	Address	City	Zip code
315597780	JONES	JAMES	141 HIGH	K CITY	34771
315697780	ADAMS	HELEN	133 LOW	J CITY	18833
314788453	BROWN	BETTY	1339 BIG	M CITY	23387

by the institution across the years. Where a number appears after a data element, it indicates the number of characters reserved for that data element. For instance, in the county field, code 07 may refer to Rockland County, 08 to Westchester, etc. Thus it is a two-character field. Dashes indicate nonuse.

For readers not acquainted with computer file records, the data elements, when strung together, form records, one for each individual—just as they would in a manual business file.

These files and records are carried on computer tape in older systems and on disk devices in contemporary systems so as to permit immediate changes. A typical computer file can be visualized as in Table A1.2.

In order to visualize how much data are actually carried for each person, Table A1.3 displays one record for one person as carried in computer files in 1966, 1972 and 1980. Notice the increasing amounts of data which are carried in the evolving systems. The increase from system to system is totaled and summarized

Table A1.3
Totals of payroll data elements

Type of data		1966	1972	1980
Biographical data elements		10	13	68
Financial data elements		67	139	139
Appointment data elements		0	0	43
	Totals	77	152	250
Biographical characters carried		78	105	639
Financial characters carried		361	1847	1874
Appointment characters carried		0	0	203
	Totals	441	1955	2716

in Table A1.3. More data may have been carried in paper-based file folders, but the possibility of creatively searching through all employees for ad hoc queries was too costly and time-consuming to be considered feasible. As shown in Table A1.3, 250 data facts on each employee can be sorted or compared to other employees and creatively reported, on demand.

Governments would not request so many facts, reports and surveys unless they knew that most institutions could utilize computers to obtain the information. Thus institutions which have not yet automated their information handling are strongly motivated to do so in order to keep up with the ever-increasing government reporting requirements.

Appendix Two

Media Case Study: Federal Files on Citizens

The Privacy Act of 1974 (Public Law 93–579) required federal agencies to publish the existence of files which they maintain and to provide a clear means of contact for citizens to inquire about their records in each file. As a result the government published the 737-page volume *Protecting Your Right to Privacy*, edited by L. Greenspan (Washington, D.C.: Office of the Federal Register, General Services Administration, 1975).

In 1974 the federal government used its 3,622 business computers to maintain 6,739 files throughout its 83 agencies or departments according to the published list of files as shown in Table A2.1. Former President Gerald R. Ford stated:

> . . . it became increasingly apparent to me that, over the years, Federal agencies have amassed vast amounts of information about virtually every American citizen. This fact, coupled with technological advances in data-collecting and dissemination, raised the possibility that information about individuals conceivably could be used for other than legitimate purposes and without the prior knowledge or consent of the individuals involved.
>
> The administration of the many worthwhile programs for which this information is collected makes the continuation of these data systems necessary. At the same time, however, we have a clear duty

Table A2.1
Files kept by federal agencies
and departments, 1974

Department and sample file names	Number of files
1. Department of Agriculture	225
Employment history records—licensed nonfederal persons	
Supervisor's notes on employees	
Food stamp program inquiries and complaints	
State farm census	
Telephone, electric and LP gas survey	
2. Department of Commerce	96
Petitioners for licenses to file for foreign patents	
Individuals engaged in weather modification activities	
Participants in psychoacoustic experiments	
Travel records of employees and certain other persons	
Population census records for 1900 and all subsequent	
Medical records of seamen treated in overseas hospitals	
3. Department of Defense (general files)	4
Employee relations: discipline, grievance, complaints	
4. Department of the Army	328
Personal clothing record files	
Blood donor files	
Personnel data-card and locator card files	
Evaluation files on cadets and potential instructors	
Informant register	
5. Defense Mapping Agency	102
Individual academic record files	
Inspector-general investigative files	
Traffic law enforcement files	
6. Defense Civil Preparedness Agency	42
7. Office of the Secretary of Defense	124
Office social roster and locator card	
Application for Pentagon parking permit	
8. Department of the Air Force	824
Religious educational registration and attendance records	
Psychiatric treatment records	
Personal property movement records	
Congressional inquiries	
Individual weight loss records	
Bicycle registration file	
9. National Security Agency	12
10. Defense Nuclear Agency	11
11. Office of the Joint Chiefs of Staff	4
12. Defense Communications Agency	84
13. Defense Intelligence Agency	114
Security violations	
Intelligence collection records	
Automated bibliographic data files	

Table A2.1
(continued)

Department and sample file names	Number of files
14. U.S. Marine Corps	112
Deserter inquiry files	
Unit punishment book	
Insurance files	
Laundry charge accounts	
15. Department of the Navy	267
Minority group identification file	
Employee grievances, complaints, adverse action appeals	
Author publication list	
Pet registration	
16. Defense Contract Audit Agency	48
Letters of commendation and appreciation	
Parking permits and vehicle registration	
17. Defense Supply Agency	76
18. Defense Investigative Service	18
Privacy and freedom of information request records	
19. Uniformed Services University of the Health Services	4
20. Department of Health, Education, and Welfare (general)	65
21. Food and Drug Administration	12
22. Office of Human Development	148
Runaway Youth Act mailing lists	
National Defense Student Loan program files	
23. Social Security Administration	179
Health insurance master record	
Employee production and accuracy records	
Medicare benefit check records	
Local school records	
Social security and the changing life ethos	
24. Social and Rehabilitation Service	3
Federal parent locator system	
Cuban refugee registration records	
25. Alcohol, Drug Abuse and Mental Health	30
Medical records of mental health patients	
Saint Elizabeth's Hospital subjects data records	
26. Center for Disease Control	115
Coal miner worker's study	
Congenital rubella registry	
27. Health Resources Administration	63
Survey of pharmacists	
Dental patient records	
Vietnamese refugee physicians and students	
Physical therapists proficiency exam results (Medicare)	
28. National Institutes of Health	82
Urinary steroid levels in breast cancer patients	
Trainees record system	

Table A2.1
(continued)

Department and sample file names	Number of files
29. Office of the Assistant Secretary of Health Motor vehicle accident reports Medicare beneficiary correspondence General criminal investigation files	161
30. Dept. of Housing and Urban Development Construction complaints file Architects and engineers Mobile home park inspection Real estate files Mortgages—delinquent/default	57
31. Department of the Interior Great Lakes commercial fisheries catch records Mineral lease and royalty accounting files Timber cutting and fire trespass claims file	273
32. Department of Justice (including the FBI) Inmate central records system Addict/abusers system Organized crime information management system Watergate special prosecution—automated investigation National crime information center (NCIC) Personal information network system Tax division central classification cards Warrant information system Prosecutor's management information system	187
33. Department of Labor Conflict of interest file Pension embezzlement file	68
34. Department of State Fine arts records Berlin document center records Law of the Sea records	48
35. Department of Transportation Motorboat registration U.S. merchant seaman's records Aircraft registration system Police warrant files and central files Driver accident record cross-reference file Memorandum of monthly performance of keypunch operators National driver register Drinking driver tracking system	260
36. Treasury Department Gold licenses Census of blocked Cuban assets Tax court judge applicants Tax court files, public affairs—treasury—IRS	913

Table A2.1
(continued)

Department and sample file names	Number of files
Annual listing of undelivered refund checks—IRS	
Collection case file—IRS	
Form 1042 index register—IRS	
Artist file—IRS	
Foreign stock ownership file—IRS	
37. Action Agency	62
Peace Corps application record system	
Congressional files system	
Talent bank	
Conflict of interest records	
38. Administrative Conference of the U.S.	6
39. Advisory Commission of Intergovernmental Relations	4
40. Advisory Commission on Federal Pay	2
41. Agency for International Development	26
42. American Battle Monuments Commission	4
43. Board for International Broadcasting	3
44. Central Intelligence Agency	53
Computer access file	
Polygraph files	
Psychiatric test data files	
Foreign map sources file	
Security records	
Professors and placement officers of selected colleges	
45. Civil Aeronautics Board	12
Consumer complaint records	
Mailing lists of persons requesting CAB information	
46. Commission of National Policy Toward Gambling	2
47. Commission of Fine Arts	2
48. Commission on Civil Rights	10
49. Committee for Purchase from the Blind	3
50. Commodity Futures Trading Commission	27
Fitness files	
Investigation files	
51. Community Services Administration	11
52. Consumer Product Safety Commission	19
53. Council on Wage and Price Stability	2
54. Defense Manpower Commission	3
55. Energy Research and Development Administration	39
Alien visits and participation	
Access to weapon data and weapons program facilities	
56. Equal Employment Opportunity Commission	13
57. Export Import Bank of the United States	38
58. Farm Credit Administration	17
59. Federal Communication Commission	66
Broadcast station ownership interest file	
AT&T witness file	

Table A2.1
(continued)

Department and sample file names	Number of files
Radio operator records	
Alcoholism and drug abuse file	
Alleged violations file	
60. Federal Deposit Insurance	13
61. Federal Election Commission	9
62. Federal Energy Commission	22
63. Federal Home Loan Board	29
64. Federal Maritime Commission	16
65. Federal Mediation and Conciliation Service	4
66. Federal Power Commission	26
67. Federal Reserve System	17
68. Federal Trade Commission	41
69. Foreign Claims Settlement Commission	31
Bulgaria, claims against	
China, claims against	
Italy, claims against	
Cuba, claims against	
70. General Services Administration	96
Fund raising campaign files	
Author files national archives	
Researcher application files	
Motor vehicle accident and claim system	
71. Interamerican Foundation	5
72. Interstate Commerce Commission	12
73. Joint Board for the Enrollment of Actuaries	9
74. Marine Mammal Commission	5
75. National Aeronautics and Space Administration	20
Aircraft crew member performance records	
History archives biographical collection	
76. National Credit Union Administration	19
77. National Foundation for Arts and Humanities	9
78. National Labor Relations Board	16
79. National Science Foundation	34
Grants to individuals	
80. National Security Council	8
81. National Transportation Safety Board	4
82. Nuclear Regulatory Commission	40
83. Occupational Safety and Health Administration	7
84. Office of Management and Budget	10
85. Office of Representatives for Trade Negotiations	4
86. Overseas Private Investment Corporation	22
87. Office of Telecommunications Policy	11
88. Panama Canal Company	134
State Dept. visa lookout book	
Customs fugitive records	
Seaman's locator list	

Table A2.1
(continued)

Department and sample file names	Number of files
Fishing pass application file	
Hunting permit file	
Marriage license records	
Fingerprint file	
89. Pennsylvania Ave. Development Corp.	6
90. Pension Benefit Guaranty Corp.	6
91. Postal Rate Commission	1
92. President's Commission on White House Fellowships	1
93. Privacy Protection Study Commission	3
94. Railroad Retirement Board	34
95. Renegotiation Board	1
96. Securities and Exchange Commission	109
97. Selective Service System	9
98. Small Business Administration	90
Hurricane Agnes disaster files	
Lessees of federally owned land on rivers in Illinois	
Potential Spanish-surnamed applicants	
99. Tennessee Valley Authority Privacy Act Digest	28
100. U.S. Arms Control and Disarmament Agency	10
101. U.S. Civil Service Commission	12
102. U.S. Information Agency	35
Artists and speakers	
Americans residing in foreign countries	
103. U.S. International Trade Commission	2
104. U.S. Postal Service	68
Philately—Ben Franklin, stamp club sponsors records	
Postal meter records	
Collection and delivery mailbox irregularities	
Customer programs—sexually-oriented advertisements	
Philately—elementary school teacher records file	
105. U.S. Railway Association	7
106. Veterans Administration	57
107. Water Resources Council	4
Total Files	6,739

to ensure that reasonable safeguards are erected to prevent the use of this personal information for purposes other than those for which it was collected.

Because of the large quantity of material involved, the Office of the *Federal Register* has published in this one volume a digest of all the systems of records and the full text of all the implementing regulations previously published in the *Federal Register* under the Privacy Act. The purpose of this digest is to assist individuals in exercising their rights under the Act. It is designed to help the reader determine the following:

The names of the various record systems maintained by the federal government;

The various categories of individuals about whom the individual record systems are maintained; and

Procedures whereby an individual can obtain further information on any record system covered by the Privacy Act.

The files for all the agencies total 6,739. A few sample file names or file contents are shown in order to reveal the diversity and breadth of federal information collection.

Some files, such as employee files, payroll files, security files and parking permit records enable agencies to operate from day to day. Other files carry the data which the agency was created to collect. The question, "Why does so much information have to be collected?" is answered by the mission assigned to each agency. For example, the Department of Agriculture states its mission in the U.S. Government Manual:

The Department of Agriculture (USDA) serves all Americans daily. It works to improve and maintain farm income and to develop and expand markets abroad for agricultural products. The Department helps to curb and to cure poverty, hunger, and malnutrition. It works to enhance the environment and to maintain our production capacity by helping landowners protect the soil, water, forests, and other national resources. Rural development, credit, and conservation programs are key resources for carrying out national growth policies. USDA research findings directly or indirectly benefit all Americans. The Department, through inspection and grading services, safeguards and assures standards of quality in the daily food supply. (p. 102)

In order to carry out this mission, the Department of Agriculture maintains 225 files in five categories (see Table A2.2).

Table A2.2
Survey of Department of Agriculture files

1. Files on selected private individuals	167
2. Personnel, payroll and license files	49
3. Files on private businesses	4
4. Files on bidders or suppliers to USDA	4
5. Management information system file	1
Agriculture Department total	225

Thus 49 files are used to maintain the organization of the Agriculture Department and 175 files hold information about people or groups external to the department but (hopefully) in keeping with its mission. Table A2.3 lists the first 35 Agriculture Department files related to private individuals, to give the reader a view of the types of records maintained by government agencies.

Several positive statements should accompany this survey.

1. The list of government files was not published prior to 1975. The scope of information which government agencies carry might never have been known if it were not for the Privacy Act.

2. Greenspan's *Privacy* contains the address and telephone number by which each agency can be contacted for further information about each file.

Table A2.3
Thirty-five sample files on private individuals
carried by the Department of Agriculture

---

1. Persons whose training, position or achievements make them prominent in science, agriculture or both.
2. Individuals who hold key positions in agriculture stabilization and conservation service.
3. Individuals who have applied for commodity storage or drying equipment loans.
4. Individuals who merchandise commodity credit corp. owned commodities.
5. Individuals who perform consulting service for ASCS.
6. Cotton loan clerks.
7. Emergency livestock feed program.
8. Farm owners, operators and other producers (automated).
9. Farmer's name and address master file.
10. Individuals filing application for wool, mohair, milk and bee indemnity payments.
11. Individuals who are the subject of formal investigation.
12. Farm owners who file program appeals.
13. All known farmers who reside in areas served by the local county ASCS office.
14. Rice cross-compliance system.
15. Farmers who participate in shorn and unshorn wool and mohair incentive programs.
16. Farmers who participate in flue-cured or burley tobacco programs.
17. Individuals operating as agents for a warehouse.
18. Individuals engaged in the slaughter of meat or poultry.
19. Violators and alleged violators of plant protection and plant quarantine laws.
20. Records of accredited veterinarians.
21. Animal health scientists.

Table A2.3
(continued)

---

22. Scientists listed on research projects.
23. Operators of large-scale wheat farms.
24. Owners of land in Pappahannock County, Va.
25. Discrimination complaints file.
26. All FMHA borrowers, grantees and applicants.
27. All FMHA attorneys and escrow agents.
28. Housing contractor complaint file.
29. Individuals who are indebted to the federal crop insurance corporation.
30. Individuals who produce specific crops in the country.
31. Food stamp program inquiries and complaints.
32. Individuals hired to fight forest fires.
33. Pilots who have performed unsatisfactorily while under contract.
34. Parties who have applied for mineral leases.
35. Suspects and unpaid informants.

---

3. Formal procedures permit individuals to query the agency to determine whether they are personally recorded in any file and what information is carried about them.

4. A mechanism for correcting false or missing information is provided by each agency.

Other questions remain, however.

1. What is the size of each file? How many records are carried, especially on private individuals?

2. How many files are computerized and how many are carried manually? What files are merged with other files under management information systems?

3. Who can access each file? Can any federal agency access all the files of all agencies? Can information be requested from the management information systems of other agencies?

4. Can federal agencies demand information from similar (or dissimilar) state or local agencies?

5. What data elements are carried in each file?

6. What happens to the information and records when a reorganization of government occurs?

7. Who enforces the rule that record-keeping be limited to necessary and lawful purposes? Who interprets the meaning of this law?

8. What prevents agencies from carrying secret files of data which are unreported and unmonitored such as "enemies" lists?

Table A2.4
Combined statistics showing the number of
government files and business computers

Agency	Number of business computers	Number of published files
Agriculture	56	225
Commerce	82	96
Energy	285	39
General Services Admin.	24	96
Health, Educ. Welfare	82	858
Housing & Urban Development	6	57
Interior	32	273
Justice	9	187
Labor	94	68
NASA	188	20
State Dept.	5	48
Transportation	50	260
Treasury	150	913
Veterans Admin.	36	57
Other Civil	8	1,372
Defense	2,515	2,170
(Army, 703, 328)		
(Navy, 586, 267)		
(Air Force, 1,047, 824)		
(Other DOD, 179, 751)		
Total	3,622	6,739

9. How many files move from manual to automated systems
each year?

10. On what basis could an agency refuse to release certain of
its records to other agencies?

Although the list of government files does not state how many
files are computer-based, the trend can be deduced by combining
certain statistics from Chapter 7.

In 1975 there were 3,622 business-type computers available to
automate 6,739 files. (See Table A2.4.) Since 1975 the growth in
all government agencies has multiplied these numbers many times,
as the 1985 computer census will reveal.

ACKNOWLEDGEMENTS *(continued from page vi)*

World of Tomorrow (Washington D.C.: U.S. News & World Report, Inc., 1973). Copyright 1973 U.S. News & World Report, Inc. *Page 38:* Reprinted with permission, from Samuel Florman, *The Existential Pleasures of Engineering* (New York: St. Martin's Press, Inc., 1976). *Page 40:* Reprinted with permission, from L. Yablonsky, *Robopaths* (Indianapolis: Bobbs-Merrill Co., 1972). *Page 41:* Reprinted with permission, from Jacques Ellul (translated by John Wilkinson), *The Technological Society* (New York: Alfred A. Knopf, Inc., 1964). *Page 41:* From R. Buckminster Fuller, *Utopia or Oblivion: The Prospects for Humanity* (New York: Published by Bantam Books, Inc., 1969. All Rights Reserved). Copyright © 1969 by Buckminster Fuller. *Pages 42, 159, 160:* From *Understanding Media: The Extensions of Man* by Marshall McLuhan. Copyright © 1964 by McGraw-Hill Book Company. Used with the permission of McGraw-Hill Book Company. *Page 58:* Reprinted with permission, from Teilhard de Chardin, *The Phenomena of Man* (New York: Harper & Row Publishers, Inc., 1959). *Page 58:* Reprinted with permission, from D. E. Smith, *A Sourcebook in Mathematics*, vol. I (New York: Dover Publications, 1959). *Page 82:* Reprinted with permission, from Nyborg, McCarter and Erickson, eds., *Information Processing in the United States* (Montvale, N.J.: AFIPS Press, 1977). *Pages 102–103:* Reprinted with permission, from André G. Vacroux, "Microcomputers," *Scientific American* 232, no. 5 (May 1975):32. *Pages 199–120:* Reprinted with permission, from *More About the Computer* (New York: IBM Corp., 1971). *Page 151:* Reprinted with permission, from B. Lipson, "Search Warrants Without Due Process," Robert Ellis Smith, ed., *Privacy Journal* 2, no. 8 (June 1976):4. *Page 152:* Reprinted with permission of the Editor, Robert Ellis Smith, from *Privacy Journal*, 1977. *Page 164:* Reprinted with permission, from James Nobles, "Minnesota Privacy Experience," *Data Management Journal* 15 no. 4 (April 1977):25. *Pages 180–182:* Reprinted with permission, from James Martin and Norman R. D. Adrian, *The Computerized Society* (Englewood Cliffs, N.J.: Prentice-Hall, © 1970). *Pages 186–187:* Reprinted with permission, from C. L. Nystrom, "Immediate Man: The Symbolic Environment of Fanaticism," *Et Cetera* 34 no. 1 (March 1977): 26, 28, 30. *Page 202:* Reprinted with permission, from Withington, *The Use of Computers in Business Organizations*, © 1966, Addison-Wesley Publishing Company, Inc. *Pages 203–204:* Reprinted with permission, from Mowshowitz, *The Conquest of Will* (Reading, Ma.: Addison-Wesley Publishing Company, Inc., © 1976). *Page 207:* Reprinted by permission from James Martin, *Future Developments in Telecommunications*, 2nd ed., (Englewood Cliffs, N.J.: Prentice-Hall, 1977). *Pages 209–210:* Reprinted with permission, from, Don Parker, "The Future of Computer Abuse," *Computers and Public Policy: Proceedings of the Symposium*, Teresa Oden and Christine Thompson, eds., (Hanover, N.H.: Dartmouth Printing Co., 1977). *Page 212:* Reprinted with permission of the author, Robert Ellis Smith. *Page 213:* Reprinted with permission, from R. A. McLaughlin, "The (Mis) Use of Data Processing in Goverment Agencies," *Datamation* 24, no. 7 (July 1978):147. *Page 239–240:* Reprinted with permission, from John G. Kemeny, "The New Symbiosis," *Computers and Public Policy: Proceedings of the Symposium*, Teresa Oden and Christine Thompson, eds. (Hanover, N.H.: Dartmouth Printing Co., 1977):2. *Page 247:* Reprinted with permission, from W. Ware, "Public Policy Aspects for an Information Age," *Computers and Public Policy: Proceedings of the Symposium*, Teresa Oden and Christine Thompson, eds. (Hanover, N.H.: Dartmouth Printing Co., 1976):2. *Page 237:* Reprinted with permission, from Joseph Weizenbaum, *Computer Power and Human Reason: From Judgement to Calculation* (San Francisco: W.H. Freeman and Co., Publishers, 1976).

Index

2. The government should minimize the extent to which it requires information to be collected by an EFT system that is not required as a matter of sound business practice.

3. EFT systems should not be used by government for surveillance, to learn either a consumer's physical location or his patterns of behavior.

4. Law enforcement agencies should be allowed access to personal records, with a subpoena. In some instances the individual investigated need not be informed in advance.

5. The local EFT agent or bank should treat all records as confidential and should not disclose to third parties any information without the consent of the individual.

6. Certain credit grantors, credit bureaus and credit authorization services could be given access to learn about an individual's credit rating.

7. EFT records should be open for use in finding the new address of someone who owes money at an older address.

8. Consumers should have the right to see and correct their records when denied credit.

9. Consumer statements should be provided monthly when transactions pass within that month.

10. No method of stopping payment should be provided, due to the immediacy of the system.

11. Consumers should not be held liable for the loss or theft of their card unless their personal identification number was also attached to the card.

12. Banks should be permitted to install terminals anywhere in the U. S. without calling them branch offices.

13. Debit and credit services should be offered by any bank to any location nationwide, even across state lines. If a New York bank has a terminal in Nevada, a card holder may deposit (credit) or debit his account in Nevada.

14. Security regulations should be developed uniformly from state to state. Heavier penalties for computer crimes should be legislated.

There were many open issues which the commission did not resolve:

1. Debit collection agencies, which trace missing persons, remain unregulated.

2. Reasons why credit has been denied can only be elicited by writing to the bank. Travelers are not secure under such a system:

c. Wholesale and retail trade
d. Services and education
e. Transportation, communication and utilities

Computer vendors such as IBM, UNIVAC, Burroughs, Digital Equipment Corporation and Control-Data divide the nation into geographical marketing sectors which become the territories for sales representatives. Sales personnel are trained to market to specific audiences. Commonly, these groups are government, education, industry (business) and others.

The Association for Computing Machinery publishes the following categories of computer users in its conference book *Computers and Crisis:*

1. Education
2. Finance (Securities, Insurance, Banking, Accounting)
3. Government
4. Health and Welfare
5. Industry (Apparel, Automotive, Food distribution, Petroleum, Plant automation, Power, Printing and publishing, Retail)
6. Transportation
7. Urban Development
8. Engineering
9. Humanities
10. Law
11. Management
12. Medicine
13. Science

Divided according to dollars spent, up to 1975 the biggest spender was the government, followed by business, education and other users.

Government

The federal government was by far the major user of computers in the country, until about 1975, after which trends changed. Within government the military ranks as the biggest spender. The U. S. military, unlike those of Japan and Canada, whose use of computers was negligible, utilized more than 8,000 computers in 1976, twenty of which cost more than $1.5 million. (*Inventory of Automatic Data Processing Equipment in the United States.*)

Infosystems Journal observed in 1976: